THE
TEXAS
SAMPLER

A Stitch in Time

By Donna Bearden
and
Jamie Frucht

The preparation of this report was financed in part through an
urban planning grant from the Department of Housing and Urban
Development, under the provisions of Section 701 of the Housing
Act of 1954, as amended.

A word of thanks to the Governor's Committee on Aging and the Governor's Office of Budget-Planning for supporting this project; to the Texas Historical Commission for their help on various topics; to Mary Sherwood for donating her time and photography skills; to Cherilyn Wilson for typing, proofing and art work—especially for designing the sampler for the book jacket; to Hubert J. Miller for his taped interviews with Dr. Octavio Garcia; to the C. J. Woodson Junior Historian Chapter (Houston) and its sponsor Mrs. W. L. Gay for their help (ninth grade student Jackie Swindle prepared much of the material on Christia Adair); and to all of the individuals interviewed, their families and communities—Thank you.

D.B. and J.F.

Table of Contents

A Stitch in Time

It is the Bicentennial year and everyone is looking for history. The Governor's Committee on Aging has a hotline to the past. Many of the older citizens of Texas have fascinating stories to tell about growing up in Texas when she was half-wild. Some of the people are knowledgeable in old-time skills or handcrafts—bootmaking, beekeeping, moonshining. Others were involved in building Texas' industries—lumber, ranching, oil.

In April 1975, nomination blanks were sent throughout Texas—to libraries, senior centers, aging programs, county officials, bicentennial committees. This was our bicentennial bait by which we hoped to eventually catch a part of the lives of Texas' older people. Over 2000 nominations were submitted, proving that the wealth of stories at least is evenly distributed. Obscure locations were not immune from rich lives.

It was no easy task to select a variety of people who could represent a cross section of background, occupations, locations and, hopefully, temperament.

The one page application had room for one-liners of vital statistics. One page is only enough to tantalize.

The nominations offered intriguing fragments:

"This man is representative of my father's generation of cowboy-rancher. . .resourceful men who met hardships head-on and simply outlasted them, enduring whatever came. . . ."

"If you need help or good advice, call him. No room to write all his good traits. . . ."

"This man never knows a stranger, epitome of true Texan. . . ."

"A typical specimen as people think of Texans, being 6'4" tall, dark complexioned and very wide awake mentally."

"She doesn't have a tame story to tell. . . ."

Despite the resolve and preparation used in the narrowing down process, our final selection was haphazard. Like the ponies, chance helped us pick the "winners."

When people heard what we were up to, they added their own nominees right on the spot. We occasionally went after these leads. Or sometimes an older person would innocently catch our eyes and ears, as did Mrs. Hughes in the museum at Marshall. Not being able to forget her, and throwing the nomination process to the wind, we found her again and got our interview.

Coincidence entered into the selection process. In one town, after traveling three hours to interview one man who was not at home, we called another man, who turned out to be equally wonderful. This happened to Fish Martin. On the evening of February 26th, he was sitting peaceably on his porch when the phone rang, and a breathless voice just released from hours of driving explained about the Governor's Committee. Would he mind being interviewed? "Come on over, you bet,'' said Fish Martin, and from 7:30 to 11:00 p.m., he unravelled 92 years worth of experience.

These near-misses only proved that for every person we selected, there are countless others just as deserving, dynamic, and interesting who got away. We experienced great frustration over the limitations that kept us from interviewing every older person who was nominated.

Letters were sent out to those who were selected. We received surprising, paradoxical answers. Although Texans love to brag about Texas, Texans are reluctant to brag on themselves. We received letters that tried to discourage us, but were too polite to refuse us. Some of our people didn't think of themselves as the stuff history is made of.

"If you are making the trip just to interview me—it's a waste of your time and money. I am neither important nor interesting."

"Don't expect a lot from me, for I am not good copy, even for a good writer."

"I have your letter of the 16th of January regarding your coming out February 14 at 3:00 p.m. I want to say **No.** However, don't know how to in fairness to the woman who nominated me. So come ahead and I will do what little I can. Looking forward to meeting you. Ha!"

In the interview process there was some premeditation involved. You cannot drive 200 miles toward the "epitome of the true Texan" and not build up expectations and questions. After the preliminary questions that any Joe Friday might ask, the interview took off on its own, adapting to time, place, climate and characters. We came as freelance "grandchildren" longing to sit at the feet of our storytelling "grandparents."

The tape recorder sat in the room, like a snare. Whatever sounds tried to get away, it grabbed.

But sometimes our subjects were too strong for the trap. Chief Red Fox, for example, could outlast the Sony. Nine hours of talking only scratched his surface. He was still going strong in a marathon of monumental talking.

After several hours, we examined the tape to see if we had gotten anything valuable. We wanted to take the creature alive, we weren't interested in pelts. But we were lucky to get even a paw.

Our people were all good sports and submitted to interviews that, despite advance warning, still seemed to come out of the blue. They even abeted us, hauling old photos out, releasing precious mementos that had carefully been kept in wallets and family albums for many years—to be taken back to Austin to be photocopied and included as exhibits a, b, c, etc. And fresh photographs were taken as our people remained candid even with close-up lenses staring at them.

The tape recorder also had a benevolent side. It doubled for the interviewer and, in fact, had a presence and sensitivity all of it's own. The Sony magnificently picked up all the sound from the air, so we not only got the grandfather but the grandfather's clock. Sighs, oven doors opening, birds singing, the wind of Corpus—all were captured.

The tape recorder was set at 15/16 inches per second—the slowest speed possible. It was like going effortlessly down a lazy afternoon river. Only instead of canoe and paddles it was wicker chairs and voices. Replaying the tape, though, was like going upstream against tremendous currents of time. The foolhardiness of the voyage became apparent—we had covered such great distances.

The field work, completely enjoyable, was over. Now there was the task of writing the stories—two months with which to describe over 2000 years worth of living. How to transcribe hours of tape, and also how to equate that with a life?

If you write about these people, you have to include their environment and problems, their coyotes and mules, their bitterweed and weather. We recalled the story of the man at Guadalupe Peak who stood hunched against the sunset. When someone asked to take his picture, he said, "If you take me, you'll have to take my mountain."

So too, with our people. We have tried to include their towns, their flowers, shrubs, barns, whatever is part of their world picture.

When the writing was complete, the copy was sent to those interviewed to see if they could recognize themselves. They were invited to offer suggestions, corrections and deletions that might or might not be heeded. One man who, at the age of four, had listened in on a party line, felt that if this were revealed, it would discredit him before the community. Never mind that he was the cornerstone of the community and into his 70's. We reckless outsiders persuaded him to let us keep his "faults." His wife, who shares his good humor, wrote, "Joseph has decided that rather than the court costs of suing you, he will agree for you to use the controversial items."

Other people thought we had exaggerated their good qualities, made them bigger than their lives. "I liked your article. It flatters me, but of course, that does not offend me." Their own voices on the tape, however, are the accomplices to any claims we made.

In the end, these are not histories, but sketches. A sampler of sorts, having the colloquial words, family names, dates, and faiths by which our people lived. A collection of golden rules. A stitch in time. . . .
A small work to show the larger work that has already been accomplished by the men and women who lived and survived their hard times. These lives are part of Texas' great mythology. Our people are the sons and daughters of the young men and women who went west. These are the children who grew up with Texas, living her dreams and opportunity.

We sing the praises of the "Mexican kid" who was determined to fly; of the gentle beekeeper and rugged sheep breeder, who both had a vision; of the civil rights "fighter" who refused to accept second place.

But this is just a sampler of a diverse and beautiful generation. We sing the praises of "old" people. You have given us so much.

DB and JF

"*. . . . .rich man, poor man, beggar man, thief; Doctor, lawyer, Indian Chief. . . . .*"
Plus ploughman, cowboy, lady bootmaker, mule trainer, musician, actress. . . . .

"I sure been around, done a little of everything."   *(photo courtesy Fish Martin)*

The Saga of This, That and the Other

by Jamie Frucht

On the 4th day of May 1884, J. Fisher Martin came into this world. He is still very much in it. His episodic life has transpired in the West under many guises. On foot, on horseback, on mule, with a wagon team, in a pick-up, he's been transported. The best explanation of Fish's adventures is Fish himself—a powerful small man with an exuberant outlook on life.

Fish almost didn't get born. His father, James Shepherd Martin, a "little bitty man," who shed his larger name for the nickname 'Bit,' came to Ben Ficklin from Gonzales County in 1872. He built a hotel there with lumber freighted from Austin by ox team. Ben Ficklin was three miles downstream from San Angelo on the South Concho River. Since San Angelo was an important stage station in the cattle drives, the hotel seemed like a good idea. But unfortunately the town of Ben Ficklin flooded away in 1882.

In the midst of the fateful flood his Uncle Billy came and rapped on the bedroom door. "Bit, are you going to lay there and let your folks drown?" So his father went out into the flowing street, got the hack and team ready, and put his family in it. They tried to persuade old lady Metcalfe, who lived near them, to flee into the little hills with them. They begged her to go but she wouldn't, and so washed away with 64 other Ben Ficklians.

By the time the whole family was bundled up in the wagon, the horses had to practically swim to the safety of the hills. That storm washed even the dead away as cemeteries came apart. It cleaned the town out, taking everything except the old adobe courthouse which dissolved several days later. It was a close call, but not for Fish. He wasn't born yet.

Two years later, in 1884, he was born between Christoval and Knickerbocker. When he was three months old, the family moved to the town of Sherwood which had just been founded. It was the only town between San Angelo and Fort Stockton and lay serenely in the bend of Spring Creek. When the town of Mertzon sprang up across the river, the population deserted Sherwood for the newer town. Bit, however, stayed in Sherwood where he had several ranches and a farm.

As a young boy, Fish, as he's always been called, was afflicted with awfully curly hair way down to his waist, and he worried about it. "All the children ahead of me was girls. When they was aggravated with me 'cause I wouldn't quit squalling, they would pull my hair purposely; they used to comb and brush it for fun too. I was sure glad when my hair was cut off." Fish survived being a curly-headed boy in a family of five girls. Later he got another sister and brother. Today, only an echo of the long brown curls exists—Fish has fluffy short white curls that look like smokey wisps of a harmless fire.

Fish's daddy, as county inspector of cattle, traveled to all the area ranches. Fish got to ride beside him in the buggy. Growing up on his daddy's ranch was a real education. He saw his daddy catch wild mustang colts. "That was easy work. You just ride into them. A good horse can overtake them and you just go down in them and hold one till the rest of the mustangs are out of sight." One day his daddy brought home two mustangs at once, having roped one and reached down and caught the other around the neck.

"Those little old horses, they had big tails that dragged the ground. Those tails would pick up cockleburrs and burrs of all kinds and sometimes make a big ole hard roll that big around, that long. Their mane came way down to their knees and the foretop came over their eyes. I saw them running where they had to sling their head to see where they was going."

Fish remembers the mustangs the way some kids remember childhood pets. He raised five mustangs by bottle feeding them. "They was plum gentle pets, those little round-bodied horses, gentle as a cat" (even though they weighed 700 pounds apiece.) Because they were Fish's ponies, his daddy gave them Fish's very own brand. FI on the shoulder, SH on the hip in big Boxcar letters.

One of Fish's favorite colts was a little horse named Billy who was worked to a buggy, peddling produce—butter, eggs, milk. Fish remembers the day he visited the little irrigated farm with his daddy. That was the day the joke was on Fish.

"We drove up there. We was in the wagon. A little ole speckled chicken kept running about, and I kept punching my daddy and saying, 'Pop I want the little old speckled chicken.' Mrs. Woods who worked the farm for my daddy heard me and said, 'Well Fish, what will you give me for that speckled chicken?' 'I'll give you Billy.' (The chicken was worth about 10 or 15 cents, the horse about $10.) My daddy said, 'All right, get out and catch that chicken.' "

When they got home, Fish couldn't wait to run out and show his mother his prize chicken. She looked and said, "What did you give Mrs. Woods fot it?"

"I give her Billy."

His mother said slowly, "You mean you give a horse for a chicken?" Then she was after Fish's daddy. "Bit come here! You take this boy and this chicken and get in this buggy and go back down, trade back this chicken! Mrs. Woods don't want to beat a boy out of a horse."

But Bit wouldn't budge. "Oh, no. That horse belonged to that boy. He made his own trade and it's going to stay just that way." And it did. The chicken went into the pot and Mrs. Woods got 27 years of service from that little ole pony, Billy. Fish has a fresh laugh for that story each time he thinks of it.

Fish has got a longer job history than some men have lives. Since he was 16, he had an odd assortment of jobs. Sometimes he had simultaneous jobs. Sometimes he had one job in the morning and a new situation in the afternoon. He was never afraid to try anything and didn't waste effort and nerves worrying over outcomes. He worked off and on, lived around "here, there and up yonder," did "this, that and the other." Just so he was working.

At the turn of the century, Fish got his first steady job. It was only natural, given his ranch upbringing, that he would be cowboying. At 16, with a roll of bedding, a good tarp, saddle, boots, spurs, cowboy hat and high spirits, he started in as a horse jingler on Ed Jackson's 09 Ranch. A horse jingler takes care of the cowpunchers' saddle horses, or **remuda.** In an outfit like the 09 that meant some 100 horses. Each cowboy would have seven horses, only riding each half a day, giving the horse three and a half days of grazing. As the round-up moved from windmill to windmill over the 100 section pasture, Fish would move the **remuda** and help the camp cook. At night he'd tie a rope around mesquite trees to form a little ring for the **remuda.** Fish can still remember some of his charges names—Brownie, Alamogorda, Conger and Cowboy Dun.

Fish progressed from jingler to cowpuncher and to a salary of $20 a month or 83½ cents a day. That for being up before dawn and sometimes, when two or three would have to stand guard duty, up all night long.

The rhythm of the round-up and the drives is still with him. "Night overtakes us. Those on guard duty ride circles around the cattle to make sure they don't graze off or get up and walk off. If you stand guard right, you're moving all the time cause the cattle got to hear the horses' feet. But when that quits, and they all go to sleep, then's when you got to be most careful. If you get an ole green boy who don't know much about cowboying, he's liable to stampede the cattle, accidentally. Like he might just ride up, maybe get to talking, might roll a cigarette and strike a match. Worst thing is to strike a match. Those cattle just run, dead run."

Many's the night Fish has been stampeded out of his dreams and had to circle those running herds for five or six miles, for three or four hours, "till directly they get quiet."

Fish can forgive those all night incidents when he remembers the rewards of the chuck wagon. "Cow camp cooking is fine. Fine good ole frijole beans, big thick bacon, and great bread." The cook carried a sack of flour in the chuck wagon and would make up "a great bunch of dough with baking powder and water and pat it down pretty thin in a dutch oven, then it'd come up fluffy." Every once in a while they'd kill a beef and barbecue the sides of beef. Using the rods that went through the wagon bed, they'd skewer the ribs or shoulder on them, sticking the rods in the ground "in a big ole fire, with a big ole bed of coals."

Then standing guard wasn't so bad. "You just go to the chuck box, break you off a piece of pone bread, eat off of those ribs, and break out a little bit of coffee."

On the twelfth day of the twelfth month of 1912, Fish went to work bossin' for the Cargile Brothers at Rocky Ranch and stayed 18 years off and on. There were eight ranches to take care of. His job description was everything—round-up, branding and dipping sheep, you name it. He moved his last herd of cattle in 1914. The kid who had started as a horse jingler had made it to boss. Not bad.

In 1905 he got out of his saddle long enough to get married. For a wedding present, his daddy gave him 32 cows and calves. He traded them in for his own water well drilling outfit. In 1906 his son, Otha, was born at Sherwood. Fish had leased out his well drilling outfit and was horse-trading while he was Sheriff's deputy. Another time, a rancher, Jesse Cargile, staked him to some sheep and he was in the sheep business, in partnership with Jesse, separate from Cargile Brothers.

Fish was in the West when there was still open range. He remembers the country "way back yonder" when it was full of wild burros, prairie dogs, mustangs, antelope, coyotes. Because of the fierce competition for grass on the prairie, there was conflict. Then they used the verb "to get shed of" as in "to get shed of the wild burros, to get shed of the dern coyotes."

Those animals were wild and "weren't worth nothing."

One particular coyote gave the ranchers a lot of trouble. He had already eluded one trap and had three feet and a stump to prove it. A Mexican sheep herder came to Fish. "Fish, there's a three-footed coyote killing my sheep." Fish, ever confident, took on the job of getting shed of the wily coyote, even though another rancher, Louis Farr told him, "You can't catch that coyote. I've tried poisoning him. I've tried trapping him. I've tried every way in the world. He's too slick."

Undaunted, Fish asked for "one night at the coyote," and warned the ranchers to keep their dogs in. Then he gutted a jack rabbit, making four little baits and whittled four little pine sticks. He saturated the baits with strychnine. Tying the rabbit to his saddle, he dragged it to the windmill where he knew the coyote would go for water. Then he hid the baits separately along the path.

Next morning he rode out. He picked up the first bait, then came to the second bait. It was gone and Fish said, "All right Mr. Coyote I've got you." Predictably as the strychnine took effect the coyote had gone to the well and drunk water. Fish could see the yellow figure on the hillside on one of the cow trails. He tied him behind the saddle, then called his neighbor Louis Farr. "If you don't mind coming over I'll show you a three-footed coyote laying on my front porch dead."

Fish's confidence often went a few steps ahead of his common sense. Consequently, he admits, "I've been in some narrow places." There was the time he was going to Kansas City with a full car of four-year-old steers. He was anticipating the train trip home since the train companies gave cowboys free passes on return trips. Fish had a suitcase with clean clothes. He almost didn't get to use the free pass and narrowly escaped coming home in his Sunday Best as frozen human remains.

His job was to take the prod pole and, when night came, make sure the steers were up so they wouldn't stomp one another in the long dark night. If they weren't up, you wouldn't see them anymore till daylight when the damage would have already been done. They were stopped at Enid, Oklahoma. "It was sleeting and raining out of the northeast. We stopped there and I got off and was up in front seeing about my steers, getting them all up, when the brakeman came to me. 'Fish, when we leave here, you be pretty close to the caboose cause we leave downhill and we'll be going pretty fast.'

"Well, I thought I knew how to hop a train. So I kept messing with the steers. And directly the train started rolling. When that caboose got to me, it'd be a flying so I started running down toward it. I jabbed my prod pole on a car and hoisted myself on top. There were big boards on top of the cars to walk on. We were going northeast, facing the sleet. You talk about cold. It was solid ice. I just sat down. I was wearing my old Stetson which had been worn so much it got plum black around the band. Directly my hat began to ease up so I just give it a little tug and pulled the front half of the brim down under my chin. I didn't know when they'd ever stop or where the next town was. I nearly froze to death. And all I could do was just sit there and take it."

Another time Fish was working for a man who had 800 mules. There was one "great-big-ole-hungry-raw-bone-brown-mule" who really had it in for Fish and all human folks. Three men from the penitentiary had come to the ranch to buy 100 mules. They got their pick of the bunch. Since mules run with their heads together, Fish had to throw his rope and pick up their forefeet. Suddenly he noticed that hungry mule eyeing him, picking him out of the bunch of cowboys.

"I dropped my rope and ran for the gates. But he charged and reached up and got me off the gate and just walked around there in the corral with me in his mouth, like a dog with a rabbit." Fish still has the flank scars to show where the man-eating mule got him, but the penitentiary men bought the mule anyway. They said, "We've got a convict that can chew both his ears off."

Not all Fish's jobs were so demanding or roughed him up quite so badly. Once, for a time, he was a flag man in a surveying team with his nephew. Tom Green had once been a big county but every time they cut off a new county, Tom Green shrunk.

His nephew told him the surveyors needed a couple of men on horses to run the front and back flag on the Reagan county survey. "If I was setting here with my flagpole, well then my nephew would come up from back yonder with his flag and sit down where I was. Then I'd look through that transit machine and pick out an object maybe two or three miles, and go to it on horseback. The surveyors were on foot, chopping the right of way, and running a chain. When they cut a right of way, they put up a milestone with these big flat rocks at the corner of every section. Sometimes it'd be a couple of days before they ever got up to me again. All I had to do was just lay around. My nephew and I, we had it pretty good."

Another good job he had was selling real estate in Angelo during the Depression. In 1910, in Styles, he had had a blacksmith shop and sharpened the tools used to make the courthouse. That little town boomed for a few years, then went out.

Twice he lived "way up yonder" near Roswell, New Mexico where his daughter Cleo was born in 1909. The sequence of events is Horatio Alger all over again. Only Fish never got fully rich. But he did walk into lucky coincidences and worlds of opportunity. He bedded down with the unexpected, not knowing from one hour to the next what he'd be doing. He was only sure of one thing—that he was willing to work, be it as laborer or boss. Sweat is something Fish has always had plenty of.

Land in the Toya valley had gone from Indians to Mexicans and now to three men who bought 10,000 acres for speculation. The three men's names were Balcolm, Marrow and Rhea, and hence the town was named Balmorhea.

"The first thing they did was get a blazer and just made them a road. They didn't pay any attention to any other roads, they just leveled off the sand dunes. Then the bunch of them would go north and get the excursionists to come down and buy this land. Thirty-five cars of people came down to buy, three or four priests among them. As soon as somebody bought some land, they wanted it in cultivation. The water was there in springs if you could get it out down irrigation ditches.

"Well, I met this old boy who was contracting. I was broke. I didn't have any money but had a wife and kids and I hit this ole boy up for a job."

The contractor said, "I have all the men I want but I'll sell out to you."

"Shoot, I couldn't buy nothing. I'm just looking for a job."

"I'll still sell it all to you on credit."

"All right, and after you sell it to me on the credit, then where am I going to get money to buy the feed for all these mules and horses and how am I going to pay these men?"

"I'll fix that for you. I'll speak to a German who owns a store."

"Sure enough the German said, 'I'll furnish you groceries and feed.' So we made a trade. I didn't pay a nickel down and I went to work and made a bunch of money and paid him back in just a little while."

In time, Fish sold out from this contracting firm, and took a wagon and a big team of horses and a big bay mare. "I built me a regular ole chuck box to put on the back of my new big wagon. I extended the wagon bed wider and made me an old frame on top of the wagon boards and put a mattress inside and had a place for my wife and baby and kid to sleep. I filled the chuck wagon full of chuck at old man Schurtz's store and I pulled out of Balmorhea.

"Well I got up to Roswell and camped out there in the flat. In the morning, I told my wife, 'I believe I'll walk over and see about picking up a little work.' I still had a little money but I was always a great hand to make a little more. I saw where they were building a three or four story brick building. I hit this fellow up for a job. 'Be here at 1:00,' he said. 'And you can go to work.' "

Fish was stout and strong. (All his life he's weighed a cheerful 200 pounds.) But the job was stronger than he was. He had to put a big hod on his shoulder, lower it down to a hole where the men were mixing the bulk of mortar by hand and get great scoops that often knocked him over. Then he had to go up three or four stories at a time to give it to the men on the building. Fish said it reminded him of a joke he'd heard about this Irishman Pat who got him a job carrying brick and mortar, and writes to his friend Mike. "All I have to do is carry that brick and mortar up eight stories. The man up there does all the work.''

He went home, cooked dinner and got to talking to a young boy. "I told him that I had a big team of horses and a wagon and I wanted to get a job where I could use them. He said, 'You know I may find you a job.' And sure enough, the word-of-mouth employment agency came through again.

"He got me a job with a man in Roswell who had contracted to put in a sewer and water system. It was a big job. For a few days I hauled water for him, using my wagon and team. After asking if I could run the ditching machine, we agreed for him to pay another driver for my team so I could be free to be running one of them big ditching machines. It was run by steam. Had a boiler way up yonder in front and a 28 foot wheel that dug the ditch. Until I leased out my wagon and team, all I had to do was every two hours or so, drive up a little piece and put water in the boiler and sit there."

One thing always led to another. Fish seems to have a propensity for tripping over schemes. While he was feeding the boiler he met a man by the name of Jim West who had a team of mules and was pulling in work filling ditches.

His new friend said, "Say, Fish, there's a company putting in a railroad from Oklahoma to El Paso and they're going to come right through Roswell. I've contracted ten miles of railroad out here. Why don't you contract ten miles?"

Fish said, "Me with one team of horses and a wagon, build a railroad dump?" (He laughed, though he shouldn't have. Nothing should have been incredible to him.)

Jim West persisted. "I know a place out here, a big trading yard, Charlie Franck's, where you can buy all the horses and mules you want."

But Fish wasn't convinced. He argued, "If I had the teams, that'd be lots of men to feed and mules to feed and feed for all them horses, and what about the plows and slip and scrapers and fresnos and stoves and harnesses?"

"Don't worry," said his friend. "We'll get that all right. People want railroads so bad, they'll furnish anything you want. They'll just open the doors to you."

And his friend was right. Fish bought ten teams of mules, going for credit, putting up his wagon and team for security. Then he leased about twenty teams more at $20 a month. That gave him about twenty to forty men, and thirty teams of mules and three dump bosses.

The fact that Fish had never built a railroad didn't faze him. "I didn't worry about it. I sure been around, done a little of everything." (Ulcers must be a modern disease that didn't fester in the pioneer stomach, at least not in Fish's.)

"The work went a whole lot faster than a body would think. We'd plow up a big lot of dirt. Then pile it up to the stakes the engineers put in. I was building that dump fine."

One day, Charlie Frank, who'd furnished him the teams, came out. "Say, Fish, you'll have to look after Jim's ten miles of railroad for a few days."

Fish said, "Shoot, Charlie. I've got all I can do to get my ten miles, what with all these 33 men."

Charlie said, "Oh you can run it all right."

His friend Jim came and explained. "Fish, I got to run over to Santa Fe and stand trial for horse stealing. I won't be but two or three days."

Jim West was gone two or three days and several years, for they stuck him in the pen.

Fish was only momentarily stunned. "There I was with all that mess." But again things went well and Fish had all his done except for the last stakes. "That's where you go along and smooth it out and put the ties on."

One morning the resident engineer came out very agitated and said, "Fish, we're blowed up. The president of this railroad's skipped the country."

"My God, what in the world will we do?" Fish asked.

The engineer said, "Well they owe me $1000 for wages, but the lawyers say that if you boys will go ahead and put your dump up ready for the ties, it don't make any difference how many years it is, if anybody ever uses this dump or builds a railroad five miles of this one, they'll have to pay you for your work."

Fish was dubious, not his ordinary state. "I never heard of no law like that." But Charlie Franck when he heard about the snag said, "All we can do is build it up. We can't quit now. We've got too much in it." So they went ahead and finished their dump. "And we got all the papers drawn up and put them on record in Altus, Oklahoma. That was 67 years ago and I guess they're still there." He was never paid for the work.

Experiences like that didn't stop Fish. Good and bad jobs just washed off him like water off a duck's back. He still swam as strong as ever. "I started myself a tourist court and truck stop cafe way down yonder in Arizona." His wife died so he sold out. "I bought me a big pick-up and trailed a station wagon loaded inside and up on top with personal stuff and came back to Angelo to get rid of it."

Fish had every intention of leasing him a little ranch with about 1000 ewes. The fact that he was 84 years old didn't enter into the picture. After all, he was in good health. When he got to Angelo, however, he had a sad awakening when he saw how prices had risen. Sheep were $30 a head as opposed to $8 and $10 when Fish had been in the business. The grass leases had gone up from 25 and 40 cents to $2 and $3 an acre. So Fish decided that maybe a ranch wasn't such a good idea.

As he was driving around Angelo he saw a little store front and decided that it would be suitable living quarters for a bachelor like himself. But as he was unloading all his stuff from the station wagon and pick-up, people came driving up.

"People wanting to sell me something or wanting to buy something.

So I got to selling and I got to buying. I made good money. Now I didn't aim to get in that second-hand business at all. I just wanted to sell my stuff out, to get shut of all that.''

What Fish aims to do and what actually occurs, are two different things. For instance, he didn't aim to get married again. But Fish Martin seems to live a life of spontaneous happenings.

He visited his recently widowed daughter, Cleo, in Mississippi. "I liked to went crazy. There was nothing to do over there.'' He and his daughter came back to Angelo where Cleo hunted up an old school chum, Virginia, who was also recently widowed. Virginia insisted that Cleo and Fish stay with her. Fish never left.

He explains it this way. "Then of course, we got acquainted and went on and on, and then her and I decided we'd just get married.''

Virginia interrupts, **"Her** didn't have anything to say about it. He decided he was going to take care of me.'' (Then softly) "And he really does.''

That was seven years ago. The age difference (Virginia can remember being a schoolgirl over at Cleo's house and talking with Mr. Martin) has been softened. Fish seems to have stopped aging.

"I'm just as healthy as I can be. Oh I can't get around as fast as I used to, but I can get up and go and do what I want to do.'' He even drives without his spectacles.

Once, two years ago, Fish broke down with rheumatism and had to sell out his other second-hand store. Rheumatism in a 90-year-old man would seem to be the end of the race. But not for Fish. He was down in bed for two months. "I couldn't walk, couldn't stand up, legs wouldn't percolate. One-hundred-and-twenty-five people tole me what to do. I just done a little of everything, this, that and the other. I guess I just outlived it mostly, wore it out.'' He couldn't tell you which remedy did the trick, but he's back in the running. Fish is a stayer.

The only time Fish gets down now is when he's dormant. A few weeks ago the flu kept him bedridden. "I like to gone crazy.'' Even in his sleep, Fish is a doer. His wife recalls listening to him. "He worked in there in his sleep. You could just hear him, plain and clear, repairing furniture, chairs and tables and teaching a young man how to start a farm. 'Start out early,' he said. 'to start out right.' '' In his feverish state, he walked out the front door, hat on, pockets loaded with tools to go to work, then stopped as though in the middle of a dream. "Well dad blam, where was that workshop where I was going to help this young fellow?''

Fish and Virginia live in her home on Cactus Lane. It's a long lane that's somehow immune from the traffic and destinations of the city. Their house is perfect—haphazard and comfortable like Fish's life. The front porch has easy chairs and a view of a small rodeo field where children ride and scream across hellos and jibes to Fish. Fish has a front row seat of the sunset.

Inside the house, an old clock ticks the reassuring minutes. Between the click of the clock and the clop of the horses hooves, there is momentary silence.

Fish and Virginia live a life attuned to each other. Fish is an

(photo by Jamie Frucht)

appreciative man, accepting his good luck. Sometimes he boasts a little, admiring his marriage, concocted at the end of his life. "Neither of us in seven years has ever had a cross word to say to one another. Nothing to be cross about. I've never felt anytime like I wanted to say anything cross to her. Virginia never fails to fix me a meal. No matter how sick she is. Three meals a day just as regular as a clock strikes." And sure enough, though she's one week into the flu herself, homemade currant cookies compete with Fish's pipe for dominant fragrance.

Fish's personal habits have not diminished with age. Oh, once he enjoyed cigars, hoarding them in a leather pouch in his vest pocket, enjoying five before the noon meal and several more after the evening meal. As a cowboy he consumed cigarettes. Now he concentrates on the ritual of the pipe smoker. He also loves to dance. "You should see me and my wife get on the dance floor in a big ole long sweeping waltz or schottische. Aren't we something, Sweetheart."

While Virginia serves up cookies, Fish gives away his stories. Virginia is his captive audience. "He told me something. It was old, old, old. I mean it was **old.** He tells me old things all the time." But that's no criticism. She gives him cues to start the stories she wants to hear. There's no way to exhaust his repertory of 92 years. Usually they stay up to midnight.

Fish laughs a lot, punctuating ends of sentences with his pleasure. He remembers everything so well because he enjoyed everything so much. Fish talks in details. Describing an old friend whom he'd punched cattle with here and there—"He's a tall fellow, hair pretty grey, walks with a cane, if he's got a hat on it'll be white."

Fish never held back with his energy. Every particle of his short, stout body seems to have been engaged, except maybe his nerves. If he's got worries, they're buried under tons of good spirit.

Fish has always provided for himself and family and still does. Keen to do things, he leads with the philosophy—"Give it a try. You bet." Out of odds and ends, this and that, Fish has whittled himself an incredible life.

Tomorrow is another day and Fish Martin will be there to grab it.

A Labor of Love

by Jamie Frucht

Bees are marvelous creatures; so too are beekeepers, who are a little breed of their own. Roy Weaver, on October 13, 1892, was born into a family of beekeepers and honey producers. Beekeeping is Roy Weaver's history and also his present. The Lynn Grove location of Weaver Apiaries, nine miles south of Navasota, has had bees and Weavers since 1888. Mr. Weaver works where his father Zack worked. He inhabits the same region.

Despite Mr. Weaver's assertion that the Lynn Grove location is not as good as it was in 1888 when Zack lived there, it's hard to believe that Paradise was diminished. Gulf storms have taken their toll in Lynn trees, and development has thrown a house here and there; nothing serious.

Mr. Weaver is two roads removed from any big highway. A farm-to-market road narrows into a dirt road that goes past a red dwelling and finally curves at the rock church on the site of the original church that his father helped build in 1889. (The lumber and benches are from the old church.) About the only parishioners there on a weekday morning are cows grazing on the grass. Mr. Weaver's place is just past the church.

His old white frame house is bright and meandering. Giant oak, pine and magnolia make live pictures through the window panes. Strawberries veiled against birds grow so abundantly that their excess has been used for edging. Dogs lay at ease in the shadows, as Mr. Weaver, his son, grandson, and other workers (and the bees) go about their business.

Beekeeping is the art of small details. A person can know one or two of those details and still be a big failure as a beekeeper. Mr. Weaver, whose apprenticeship with beekeepers and bees has been lifelong, knows the little details and delights in them. The details are housed in four or five old apiary buildings that graze near his house. Each building is sweet smelling from honey and wax.

In the extraction area, the tops of the combs are sliced off and the combs whirled about. The honey is spun out by centrifugal force. It then descends and ascends through systems of pipes until it is finally "put up" in jars and drums. The labels on the bottled honey read, "Put up by Weaver Apiaries. Beekeepers here, since 1888."

Removed from the other buildings is the queen yard—little white mating boxes, nuptial suites forming white rows that curl back to a sunny ash tree. Mr. Weaver, haloed in the sifted light of the tree length vines of the mating yard says, "Beekeepers run into numerous beautiful places like this. For outdoor life, beekeeping is hard to beat." Here the queens live during their mating. The actual mating is a real aerial show and can take place fifty feet in the air when the queens keep their instinctual rendezvous with the drones. Then it's goodbye, Mr. Drone.

The Lynn Grove location has had bees and Weavers since 1888.

(photos courtesy Roy Weaver)

The apiary location has been home to Mr. Weaver for 84 years. He moves about it with the utmost ease. He is a small man who wears a loose cardigan and baggy pants that swallow him up past the shirt. His countrified fedora sits on his head like an old companion. In a more extreme season it might have sheltered the beekeeper from the elements, but now it seems to be worn from sentiment. His fingers are strong, thick and weathered. They look like they could have sculpted pink granite; instead, his medium is honey.

The steel-rimmed glasses that are now so popular with every near-sighted 20-year-old seem unique and authentic on Mr. Weaver's nose. His serious eyes often slant into a prize-winning smile. When he laughs he means it and the pleasure takes over his whole face.

Although Mr. Weaver has been in Texas all his life and has a meandering but original accent to prove it, there is a touch of New England in him. Perhaps it is just that small country towns produce people of integrity who take hard work for granted and who don't brag about themselves; but who, if you express an interest, will quietly go about showing you the things they've done. The word that comes to mind is industrious. Just like the town in that neck of the woods—Industry—not named for factories and smoke stacks but for early rising, hard-working folks.

Roy Weaver certainly comes from such folks who worked hard, as hard as their bees did. His origins and history are not lost in genealogy vines, but are the backdrop of his daily work. It was in Lynn Grove in the spring of 1887 that Roy's father, Zack, let Walter Somerford use some of his land to establish an out-apiary. Walter was the first person in Grimes county to subscribe to a bee journal and one of the first to keep bees in a movable frame hive. He was an enthusiastic beekeeper and, through his proselytizing about the wonders of bees, managed to talk Zack into becoming a commercial honey producer.

Zack was not taken by the bees at first, but he was taken by Walter's sister, Florence. Since he was handy with tools, he found excuses for coming to the Somerford house to help build honey carts. Courting Florence, Zack also had to court the bees, as she had three brothers who were beekeepers.

Zack and Florence were married in 1888. It's only fitting that Walter gave them ten hives of bees as a wedding present. The bees multiplied, and so did Zack and Florence. They had nine children. Roy remembers going with his mother and father by wagon to bring the honey in from the out-apiaries seven or eight miles away. Zack used his carpentry skills to build a honey extractor and small houses at all the out-apiaries. These houses were built on two levels. A ramp was used to bring the honey onto the extracting floor. The extracted honey ran by gravity.

As a young boy, Roy remembers hearing of a young lady school teacher who came from a nearby village to see the honey extracted. She was dressed from head to toe as was the custom before the turn of the century. The honey was rushing out of the extractor through a strainer and into a barrel. This strainer was on the lower level; however, it was almost level with the upper floor. It was covered over with an "oil-cloth." The young lady, in trying to see, stepped off into the honey strainer and went almost up to her knee in honey.

Roy describes the early "packaging" of honey. "Honey was shipped in wood barrels to some of the larger stores. The customer would bring his jug to be filled from the barrel. At times when honey was shipped to Dallas in barrels, Zack would go by train and buy lard buckets and peddle the honey directly to the customers." Honey fetched a relatively high price in those days. In an old account book honey sales are listed at 50 cents a gallon. Also listed are such things as a suit for Roy—$2.00, and three pounds of coffee, 25 cents.

It was natural that Roy Weaver would grow up and become a beekeeper. He resisted for a year, trying his hand as a rural mail carrier. His interest in bees, however, got the better of him. "I used to stop on my route whenever I'd see flowering plants and look to see if the bees were on them, working the pollen." After a frustrating year, Mr. Weaver went to work for a large beekeeping operation in West Texas in 1914. Later he went to Cuba for six months to work with his uncles who had established apiaries there.

Within the year he was back at Lynn Grove working as a small farmer and beekeeper. Nineteen-sixteen was the year Roy Weaver became a professional beekeeper. It was also the year he married a "certain black-haired neighbor girl"—Lela Binford.

Getting started was difficult, as bees are dependent on climate and crops. In 1917, a late frost hurt the crops. The prospects for beekeeping in Lynn Grove looked grim. Being a beekeeper and a farmer, Mr. Weaver was hit doubly hard. Lela and he were forced to leave Lynn Grove and seek employment with a large honey producer in El Paso County. This was a pattern the Weavers were to follow until their business finally took hold—packing up their four children in their Model T and searching for work with large commercial honey producers.

It wasn't until the fall of 1926 that Roy Weaver's luck changed. In that year, rainy weather and new customers combined to help the bee business. A Mr. Graham, a large package bee shipper, visited the Weavers and persuaded them to produce queen bees. To sweeten the pot, Mr. Graham guaranteed to buy at least 1000 queens a year. He was true to his word and bought more than the 1000 queens he'd promised. Another customer, Mr. Burleson of Waxahachie, also bought queens. These first "queen" customers helped in the early years as Mr. Weaver was building his business. (Both Graham and Burleson remained faithful customers throughout the years, and Weaver Apiaries still sells queen bees to the Burlesons.)

It was at this stage that Mr. Weaver devoted his full time to queen bee production since the bees were outproducing and making more money than the farm. Mr. Weaver kept a few cows as souvenirs from the farm. Years later when he stopped milking cows altogether and bought the milk at the store like everybody else, he said he felt funny buying milk, as though he were committing a sin. He still keeps some cattle on his land today.

In 1929, Mr. Weaver went into partnership with his brother, Howard. They were partners until the end of the second World War. The Weaver brothers, Roy and Howard raised two races of queens—Italian and Caucasian. Roy Weaver describes what must be one of the gentlest business splits in history.

"I took the Italians and formed Weaver Apairies with two of my sons, and Howard took the Caucasians and formed Howard Weaver and Sons with his two sons." In this way the customers were automatically divided, and there were no problems of brotherly competition. Both apiaries are within a few miles of each other, south of Navasota. A third brother, now deceased, produced honey in Alto, Texas. Mr. Weaver remarks that "there are few, if any, post offices that have had as many queen bees mailed from it as Navasota, Texas has had."

Weaver Apiaries and Weaver and Sons went into queen bee production in a big way, becoming the largest queen bee producers in the world. Weaver Apiaries expanded, producing not only the dark and hardy Italian variety, but Starline Hybrid and Buckfast Queens. Weaver Apiaries is the only licensed producer of the Buckfast variety in North America. This bee was developed by the world-renowned Brother Adam of Buckfast Abbey, Devon, England, who received the order of the British Empire from Queen Elizabeth in 1974 in London for his work with bees. Brother Adam traveled over 100,000 miles, going to such remote places as the "back country" of Turkey, Russia and northern Africa, in search of a better race of bees.

With the largest of anything in the world, you would expect omnipresent machinery, assembly lines of remote employees, and the boss—cigar in mouth, ulcer in stomach—up above it all. (No such creature exists at Weaver Apiaries.) For while Mr. Weaver is in partnership with his sons and grandson, he is also in partnership with the bees. The bees keep beekeepers honest. Mr. Weaver takes his cues from them, pacing the business to the bees' business. He has been faithful to his origins. Large cannot be equated with impersonal. The word commercial has no sting with him. He treats neither the bees nor his workers impersonally, respecting them both, sharing with both.

In commercial enterprises some people get stung by bees because they're involved in a more complex form of bee production and treat the bees more roughly, almost like objects to be hurried through processes. Bees become less important than their by-product, honey. These large commercial beekeepers wear gloves and veils. Mr. Weaver himself prefers not to wear gloves and veils because he does not handle the bees roughly. He respects them and knows not to cross in front of the entrance to their hives. He believes in not bothering the bees, or frightening them or making them angry. But Mr. Weaver does have bee veils for visitors and other amateurs. He also uses a bee smoker, a tin smoke maker with a bellows. The shrouds of smoke calm the bees so he can touch them.

There is something almost religious about him walking among his hives. He pulls out a wooden frame of beeswax which is smothered with a thick coat of bees with pollen on their legs. The bees brush gently against his fingers, too busy working to take notice. Mr. Weaver knows the moods of his bees and allows for their irritability when the barometer falls, or when truckloads of bees, brought in from out-apiaries, mix with the regulars. He listens to their buzzing and can tell from the shift in sound how they're feeling. "When they're angry, they cuss." But as Mr. Weaver walks among them, they seem to calm down and his sure hands, touching his wife's vulnerable face, is better than a veil in keeping the bees away.

"You know," he says, "if you fool with folks, sooner or later, they'll sting you and it'll hurt for years. If a bee stings, it'll nettle, but then it goes away—no ill feelings." To Mr. Weaver, bees are not bad. There's even hope for the so-called "killer bees" from Brazil. "Personally we're not worried. This very bee for many years has been in Africa and it's a good honey gatherer. It's also true that not only with bees, but with any other insects, and presumably with man, you can change the characteristics by the breeding process."

As he passes a small swarm of bees in an old wall, someone asks him why he doesn't give them a hive, a real pre-fab home. He looks at the bees who are working hard on a February morning and says, "They have a happy home. They're like some folks who don't want urban renewal. Maybe they don't want to be relocated." (Maybe beekeepers should become mayors.)

Mr. Weaver treats bees according to the Golden Rule. Any allegations that beekeepers rob the poor bees of their honey are quickly dismissed by this bee guardian. "We don't rob the bees. The beekeeper takes care of the bees, and the bees, in turn, give him the surplus they do not need. A good beekeeper only harvests the "top half" of the hive. We leave them plenty of food and, if the bees run out, we feed them in winter."

In the same way, Mr. Weaver takes care of his employees, keeping them warm in winter as well as summer, giving them good country

Bees are marvelous creatures. So, too, are beekeepers.

(photos by Mary Sherwood)

wages. He has structured his business so as to accommodate a year-round labor force of some eight to nine people. Mr. Weaver's hiring practices reflect the same philosophy he applies to the breeding of bees—he breeds for character, not color. In the spring he hires additional employees to help collect the queen bees and ship them to all parts of the U.S. and world. To maintain that year-round staff, he has made the business almost self-sufficient. For example, although he buys the parts for the queen bee and package bee shipping crates, the crates are assembled on the premises.

The same workers perform a multitude of duties. They learn the details of beekeeping and some become quite expert in those details. The women remove the larvae from the comb that is taken from the breeder queen, and "graft" (transfer) it into queen cell cups. The transfer has to be done fast or the small larvae will dry out. The surplus queens cells will be given to starter colonies. "If we leave too many queen cells in the hive, the bees will get to thinking, 'Well, shucks, we don't need all those queens,' and they'll stop feeding some of them."

The women also put the finished queen cells into the mating nuclei and cage young laying queens for shipment. In a season, there are about 1200 queen cells started a day. There is a special tool that is sold to take the larvae out and graft it into the queen cell cups. Mr. Weaver and his workers, however, prefer tools that they make out of crooked sticks.

Mr. Weaver gets genuine pleasure from working with his employees, watching them learn and master the different skills. Since the workers do a variety of jobs, their interest is maintained. It's not surprising that his staff is dedicated and some have been there twenty to thirty years.

Aside from his regular workers, there are usually people who work from a week to a season to try to break into beekeeping. Small beekeepers and big beekeepers alike have worked at the apiaries. The manager of the biggest honey production operation in Mexico stayed with Mr. Weaver a week or two. A boy from England, whose father was the largest honey packer in that country, visited and learned. A man from Honduras was sponsored by a local Hondurian bank that was trying to encourage small farmers to keep a few hives. The Canadian government sent some Indians from Manitoba to Mexico to learn about bees. En route, they stopped at the Weavers where they were entertained and "educated" for a while. Into the melting honey pot go Rumanians, Mexicans, Englishmen, El Salvadorians.

Mr. Weaver is a very good teacher, sharing his years of experience. "We have no secrets and, if we can help a person, we try to." He and his sons write for bee journals and publish leaflets that are education-oriented. In the fliers he sends out to prospective customers, he recommends that beginners read certain books. It's almost as if he wants to find good homes for his bees. "It is important that you have your beehive all assembled and ready for the installation of the bees before your package arrives. It is also important that you have a bee smoker, bee veil and hive tool and know how to use them."

Mr. Weaver is a real matchmaker between men and bees. His sons laugh and tease him saying, "We can always tell when Dad likes a young man, he tries to talk him into becoming a beekeeper." (Same as his Uncle Walter did with his own father.)

The part of the business that you can see from Mr. Weaver's house is only the tip of the beehive. Just as you could not expect to see the whole of a ranch from standing on the ranch house porch, so too with Weaver Apiaries. Beekeepers, in fact, are like ranchers. They even have their own brand which goes on the hives. (W—for Weaver Apiaries.) "We move our bees just like you move your cattle on the range." A cattleman can overgraze his land, until there is little grass for his cattle. Beekeepers also can overstock their land, to their detriment. Too many bees in one field cannot find enough flowers that secrete nectar. Apiaries need to be about three or four miles apart so the bees can range freely.

In early June or the last of May, Weaver Apiaries move a part of their complete hives of bees to North Dakota where the bees can work the clover and alfalfa fields. Then in September, they move them back down to Texas. The Weavers also have an outfit in south Texas, around Jourdanton.

To the expert, honey tastes of the different flowers the bees have worked on. Mr. Weaver's honey is a delicious blend of cotton and wildflower. Some of his queens will be shipped to Norway where they will gather nectar from Rosslyng, the Norwegian national flower similar to heather. That honey will be different from the Navasota variety.

The bees most important service is not the honey they produce, however, but the pollination of crops. (Honey is a by-product of that good deed.) Fifty-odd crops are dependent upon insects for pollination. And so bees are an asset to any farmer's field.

Occasionally bees risk their lives in pollinating crops. Mr. Weaver remembers one tough assignment his bees had pollinating sunflower plants on a farm down in the Brazos River Bottom.

"The sunflower seeds were under contract with a seed firm that sent an entomologist to tell the farmer when and where to use the pesticides. Well, just as we got the bees in and they got going good, the seed people told the farmer he had to poison the plants. We tried to coordinate it. We told him what time of day to do it but still there was a heavy kill of bees." Those are problems that Zack and Uncle Walter didn't have. There are Federal laws which help make up some of the loss of bee kills from pesticides. Mr. Weaver in his understated fashion says only, "Pesticides are **serious**." It's because of pesticides that he moves some of his stock out to Lubbock, to the High Plains, to work on the cotton plants. There they do not poison them too much.

Mr. Weaver's bees are in demand all over the beekeeping world. Weaver Apiaries is a grassroots operation that has become international. They ship queens to Alaska (they have to buy swarms yearly), Sweden, Manitoba, Mexico, Central America, Peru, Greece, to name a few countries. Iran buys 5,000 or 6,000 queens a year from Weaver Apiaries, and Howard Weaver and Sons.

When queens travel, they travel in style. The queen shipping cage is a small block of Ponderosa pine, or other light wood, with three holes bored in the wood and wire screens over the holes. A candy made from honey and powdered sugar goes into one of the holes for the queens and bees to feed on enroute. The worker bees are put in with the queen to ventilate the cage and groom and feed the queen. The entourage is shipped by air mail or sometimes by air freight. The beekeeper uses these queens to increase his own colonies, to replace poor laying queens or to improve his stock.

The swarms of bees (package bees) are shipped in a wooden box with screen wire on two sides. These boxes hold about 8,000 to 12,000 bees; the size of the box depends on the order. The queen that is shipped with these bees is suspended in her own small cage in the larger cage that contains the swarm of bees. These packages of bees are fed while in transit by a can containing a mixture of sugar and water. The can, suspended in the cage, has very small holes in its sides. Beekeepers buy these packages of bees with the queen to start new colonies.

In early spring, trucks from the northern U.S. and Canada converge on Weaver Apiaries to buy the bees. Mr. Weaver knows how important it is to make delivery on approximate dates that beekeepers want their bees. In buying queen bees and swarms of bees, ten days difference can mean success or failure. Mr. Weaver can put himself in beekeepers' shoes because they are also his shoes. "If a truck comes down from Minnesota or Manitoba on the 5th, he doesn't want to spend money for motels." Meeting delivery dates is good business whether you're selling pants, cars, airplanes or bees. The reliability of Mr. Weaver and quality of his queens speak louder than any commercial blitz.

Though Mr. Weaver has made his home within 300 yards of the place where he was born, he also has traveled all over the beekeeping world, just like his bees. Most of these travels were in pursuit of beekeepers and bees. Friendly beekeepers have driven the Weavers over the countryside to visit apiaries. The Weavers see the beekeepers' homes, as well as their bees' homes, and experience teas and home cuisines. Mr. Weaver enjoys these visits more than any of the usual tourist attractions of Europe and England, preferring apiaries to abbeys (except for Buckfast Abbey, where the Buckfast strain of bees was created by Brother Adam.)

In England, the Weavers had a little international intrigue. Mr. Weaver picked up queen eggs of the Buckfast variety in England with the intention of artificially inseminating the virgin queens with drone sperm air mailed from England. At customs, he was unsure whether to declare the queen eggs secured in his Pan Am bag. (It was perfectly legal, if not a little strange, to bring the eggs across international boundaries.) Though Mr. Weaver successfully achieved his mission, back at Weaver Apiaries, a fungus attacked the queens in the process of inseminating and the queens died.

He found himself in another adventure in a street in Tegucigalpa, Honduras. He saw a store that had a whole lot of honey in wine bottles. Naturally, he went inside. Mr. Weaver enjoys the memory. "I could talk no Spanish and the shopkeeper could talk less English, but we had a great time." Through pantomime, fingers imitating little bees flying about, they conversed—two beekeepers brought together by the universal language of bees.

Mr. Weaver has lived in a peaceable kingdom for 84 years, yet he is not a naive man. His travels have exposed him to other rural lives and societies, and often he has been deeply affected by what he has seen. His sympathies project to the plight of some of the Third World countries where the worker only draws about $1 or $2 a day. The desperate poverty moved Mr. Weaver, especially when he saw bins of weevil-eaten rice the populations must eat.

He visited El Salvador for three weeks to help a man get into queen bee production. He found native El Salvadorians to be good workers, despite exploitive work policies. One young man was especially eager to learn and, with proper instructions and the opportunity to see the different operations, he would make a good queen breeder. Mr. Weaver wished that he could get him over here to give him that opportunity.

After he lost his wife of many years, Mr. Weaver traveled. It was while traveling that he met Jean. They were both touring on the "Delta Queen" on the Ohio River when the boat ran aground. It was towed to dry dock for repairs and the pasengers were turned loose on the countryside in sightseeing buses. Jean sat down in an empty seat next to Mr. Weaver. Several months later they were married.

Jean is a retired art teacher and practicing artist from upstate New York who has taught and studied in many places including Florence. After their marriage, Jean's first painting was a portrait of Mr. Weaver. Together they share interests and energies in gardening, taking care of many shrubs, trees, flowers and vegetables that grow in their yard. They re-finish old furniture in their home, including an old cupboard made by Roy's father. Bees figure into the motif of the inside of the house, as well as the outside, with journals, bee knicknacks, and golden yellow walls. Handmade and fired leaves, modeled from ten local Texas leaves, decorate the tiled table made by Roy and Jean. He makes frames of old wood for her paintings. His first frame was made for her painting of their local church. Since then he has made six more frames.

They also love to travel and have visited Norwegian fiords, and Mexican ruins. When they come home, along with the snap shots, they also have the seeds for more of Jean's fine paintings. Their house is incandescent with lightness and her pictures of the Texas countryside, old churches, Grimes County Courthouse and European arthitecture. And, now, reflecting her new life in Navasota, Jean has drawn the Queen, Drone and Worker Bees. Mr. Weaver is especially proud of her portrait of bees.

Who are these wonderful creatures, bees, that men would devote their whole lives to breeding better ones and collecting their works? Mr. Weaver has been in the bee business since he was a small boy and he can still say, "My interest has never died. I still keep learning new things about bees every day." Perhaps that's why he wears his 84 years so gracefully.

Familiarity does not breed contempt, but contentment. Mr. Weaver is filled with a sense of wonder about his bees. "A hive of bees is quite marvelous really. When man started air conditioning a few years ago we had a tendency to pat ourselves on our heads and say, 'Look how smart we are. We can control the temperature.' Well, the bees have been doing the same thing for millions of years, very much like man does it.

"A colony of bees stations guard bees and ventillating bees at the entrance of the hive. They fan their wings to suck in currents of air. Other bees stationed in different sections of the hive fan their wings to carry the current of air all over the hive and finally out the corner of the entrance. In the spring of the year, especially when they're producing large quantities of honey that have to be cured or "ripened," a great many bees spend most of the night fanning with their wings as hard as they can."

When it's hot, bees get water and store it on top of the comb. The water evaporates and helps reduce the temperature. It might be 120 degrees on the top outside of the comb. Just one inch below inside the honey comb, the temperature is not higher than 96.

Likewise bees know how to keep each other warm. The queens start laying in February when the temperature in some areas might be zero. Then the bees form a tight cluster with the queen in the center. The muscular action within the cluster gets the temperature up to 92 degrees, so the queen and swarms can survive to produce more bees. The bees on the outside of the cluster might get pretty cold and eventually they'll work their way into the warmer regions and other bees will take their place on the front line.

Mr. Weaver has learned these many years to feel as a bee would feel and put himself in a bee's wings and hive. His ultimate tribute to bees is Buzzy, the heroine of his children's story. Buzzy is Mr. Weaver's biography of a bee. Under the guise of a children's story, he reveals the intense and delicate life of a bee.

Buzzy is born, waking up in a very dark cradle in the hive.

"Buzzy found that she had six legs and by twisting and turning she could do a very good job of smoothing out the very short hair or fuzz that was on parts of her. The next thing Buzzy knew, there was another little bee helping her. How good it felt when this helper gently brushed her all over. Buzzy found that this new friend was really a little sister of hers. She said her name was Flighty."

Flighty shows Buzzy the ropes—how to eat from the waxen cell filled to the brim with golden honey (a kind of cookie jar), and how to perform the various jobs in the hive.

Bees have a wonderful homing instinct that's very accurate. The young bee when she first comes out to fly, circles around many times and locates objects in relation to her hive before going out for field work. Flighty warns Buzzy to look carefully since the bee yard has a great many white houses sitting in long rows, and they almost all look alike.

Bees, it is believed, have a method of communication. They have scout bees that dance when they find a new source of honey or pollen.

The dance tells other bees which way to go in relation to the sun and about how far. Presumably, if it's just a short distance they make a round dance. When Buzzy finally takes her first field flight, she flies due south because the scout bees, through their dance, have told them the direction to go—by running along a straight line on the combs in the hive and also by the number of times they "wagged" their tails.

Mr. Weaver's bees seem to like their lodgings at Weaver Apiairies. He doesn't have too many escape-bees. He doesn't overcrowd them and anticipates when a hive is getting too large. Then he divides them, making a new hive. Bees wouldn't let themselves get stuffed together in slum conditions anyway. "When a hive swarms it has become overpopulated. A great many bees confined to a small place become dissatisfied. Unlike people in our society where the young pick up and leave, in bee society, it's the old queen who takes off with the adult working force of bees. And the young bees stay put and take over the old hive."

When bees do swarm, they gather on a limb of a tree, while the scout bees locate new homes. Before they leave, every bee fills up its honey sac with honey provisions for the journey. Then the whole swarm flies off in a circular motion, the queen in the center.

Mr. Weaver and his bees cooperate with each other. Bees definitely have a good effect on beekeepers, keeping them temperate. (Bees hate the smell of alcohol.) Of more importance, watching bees and their society inspires a love of nature and its perfect harmony. In a reverse of anthropomorphism, Mr. Weaver seems to ascribe bee traits to Man, presuming that Man could be as caring and sensible as bees, thereby giving Man the benefit of the doubt.

The credit for Mr. Weaver's character and philosophy, however, cannot go to the bees alone. The continuity of location and people and roots has produced a man of rare qualities and serenity in Mr. Weaver. The church that his father helped build in 1889 is the same church where Mr. Weaver taught Sunday school for 58 years. The fields where his father's bees worked, his own bees work.

Mr. Weaver is a modern man in an old setting. He laments the evolution of natural man into commercial man. "The tragic thing is that commercial man, he gets so wrapped up in what we call 'success' that he doesn't take time to learn as much as he should."

Mr. Weaver has paper certificates that show he's reached the top of his profession. He's been President of the Texas State Beekeepers Association and the Southern States Beekeepers Federation. But even without their certification, Mr. Weaver is special. He has taken the time every day of his life to learn and has shared that learning as one would a fish, a loaf of bread, or a jar of honey, inviting others to join him.

They were a team, working together, supporting each other.   *(photo courtesy Haskill Harelik)*

Yes, We Have Some Bananas

by Donna Bearden

In 1909, 1400 immigrants boarded a ship bound for America. Among them was a young Russian lad, 19 years old and eagerly looking forward to new opportunities.

The trip was a grueling one, lasting 24 days. Even today, he almost gets seasick as he recalls the mass of people living in cramped quarters, sleeping on triple bunks and swaying, swaying with the ocean.

It was a long trip and he had time to reflect on his life and what had occurred to bring him to this point.

His parents had wanted him to be a school teacher—his father was a teacher. But he was bashful and small of stature. School teachers needed to at least feign authority—he felt none. He tried though, for two years he tried to fit that mold, but it was no use. He wasn't cut out to be a school teacher. He had also tried blacksmithing for awhile, but that life was not for him either.

From the beginning he seemed to know himself, his strengths and his limitations. He accepted life as it came to him, and it came—the opportunities arose and he recognized them.

Like when he was reading the Torah for services in a small Russian village. He was very young to read the Torah, but there he was. He stayed in the village and taught the Jewish children. It was there that he met Matley Paley. With her dark hair, fair skin and blue eyes, she was the most beautiful girl he had ever seen.

He soon shared with her his studies, how he was learning about democracy and how he read that America was accepting Russian immigrants. It wasn't long until he asked if she would like to go to America when he could make enough money to send for her. And she promised to wait as long as it would take.

His parents had trouble understanding why he wanted to leave his homeland, his family, his friends. But he knew himself and he knew there was little future for him if he stayed in Russia.

And so his parents agreed—their son would go to America. They sold their little home to pay for his passage. He, his brother, his sister and her husband and baby boarded a ship bound for America. And now here he was, thinking of home, thinking of Matley, thinking of America, looking to the future.

At last they landed in Galveston. Haskell Harelik was excited to begin a new life, to be an American. It didn't matter what job. The authorities in Galveston interviewed the immigrants, trying to help locate jobs according to their skills. Harelik, who could speak no English, indicated he had some experience with blacksmithing. Sorry, no need for more blacksmiths—would he like to sell bananas? It didn't matter—anything! He wanted to be an American.

And so it was that he became a banana peddler. Based in Dublin, he would travel to Hamilton in a mule-drawn wagon loaded with fresh bananas. He stopped on the town square, right in front of the bank, opened the wagon to display his produce and hollered one of his first English words, "Bananas!"

To his amazement, people flocked to the wagon and among them were some folks speaking German, one of the four languages he could understand and speak. He lost no time inquiring where they were from and if they would help him with his English.

They lived in a small settlement about eight miles from Hamilton. Someone from the community came to town almost every day. They promised to spread the word about the fresh bananas and the young man who needed help with his English.

Harelik sold out his bananas so quickly and met so many people who wanted to help him, that he returned to Hamilton often.

Every day, when his friends came to the wagon, he would ask how to say this or that in English. He would write it down, in his own peculiar way, in a little black notebook. At night, he would lay on his cot and repeat the words over and over until he had them committed to memory.

All went well until one day, when he drove up hollering "Bananas!" so the people would come to buy, the town's banker was waiting for him.

The banker told him that he could no longer sell bananas on the square. The young immigrant was stunned. He was learning English, making friends, working hard and saving every penny to send home so his parents and his sweetheart could join him in his new country.

The banker, Ed Perry, was also the mayor. He explained that the grocers were complaining because the townspeople preferred to buy bananas from the peddler for 15 cents a dozen instead of from the stores for a nickel a piece.

But the banker went on to say that at the same time the decision was made not to allow peddling on the street, a decision was made to close down the saloons. So now there would be plenty of empty buildings and Harelik could have his pick. He could live in the back and open a store in the front. He could display his bananas in the window.

The banker also knew a fruit wholesaler from Waco and would arrange for Harelik to meet him. Still grappling with English and with little knowledge of business, Harelik agreed.

"I don't know what he noticed about me, but bankers deal with people. They can always size a person up and make up their own minds."

The town was growing and the banker was looking ahead. Somehow he sensed that Harelik, the young banana peddler, who talked in broken English and pantomime had bigger things in store. And the banker had the means and the desire to help.

Harelik cleaned his shop and displayed his bananas in the window. The fruit wholesaler showed up the following Wednesday and explained his operation. He would start him out slow, a box of apples, a half box of oranges, one crate of grapes, etc., and he'd be back in a week to see how things were going. The fruit would arrive the next morning by rail. The next morning Harelik watched the fruit being unloaded. "I could hardly wait to bring it into the house and open up each box. I was glad, I was happy, and I began to polish up everything so it would look better to the eye. I had a full window with everything displayed in it.''

Within two hours after it arrived on the train, Harelik had sold out his entire stock. "If I could have spoken English better, I could have gotten in touch with the wholesaler and told him to send more."

As it was, all he could do was close the store, deposit the money and wait for a week.

He doubled his order, then tripled it. Then one day the salesman said he could supply other things, chewing tobacco, snuff, sardines . . . The salesman would explain as best he could what the different items were and agreed to take back anything Harelik didn't sell.

But Harelik sold! He continued to expand, to learn, to study, and to save his money. Within two years he had saved enough to send for his parents and his brother. It took two more years before he could send for his sweetheart. Finally he paid for her passage and went to Galveston to meet her boat. It was a happy reunion and they were married in 1912. At first, the whole family lived together and worked together in the storehouse.

The whole family lived together and worked together in the store-house.   *(photo courtesy Haskill Harelik)*

Harelik's business continued to grow by leaps and bounds. He even became a wholesaler, providing groceries for small outlying stores.

Harelik's family had begun to grow also. He now had three sons who were each assigned chores at the store. Matley had a small kitchen in the back of the store and the boys would rush over from school at lunchtime. They grew up in the store. At night when the boys would study, Haskell and Matley worked on their language, practicing over and over to erase the traces of accents.

In those days, the farmers came to town in their wagons once a month to buy supplies that would have to last until the next trip to town. Most staples came in 100 pound sacks—flour, sugar, salt, etc. The strain of 15 years of loading wagons finally caught up with Harelik and the doctor told him that, for the sake of his back, he would have to quit the grocery business.

Just about that time, he heard of a Jewish widow in Gatesville who wanted to sell her late husband's dry goods store. But before he checked it out, he went to see his now-good-friend, the banker.

The banker advised him to go to Gatesville and look over the situation. If his judgement told him to buy, he could sign a check on the bank and it would be honored, whatever the amount.

So once again Harelik found himself in a position of not really knowing much about the business but having confidence in himself to make the best of the situation.

He bought the store and its contents for $10,000. Right off he decided to have a sale. He advertised and in a few days opened for business. He had sold about $800 worth of merchandise when a man came in wanting to buy the whole store. Harelik had no desire to leave Hamilton and readily agreed to sell the store for $15,000. He returned on the train "$5,800 to the good." First stop was at the bank to repay his loan.

The short experience was enough to open up a new avenue for Harelik. He bought a small shoe store across the street from the grocery store and soon expanded it into a dry goods store.

With the help of his parents and his wife, who was "my eyes and my hearing," Harelik's business grew. He learned about men's furnishings and she became the women's ready-to-wear buyer. She was keen on what people liked. She kept a notebook on sizes and color and style preferences, and bought to suit her customers.

The Hareliks were natural salesmen and had a built-in business sense that became sharper through the years. They had learned to waste nothing. If no one was in the store, the lights remained off. When a customer entered, the lights were turned on.

In his early days in America, Harelik's diet consisted of bananas, crackers and sometimes a can of sardines. As he traveled through the countryside, he was offered hospitality, a bed for the night and a good meal or two. Even after his business was established, his eating habits remained flexible. He rarely ate breakfast with the family. Farmers are early risers and Harelik felt he had to accommodate them by opening the store at 6:30. Harelik had seen some lean times and every penny counted. He often told his sons that "It's not really what you earn but

(photo by Donna Bearden)

what you save that counts." And he tried to save a little of anything he earned. If he earned a dollar, he might save a nickel.

Perhaps it was his ability to listen to people, to put them at ease that made him successful. Perhaps it was his perserverance. Maybe his ability to remember names and faces made him a trusted friend. Even the many families with eight or ten children—he knew them personally, fit their shoes, helped them select clothes and called each by name. Perhaps it was his wife, "his eyes, his hearing," for they were really a team, working together, supporting each other. And maybe it was partially his humbleness. He wasn't afraid to risk, to try, to ask questions when a lesser man might not.

The Harelik's three sons all attended the University of Texas, which Haskell is proud of. "They got their college education—more than I ever did. I managed to run my business. I finally learned how to read and write (English), and maybe I misspelled my words—I had to be careful. If there was anything I didn't know, I would ask somebody. And they understood what I wanted when I was selling my merchandise."

Harelik's department store in Hamilton is still there and is now run by one of his sons. The other sons own and manage stores in Comanche and Waco. They each learned the business first-hand as they were growing up. They each inherited some of that in-born business sense and skill of their parents, that confidence that enabled the young immigrants from Russia to make their way in a strange, new land—a way that started with a mule-drawn wagon and a cry, "Bananas! Fresh Bananas!"

Natural Resources

by Jamie Frucht

Joseph VanderStucken of Sonora wants to be anonymous. The expectation of an interview throws him into misery. Plaques and commendations are not to his liking. But doing good deeds is. Being charitable, open and friendly are easy for him. Joseph VanderStucken is a failure as an anonymous man.

And he's out of luck with the name VanderStucken. Maybe a Smith or Jones could recede in the roll call of names, but VanderStucken sticks to the tongue like toffee.

Someone who wants to be anonymous shouldn't be so personable. He has a handsome face that beams a lot, responding to his own inner mirth. His coloring is of a man who loves the out-of-doors. He barely tolerates rooms. His clothes and posture are well-to-do.

Like a cow who is constantly chewing the cud, Mr. VanderStucken loves to chew on stray facts, ideas and situations. As a child in Sonora, part of his education came from listening to people talk on the party line. "You knew every neighbor, all their children's names, their dogs' names, the chickens' names. It was interesting, those party lines."

His body may be seated one place but his mind can be grazing on an amusing riddle. This tendency to enjoy himself is what made his one year of college seem very long. "I would have been a good student if there hadn't been windows."

What did he learn in college? "I studied how to have a good disposition." His brand of sarcasm, so light and fluffy, has no bitterness to it, just tossed aside truths.

He's partial to the country he lives in, though you feel he could adapt to any land. He loves the west and its climate that continually surprises and evades forecasting. He doesn't even like weather to be predictable. "Anything you know for certain isn't worth a hoot. Wouldn't it be monotonous to wake up in the morning and know exactly what to expect. A cloud coming in the west and hearing the thunder—that's where you get your kicks."

He lives on the outskirts of Sonora. His house is hidden in downhill brush. Only the cynesio bushes (his favorite shrub) give a clue that human hands have sparred with the brush to give it a little organization. The house itself is spacious and more than comfortable. He lives with his wife Mabel and their daughter Jan, a drama major at San Angelo State University. They have another daughter, Mrs. James (Jo Bess) Jackson, a grandson Joseph and a granddaughter Elizabeth.

Mabel, too, prefers the shade to the limelight. But here again they're out of luck. Both come from distinguished families. Mabel is from the Mears family of Menard. The bridge over the San Saba River at Menard was dedicated to Mabel's father, Ed L. Mears, a pioneer citizen and civic leader. In the late 1800's, Mother Mears figured prominently in the life of Menard. She had four brothers, the Seiker

Brothers, all Texas Rangers—one a colonel, one a captain, and one who died while in Ranger service. Mabel's grandmother brought the first piano to Menard and taught music for 30 years. She was also principal of the public school. Her husband was the sheriff and tax collector. Mother Mears assisted him by preparing the tax rolls.

Mr. VanderStucken was born in Sonora on February 15, 1901. His parents had the delightful idea to marry at the very last minute of the last night of the century. Their timing was off by a few days, but they did other things to distinguish themselves.

Joseph's father was a pioneer merchant. He came to Sonora in 1890 and established a general mercantile store made up of five stores: dry goods, hardware, groceries, furniture, and a big red barn in back housing the feed store.

"My father successfully fought that store for 55 years. I fought it until I realized I belonged in the country. The store was a family handed-down thing that I just wasn't cut out for." He was in and out of the store, mostly out.

Understanding must run in the family since that is one of Joseph's outstanding qualities. He says of a father's relationship to his children: "A father's first interest in any child is seeing him happy and doing something half-way honest." Luckily, his father saw it that way. He realized that Joseph was not happy with the store and one day said to him, "Son, why are you fooling with that store? Why don't you sell it?" Next morning Joseph was looking for a buyer.

He was now free to do what he really wanted to do—ranch. "What I loved most was the land and productivity and the plants and not the store." His uncle had homesteaded four sections of land at a time when the State was encouraging railroads and settlers by giving land grants. Joseph, as a child, had loved to stay on his uncle's ranch.

Now on the Fourth of July, 1923, he bought his ranch which occupied 27 sections (a section being a square mile). He soon discovered that you get lonesome out there in that country with no one to make hot biscuits and beans. There were also 13 gates and a crooked road to contend with. "If you were by yourself, you had to get out 26 times. Fifty-two times in all for the coming and going." He figured out that if you were with someone you only had to get out half as many times. He needed a gate-opener. "Then I went to stirring around and found Mabel."

This is exaggerated (not the gates, but how he found his wife.) They had actually grown up together. Their parents would go to dances where it was the custom to take quilts along to put the babies on. Mabel recalls, "While they danced, we kicked. Then as we got older, we danced and they kicked." Even though Joseph no longer has 13 gates to open, he still has kept Mabel. The VanderStuckens recently celebrated their 50th wedding anniversary.

It was during their courtship that a horse rolled over on Joseph. For a week, he lay unconscious. But Joseph tends to look on the bright side of all experiences. "Anything I do off-base, or foolish, or sure I shouldn't do, well, I just say, 'Remember that horse that fell on me. I'm not right.'"

Mr. VanderStucken's life and history have to include the topography of the land where his ranch is located. Because when a man has wrestled with the land, spending his waking hours on it, and most of his dreams thrown to it, that land is more than property. It's life itself.

The ranch is situated on the Edwards Plateau which occupies the south-central portion of the state. Undulating low hills laced with rivers, some the dimension of streams, flow or don't flow. Draws, like sandy fossils of the rivers, wait for the average rainfall to come. The Devil's River, Llano, San Saba and others wind through the valleys. The country is diversified and takes combination grazing of sheep, goats and cattle. Worlds and worlds of windmills stand tall as they draw the water out of the land and into human plans.

While Mr. VanderStucken's life began in 1901, the land's began millions of years before. Mr. VanderStucken's vision is larger than his own chronology. He imagines what his land looked like hundreds of years before. He's no historian and yet he can tell you about the history of the soil, of the trees, of the grasses, and of the weeds. "Oh we must have had a wonderful land when it was virgin, we can't conceive of it."

Then the hills were covered with grass. The brush was restricted to the draws. Some brush species cowered around the large live oak trees but were unable to compete with the thriving grasses. Palatable perennial forbs were common.

All this changed when intensive livestock grazing came to the Edwards Plateau in the late 1800's and early 1900's. The livestock ate the best grasses. With the good grasses denuded and severely weakened, inferior grasses came in to take their place. The brush too came in and festered. Previously, scattered trees had sent acorns, mesquite seeds and cedar berries into the heavy tufts of grass, only to be trampled down or rotted. But with the grass grazed off the land, these seeds had a chance. Poor grasses, curly mesquite, green sprangletop, fall wintergrass, hairy grama, slim tridens (which sound like villians in a Walt Disney movie) sprung up where good grasses had been.

The severe drought of 1917-1918 was the death blow to many of the surviving good grasses. They could not recover. Quickly, the invaders—live oak, cedar, prickly pear, bitterweed and annuals spread out competing for precious moisture. While there's a trace of everything that grew once, the numbers have dwindled. Some plants have gone for keeps, especially the delicate flowering ones. But it's the deep-rooted perennials that make a ranch land.

Mr. VanderStucken's ranch was poor land compared to what it had been a hundred years before. He knows this because the people who had had it before him had grazed 10,000 sheep and goats and 1000 head of cattle. Such numbers couldn't live on the land now without coming down with a severe case of "hollow belly."

Mr. VanderStucken's vision of the gradual processes of soil and vegetation allows him to be understanding. There is no rancor against those who might have overstocked the land and left him a used-up legacy. "It's no disgrace to anybody what happened. In the early days, why should anyone have thought about conservation. The settlers would just ruin one pasture, then move on. They'd deplete it, burn it off, graze it down, but there'd always be another pasture further west. The grass was always greener up ahead. But then they hit the Pacific coast and started to bounce back."

Now the new settlers, such as Mr. VanderStucken, are trying to half-restore the land to its original productivity and vitality. "But it can't ever be done, it can't be put back the way it was when the Indians had it, because it was too abused. But people who abused it shouldn't be accused because we would have done the same thing."

Mr. VanderStucken's problems have been the problems of his land. His problems are not personal, but endemic to the Edwards Plateau. The land has declined to a rating of poor to fair condition. Grass, before the overgrazing, thrived with 15 foot roots. The fact that the roots and grasses have dwindled has a great bearing on the effects of drought.

You wouldn't think drought could be subjective, but according to Mr. VanderStucken, drought conditions for one man might be enough rain for another and his livestock to get by on. If the land isn't overstocked and the grass is deep rooted, you can go fishing during drought and survive. He also thinks drought, like everything else, has some redeeming features. Drought tends to kill the invading trees and might be nature's way of restoring balance. Mr. VanderStucken has weathered the droughts. He says, "If you're lucky, most anything will do for brains." But his success cannot be attributed solely to luck. Good grassland management is a more plausible reason.

Mr. VanderStucken's worst enemy has been bitterweed, the great villian of sheepmen and sheep alike. Bitterweed is worse than a wolf in sheep's clothing. It has a bitter smell that lingers on the hands for days, a poison that is cumulatively lethal, and a pretty yellow flower. When they were first married, Mr. VanderStucken almost ran off his wife because she innocently put bitterweed in a rose bowl for a table decoration.

Bitterweed comes up in the fall with the rains. Its effect is seen about Christmas. Mr. VanderStucken recalls, "Nothing in anybody's lifetime has ruined as many Christmas dinners as bitterweed has mine." He and his wife would be driving along to a Christmas dinner and see a line of sheep crossing the ranch road. Mrs. VanderStucken would say hopefully, "Well, Honey, those sheep look fine." Mr. VanderStucken would answer knowingly, "Just wait till the last few come by." And sure enough, as the stragglers would file by, they'd be doing the "bitterweed flop" with the last one hitting the bar ditch and falling over. The "bitterweed flop" usually ends in death.

Like everything else, Mr. VanderStucken can see some vague benefit to bitterweed. "If you've got a lot of animals and one gets sick and bad and knocked out, your normal reaction is to get a vet; and if a vet isn't handy, then you worry and wonder what it is. If you have bitterweed, well that just solves all your problems cause you can say, 'Well that's bitterweed.' " He also thinks that if bitterweed weren't there, something worse might come along.

Despite the show of humor, Joseph has fought bitterweed. First, by observing it. He saw that it grew on southeast corners of large pastures where the sheep like to graze most intensively. To make it harder for the sheep to congregate in the bitterweed patches he cut live oak brush and piled it across the bitterweed's path. Then to confuse the bitterweed, he changed his fences, "throwing southeast corners in the north sides of other pastures."

The land itself gave him one of the important answers. He had a small cultivated field fenced off from the others. The fence kept getting destroyed by the rain running in the draws so he moved the fence back to where the rain couldn't take it. Because there were crops in the field, during the growing season that pasture was off limits to the animals—spring, summer and fall. That wasn't too much of a sacrifice as bitterweed was rampant there. When he retired the pasture, a remarkable thing happened. The grasses began to grow well. In the winter he let the sheep in in great numbers to graze on the dry forage from summer's growth. The fall rains had started the bitterweed germinating, but with so many sheep, not one could eat enough bitterweed seedlings to be serious. This deferred grazing became a winning strategy in the bitterweed battle.

He also tried to divert the sheep by hiding cotton seed cake in the tall grass. As sheep love cotton seed cake, they determinedly looked for that, ignoring the bitterweed. However, he had to give up this ploy because the grass was trampled by the foraging sheep.

Grassland management has been the key to his bitterweed control. The good grasses will triumph in the end, if you only give them a chance to thrive. The only trouble is all creatures, including sheep, are attracted to the good, so the good grasses get eaten first, leaving the bad to flourish. The bitterweed goes out if you rest the land and the better grasses have time to take hold.

His battle with bitterweed has been so successful that Mr. VanderStucken can no longer count that as his number one problem. That honor goes to the live oak invasion. He's trying to win that fight by enlisting the aid of goats. He gives them sprout detail for a few weeks at a time during the growing season. The emphasis is on 'few weeks at a time', for the goats eat so heartily that they devastate the grasses, till the solution becomes the problem.

Mr. VanderStucken is a natural conservationist. He's a self-made one with no technical background, but with worlds of experience on the ground floor of nature. You might say he's done all of the field work, but none of the academics. The academic community, however, has come to him and ranchers like him, to learn the home grown methods.

In 1939 the Extension Service of the Soil Conservation Service made a cooperative agreement to use his ranch for experiments to measure the quality and quantity of vegetation. A&M takes samples of the grasses to analyze them. (The livestock has been doing that for years, selecting the best grasses).

The "Experiment Station Boys," as Mr. VanderStucken likes to call them, can circulate information to the landowners. Working with local folks, the Experiment Station has collected tons of data, some never to be worked up, but the important findings have been published and disseminated. Ironically most of the worthwhile things have come from what landowners had found out on their own—the hard way.

Mr. VanderStucken practices all forms of conservation—soil, water plant, wildlife. He helped to found the Edwards Plateau Game and Wildlife Association. On his land he's "planted" bob-white quail. The word must have gotten around that the VanderStucken's give free room and board to wild things. Every evening on the bare pecan limbs, large shadows can be seen roosting. These are 70 wild turkeys that have adopted the VanderStucken's premises for awhile. Mabel encourages them by throwing corn, perhaps out of sentiment for she remembers how some of her tame Thanksgiving turkeys ran off with the wild ones before they could get to the table. Near the wild turkeys are 17 peacocks efficiently roosting in the covering of cypress boughs. One peacock was an accident, the rest were on purpose. After the first one landed, Mr. VanderStucken's daughter Jan bought 16 more to keep the lone peacock company.

In 1948, Mr. VanderStucken helped to organize the Edwards Plateau Soil Conservation District. He served as chairman of the district board of supervisors from 1948-1953. The Association of Texas Soil Conservation District Supervisors gave Mr. VanderStucken a big silver tray for his outstanding cooperation and work.

Despite sterling silver trays and offices held, Mr. VanderStucken scoffs at any big deal, singling him out. He says, "Everyone in Texas who depends on land, whether he be a beekeeper, farmer, rancher, or a fisherman with water rights, has got to be somewhat of a conservationist if he's to exist, and an unofficial member of the land use committee, or else he goes out of business."

This is not the same as advocating government control. Mr. VanderStucken says "When we're too many people and not enough land, a situation that we're approaching somewhere down the line, something will have to be done." While he doesn't think you can let folks be too unproductive with the land, he's sure that people don't want government telling them how many sheep, cattle, goats, or peacocks they can have.

He is not a rabid conservationist. "It was a gradual process downhill, taking hundreds of years, and it'll be a slow gradual process uphill." Mr. Vanderstucken, in his lifetime, in a small way, has contributed to the uphill process. Since he started practicing intensive grassland and livestock management, the ranch has improved from a rating of "poor to fair" to "fair to good"—meaning that 25 to 75 percent of the vegetation is good grass. Conservation is its own reward. The vitality of the grasses allowed him to stock more animals without resorting to supplemental feeding.

When Mr. VanderStucken first went down to his ranch in 1923 he made a promise to himself that after 35 years if he were economically able, he would slow down. He did, retiring 15 years ago. He leases 15 sections to his cousin who continues to practice good conservation measures. Mr. VanderStucken is still vice-president of the First National Bank of Sonora, which his father helped organize in 1900.

He hasn't deserted the out-of-doors, just changed his activity. He's an avid fisherman who retreats three days a week with a friend to Lake Amistad. He says gamely, "What fun would it be fishing alone—catch something and no one to hear you holler."

He also hasn't retired from being a kind and caring man. Mr. VanderStucken loves land so much. He likes to collect it, just small pieces. It doesn't matter what kind of land it is, just as long as it's used for the purposes it was made for. In 1963, he donated one of his small pieces of land in the heart of Nueces Canyon for a Girl Scout Camp. He was inspired to do this by his two girls who only got the dusty leftovers of the local boys' camp. "Only when it got so cock-eyed hot that boys wouldn't go anymore did they let the girls use it." The camp on Bullhead Creek, with two swimming holes and 200 acres of live oaks, is called JoJan Van Camp after his two daughters.

Mr. VanderStucken doesn't play favorites, helping the boys as much as the girls. He served as president of West Texas Boys Ranch (1965-66) and is a life member of the executive committee. He is also on the Boy Scout Board.

The VanderStuckens have a long record of service to their community. For many years, he served as Chairman of the Hospital Board. Mabel now is a member of the Hospital Board and is president of the Hospital Auxiliary and served on the Sonora School Board. The VanderStuckens donated a chapel to the local hospital in memory of their parents, Mr. and Mrs. Ed L. Mears, and Mr. and Mrs. E. F. VanderStucken. They are also active members of St. John's Episcopal Church. He has served as senior warden and has been on the vestry for many years. Mabel has been president of Women of the Church.

The only troublesome part about doing good deeds is having people notice and make a fuss. In 1975, Mr. VanderStucken was named outstanding senior citizen of Sutton County.

Joseph VanderStucken is into his 75th year, and just this year the land gave him another surprise. There's natural gas on his property. All of Sonora has had a natural gas flurry and is in the middle of a boom.

On top of his father's mercantile store was a silver tin sign with orange flourishes. The sign weighed heavily on the roofs of the stores, just as the stores weighed heavily on Joseph. After the stores were sold, it was quietly moved to the ranch. There it sits on the sloping ground—no merchandise anywhere around, only grasses and cedar, stones and weeds. Somehow, the sign is where it belongs, just as Mr. VanderStucken is where he belongs. He is a happy man.

Miracle Man

by Jamie Frucht

If Hollywood were casting a doctor to ride into the brush country in the early 1900's and treat the population on both sides of the border, they'd probably cast a tall, brave man, such as Gary Cooper. But the tall, brave man might wear out, whereas Dr. Gates is still going strong at 90 and showing no signs of subsiding.

'Apa' is the affectionate name thrust upon Dr. Gates by his grandchildren and great-grandchildren. They originally called him Opa, German endearment for grandpa, but during the war it subtly shifted to Apa, the Mexican pronunciation. Most citizens of Eagle Pass, lovingly and respectfully, call him Dr. Gates, though some of the youngest citizens call him Dr. Chiquito, acknowledging the fact that he is a short man. But Dr. Gates doesn't act his age; he doesn't act his size, either. And as one close friend said, "He sure is the biggest little man and most active man ever."

Ellis Franklin Gates was born February 6, 1886, on the Gates ranch near the town of Lytle in Atascosa County. He was one of nine children. Ellis went to school in Benton City. His father, Franklin, was a rancher. At an early age, Ellis began working on the ranch, learning just about all there is to know about cattle and horses.

It was on a trip to a nearby ranch, representing his father in a business meeting, that he met his future wife, Frances Adams. Though she was only 13 years old at the time, she later often said that she knew immediately it was Ellis she would marry someday. Her father, Walter Benjamin Adams, was a rancher and also the owner of Adams Mercantile ("We sell anything from ratskins to ranches"), as well as the Adams Bank and the Adams Cotton Gin in Devine, Texas. Against the backdrop of business between the two ranching families, there were many opportunities for Frances and Ellis to meet.

Ellis' father, Franklin, had great plans for his son to become a pharmacist. To that end, Franklin sent him to pharmacy school and bought him a drugstore. But Ellis, who knew his own mind, had greater plans for himself. He wanted to become a doctor. He never worked a day in that drug store and his father had to sell it. Ellis, on his own, with no blessings or income from his family, went to the University of Tennessee to pursue his medical career. He received his degree in 1908.

In that same year he and Frances were married. It would seem that Frances' young instincts were well founded, because these two remarkable people shared a beautiful marriage of love and respect for one another every day of their 55 years together. They had three children—two daughters, Susie and Frances, and a son, W.B., who died at seventeen in an attempt to rescue his sisters and father who, he thought, were trapped inside their burning house.

When they were first married, Dr. and Mrs. Gates moved to Aguas Calientes, Mexico. A United States mining company operating in

Aguas Calientes, having heard of the doctor's medical talents and his fluency in Spanish, invited him to practice there. They lived quite happily in Mexico for two years—until the Revolution began. Dr. Gates, who kept the hours of a local bandit, riding all over the countryside on house calls, found himself the target of an occasional potshot. The increasing danger made it impossible for them to remain in Mexico and so the couple returned to South Texas.

In 1917 Dr. Gates was conscripted for World War I and assigned as Regimental Commander of the hospital at Ft. Duncan in Eagle Pass. Ellis Gates was a doctor first, a military man not at all. But he played the part, putting his patients first. Military protocol ran a distant second. On the day before he was to report at Ft. Duncan, he went to San Antonio to be outfitted for the part of Regimental Commander and to catch the train to the post at Eagle Pass.

Waiting for his train to leave, he spent the afternoon walking around the city in his fine new pair of boots. As a result, he boarded the train that evening with a pair of very tired and sore feet. When he tried to remove the boots he discovered to his dismay that no amount of pulling and tugging, by him or the porter, could rid his aching feet of the boots. So the doctor slept with his boots on, using aspirin to grab a little fitful sleep between shrieks.

At 8 o'clock, on the morning of March 15, 1917, the train arrived in Eagle Pass, and Dr. Gates was driven by horse and buggy to Ft. Duncan. Outside camp headquarters he was met by a young man, Sgt. Harvey Pollay, who, in proper military form, asked, "Does the lieutenant want his baggage taken to his quarters?" The doctor is said to have replied, "To hell with the **lieutenant!** Let's take **me,** and get these damn boots off!" Pollay, by pouring warm soapy water into the boots, slowly managed to work them off. Dr Gates never forgot those boots or his friend Harvey Pollay. Many years later, when Harvey Pollay was an old man and quite ill, some say Dr. Gates kept him alive a year longer, just from sentiment (but mainly from skill).

The Army kept Dr. Gates until 1919. His pre-war plans had been to open an office in Laredo. But after two years in Eagle Pass, he and Frances had made many friends. The community needed another doctor, and by then the citizens knew Dr. Gates and didn't want him to leave. You might say he was conscripted by the citizens. But this time he willingly went into service, moving into town and setting up his first office. The people are still keeping him, not letting him go even now after 57 years of service as Doctor of Eagle Pass.

In 1919 when the Doctor set up practice, there was no hospital in Eagle Pass and much need for one. Dr. Gates was operating on kitchen tables. An older and much respected colleague, Dr. Evans, came to him one day and offered him a loan, saying, "I think I'll take a chance on you if you want to put up a little hospital." And so with borrowed money and some assistance from the local lumber company, Gates Hospital came into being. It was a small hospital, six or eight beds, with French doors which were left open in the Summertime. Screens and a skylight added to the openness of the surroundings. The operating room was truly an operating theater where people could come and watch through glass windows. Often they heard Dr. Gates singing "Sweet Adeline," or some other melody he could not suppress, as he worked joyfully. In his small hospital the Doctor performed surgery and, according to the townspeople, miracles.

From the day that Dr. and Mrs. Gates made the decision to stay and work in Eagle Pass, their lives and the life of the town have been joined. Many individual histories of the townspeople include Dr. Gates. Not only did he bring them into the world, but once they were here he kept them healthy. But the stories are more than medical records. They are histories of love, dedication and hard work. Some of the stories are "Dr. Gates" stories, some "Doc Gates" stories, some "Apa" stories—but whatever the name, elements of compassion and humor run throughout, despite often tragic circumstances of illness and pain.

One such story is set in those early days of Gates Hospital. A man was brought in whose leg was badly mangled in a drilling accident. There was little hope that the man could keep his leg, but Dr. Gates worked on it long hours, piecing it together like an organic puzzle. He told the man, "If your leg doesn't develop gangrene by morning, I think you'll be okay, but I can't promise how it will look." The grateful man replied, "Don't worry, Dr. Gates, I'll wear long pants." The man had no money but he walked out of the hospital on two working legs. Twenty-five years later, he sent the Doctor $30 which he had been gradually saving up all those years.

Another story involved a man called Nacho, who had worked from the time he was a boy for Dr. Gates. He did odd jobs—keeping the yard, feeding the doctor's hunting dogs, occassionally babysitting. One of his duties was sweeping up at the hospital. A patient in the hospital at the time had been terribly injured in an accident in which he was pulled through the six-inch space betwen the cab and tractor of a caterpillar tractor. His bones were crushed and much of his skin was just "peeled" away. The Doctor's efforts had kept him miraculously alive, but the patient was dressed in gauze from head to foot. That day, as Nacho was sweeping up, he noticed the poor fellow lying in his room. He looked him up and down, then approached his bed, leaned over, and said, "Que fue? (What happened) Futbol?"

Nacho got no answer from the injured man, who peered at him helplessly through red eyes. Many weeks later the Doctor's daughter, who was helping out at the hospital, heard strange sounds coming from the man's hospital bed. Very concerned and believing he must surely be dying, she went to the man's bedside to give whatever comfort she could. The man, with a pained smile on his face, looked up at her and said, "I've been waiting for weeks to laugh at that fellow who sweeps up—Football!"

People who were given an 80 percent chance to die, survived. As one of his nurses said, comforting a woman whose husband was being operated on, "Don't worry. He's got Dr. Gates and God on his side."

Dr. Gates has always displayed an amazing capacity for hard work that kept pace with his skill. In those earlier years he had simultaneous offices in Eagle Pass, in Piedras Negras, Mexico and in Quemado, Texas, in addition to the hospital. He was also the doctor for the county jail and the International Bridge doctor.

The Doctor, in fact, went wherever people were sick, believing that it is a doctor's obligation to go to sick people whenever necessary, rather than asking a sick person to come to him. Today, in a time when most doctors across the country won't go on house calls, Dr. Gates still does.

"House calls" doesn't adequately describe the conditions he had to work in. Behind warehouses, in shacks, or right out in the open, Dr. Gates tended the sick. Once some men called him from Carrizo Springs, where there was no doctor, and told him a friend of theirs was complaining of severe pains in his side. Dr. Gates, diagnosing it immediately as acute appendicitis, replied that he would come. He told the men to bring the patient and a cot and meet him halfway. When the two cars met, the men laid the patient on the cot beside the road and Dr. Gates took out his appendix then and there—and saved his life.

The Doctor's house calls were sometimes vigils. He once visited a dirt-poor family who lived in a small crowded shack. A girl of about sixteen had pneumonia and, although the child needed private care, the family couldn't afford a nurse and did not have a telehone to get word to the doctor. So every night Apa backed his car up to the child's window and slept on the seat, since there was no room for him in the overcrowded shack. The mother would knock at the window if the Doctor were needed. After two weeks of this, the child was sufficiently recovered for the Doctor to leave. The miracle was that Dr. Gates did not come down with pneumonia himself.

For his house calls, Dr. Gates' first transportation was a pair of sorrel horses hitched to a buckboard. One night he went out to assist with what he expected to be a routine birth. He thought he would get home early, but the baby had other plans. The ordeal dragged on all night until finally, shortly before dawn, the baby was born. The doctor went out and climbed onto his buckboard. He had trained his horses so well that as soon as he got them onto the road, he wrapped the reins around the brake and went to sleep and they took him home. Once there, they snorted and made a fuss to wake the Doctor up, for they were tired, too. He unhitched and fed them and then went in for a short sleep before morning.

Later he acquired a car, but this was not always an improvement. Cars need roads. A baby once decided to be born between a tornado and a rain storm. Dr Gates started out in his car and went as far as the road went—to the bank of a little stream which had swelled into a raging torrent. He navigated that in a boat. On the other side, the family had a mule waiting for him. Five miles later he arrived at their home, where he spent the whole night with his patient and delivered a fine baby. The Doctor's only complaint about the long night was the coffee the man gave him. "Worst coffee I ever tasted."

Feeling indebted to the Doctor, the patient's husband said, "I'm going to give you every cent I got." In spite of the Doctor's protests, the man reached into his pocket and brought out every cent he had—75 cents.

Dr. Gates is a would-be millionaire—that is, he would be a millionaire if he had collected even half his fees. But money has never been his motivation. Doctor Gates treats only one kind of people—sick people. He is not a greedy man. All are equal to him; one person is as good as another. People pay him what they can. Payment, when it came, was not always in cash. A cow tied to a palm tree in the doctor's front yard with a note around its neck was one fellow's way of paying the bill. Others gave baskets of spinach. A fee of fruit and vegetables was common. The Doctor would redistribute this food to poor families. He also gave away pharmaceutical samples to families who couldn't afford to buy medicine.

One family amassed a bill of $1,700. The man finally appeared and said, "Well, Dr. Gates, I've come to settle up with you. Here's $100 and you can come down to the ranch and pick out any horse you want. Take it or leave it." The Doctor agreed, much to the horror of his family, who thought he'd come out short in the bargain. Dr. Gates philosophically explained, "Now, I'd much rather have $100 and a real good horse than nothing at all, and that's exactly what I'd get."

The Doctor has more than a big heart though. He has skill and imagination. In the beginning of his practice, when his hospital facilities were minimal. he often had to improvise to make up for lack of equipment and personnel.

In one case, when a pregnant woman was brought into the hospital dead on arrival after a terrible car crash, the Doctor had to work fast. He laid her down on the table, opened her up, and took the child. The baby had to be put in an incubator, but there was none in the hospital. Dr. Gates fashioned a makeshift one out of hot bricks and hot water bottles. The baby lived and now has her own family.

Dr. Gates trained his wife and his daughter Frances to work as his nurses. There was always one registered nurse in charge, as well. Granddaughters helped with the clerical work.

The Doctor's favorite patients and biggest fans are children. He thrives on babies and vice versa. Just in his own brood he has ten grandchildren and fourteen great-grandchildren. You can spot him driving a jeep full of kids into some adventure or ambush of bears. The din of children has never disturbed him. Probably their absence would. He's been known to take a nap with "little ankle-biters" crawling all over him. Once after he was firmly instructed not to take his grandson, Jerecito, out of the playpen, his daughter found Apa curled up in the playpen with Jerecito, happily reading **The American Medical Journal** while the child slept blissfully.

When Dr. Gates first became a doctor he intended to go into pediatrics, but soon realized that a life of "poking and punching and shooting" little babies was not for him. As a compromise he settled on a general practice.

He calls all little boys "Pancho Villa" (or "Guy" if they don't understand "Pancho") and all little girls "Panchita." Dr. Gates considers shots an absolutely last-ditch measure. But he doesn't hesitate to give them when necessary. On such occasions he goes to comic extreme to minimize the pain.

Inspired by children, this serious but witty man will transform himself into a subtle clown if that will help a child through a painful time. Buster Keaton with his acrobatic dignity would have a rival in Dr. Gates. He often costumes himself with yellow prescription pads in his collar until he's bristling with them. Each child gets the empty syringe, with needle removed, and a quarter as a consolation prize. After he has given the children their shots and tears are running down their faces, Apa, visibly pained himself, will run out saying, "Your mommy made me do this! Your mommy made me do this!"

During the war when his daughters' husbands were away, the sisters and their families lived together. Apa was grandpa, father and family doctor, all in one. The seasonal shots for the kids were a real maneuver. The mothers would take one child into the bathroom. If it were a diapered baby, they would take the diaper off, holding the baby to the window to look at all the wonderful sights. Meanwhile, Apa would climb into the tub, tiptoe to the end, peek around the shower curtain and pop the child in the arm or bottom, while the mother kept the child occupied. Then Apa would get out of the tub, put his hat on and come running up to the now crying child, exclaiming "Que paso? Who hurt the baby?" The baby would grab for Apa's hug and sympathy. Then Apa, holding the baby, would say, "Goodbye, everybody; goodbye, baby." The soothed baby would wave bravely, "Goodbye, Apa." Then Apa would go outside, get a needle ready for the next child, tiptoe back through the shower curtain and pop the next baby, and so on until all the children had been vaccinated.

In Eagle Pass the kids have a real champion in Apa, and common childhood illnesses are entwined with good memories as well as bad. There was great competition to be sick. In a family of more than one child, the well child would get to carry the Doctor's bag so as not to feel left out. Once a young mother had two sick children. The Doctor came to visit every day for a week. When the children were up and about, they asked their mother, "Why didn't Apa come today?"

The mother said, "Well, you're so much better."

The crestfallen children pleaded, "Well, call him and tell him to come anyway."

"I will not," protested the mother. "It costs me every time he comes here."

The children's mouths fell open. "He **charges** to come and see **us**?"

When the mother laughingly recounted the story to the Doctor, he didn't laugh at all. "You are the meanest woman I've ever met in my life. How could you dare tell those children that?"

Those children all over town have grown up. The "Panchitas" grew up into lovely women with babies of their own, the "Panchos" grew up and became fathers, but they all still love Apa as deeply as when they were feverish children. One beautiful woman, according to the amused account of Apa's daughter Susie, "every morning in the world would go up to the doctor and say 'Good Morning, Guy' (as she called him), and plant a big kiss right on his bald spot. Apa would go cheerfully off to town with those perfect red lips shining on the top of his head. And everyone could see it because he's so short.''

You don't have to be a child to love Dr. Gates, either. Dr. Gates inspires hope in all his patients. He is a man of few words, yet he takes time to chat and reminisce with older patients who depend on him, knowing he is one of the only doctors who will visit them at home. He neither sermonizes nor delivers inspirational messages. He simply walks into a room and his patient begins to believe he will recover. Those in his flock feel the unspoken commandment, "Thou shalt get well."

Dr. Gates' presence is sometimes prescription enough to cure the sick. An old man who was very sick called in the Doctor. "Now, Amigo, don't leave me. I'm afraid I'll die if you leave me." The Doctor held his hand and reassured him, "Now, you go to sleep and get a good night's rest. I'm going to sit right here and hold your hand and **you're not going to die.**" And Dr. Gates would sit right there and hold his hand until the sick man went to sleep. Then Dr. Gates would drive home, sleep a few hours and come back to his patient. When the old man would awaken, Dr. Gates would be there holding his hand. This continued until the old man got well. As one friend said, "He had Dr. Gates holding him, so he couldn't die."

Another person who became deathly ill, refused to die because Apa was out of town. "I can't die while he's out of town! I am **not** going to die!" And he got well.

Dr. Gates, despite work which has no boundaries, finds time for his fine family. It all fits with Dr. Gates and his wife—lovely children, grandchildren and great-grandchildren.

Dr. Gates himself is not a talkative man but his family is. As one of them confessed, "He spawned people who chatter incessantly." But it is some of the grandest chatter ever, drawing energy from both Spanish and English, as well as a dialect of childhood. Often the voices fall into adoring tales about Apa who got them young, put them on horses before they could walk, taught them to drive at an early age, teased them, loved them and helped them to be strong and independent.

In these family stories, it is always Apa and Ama (his wife). Although it has been 13 years since her death, Ama's presence is still felt by friends and family. Like Apa, she had a fantastic sense of humor. Theirs was a quiet, sharp and intelligent wit. Ama had been raised in an age and an atmosphere in which grace and hospitality were at their zenith. Ama excelled in both those qualities but also went beyond them in her strength of character and intelligence. She loved to read, she was an excellent bridge player, and she may well have been the best nurse Apa ever had—quick, calm and, most important of all, warm and caring.

As well as being a fine surgical nurse, in later years Lizzy, as she was called by her husband, also screened his night calls. In this way she protected the Doctor from unnecessary burdens but always awakened him in emergencies. Once, answering a frivolous night call, she overheard the caller tell her husband, "I understand if you don't tell her it's an emergency, she won't wake him up." Ama held the phone for a count of five and then said into the receiver, "The Doctor says to give him a couple of aspirin and if he's still alive in the morning to bring him to the office."

Ama had great style. On a visit to San Antonio she spied a grand piano that she knew she must have. She bought it and had it shipped to Eagle Pass by train, but then realized that Gates, as she called him, when faced with an unknown piano, might very well say, "I have not ordered that piano. Take it away." So Ama raced to the Southern Pacific train depot in time to see the train pulling out. She hailed a taxi and told the driver, "Beat that grand piano to Eagle Pass."

As usual, Doctor Gates met the train but, this time, there was no Lizzy. When he got home she gently reproached him, "You didn't meet me at the train."

"I was there, Lizzy, Funny, I must have just missed you"

"Well, here I am," said Lizzy, laying the matter to rest.

"By the way, Lizzy, do you know whose car that is parked in front of the house?" he asked.

"What's it look like?"

"It's bright yellow, Lizzy, and it has 'Yellow Cab Company of San Antonio' painted on the side."

"Well, by all rights it should be yours, but it's not. And, please, don't ever ask me how much it cost." And Apa never did.

Ama's personality seems to have been a totally individual blend of intelligence, compassion and spontaneity. Though like Apa she was serious-minded, she had a penchant for falling into funny situations. One such occasion was the visit of General Jonathan Wainwright, who came to visit Dr. Gates and some of his other polo-playing buddies after the war. The General had been on the 70 mile Bataan Death March and, having survived the Japanese concentration camp, had lost his wife.

It was a sad reunion until Ama, who was seated next to the General, in leaning back to listen to the General's aide, somehow fell underneath the table. Apa, who had just been called to come to the hospital for an emergency, left only after he saw Lizzy's laughing head re-emerge from under the table. She had a lively and easy laugh, and as the guests dragged her up, everyone, including the General, was laughing with her. Later Ama said she was proud of falling under the table, since it broke the General's grief.

Apa and Ama were equals in every way. Apa is famous for a humor which usually comes after a dead-serious volley of words. His one-liners come so quietly and surely that you have to be on your toes to get them. Jerecito, his grandson, did stand on his toes to catch them.

Jerecito gives lively eye-witness accounts from a pair of eyes that could just barely peer over his grandpa's desk at the goings-on in Apa's office.

Jerecito, who was raised by his Grandpa while his father was off to war, is one of Apa's many historians, and the history is still unfolding. His stories are definitely "Apa" stories and are repudiated by half the family, who judge them to be the exaggerations of a child and the workmanship of a good storyteller.

Once a man who was trying to enlist came into the Doctor's office. He was awfully worried that he might be color-blind. Color-blindness wouldn't have disqualified him for the particular job in the service he wanted, but he was still worrying. Apa reached into a big box containing discs with colored yarn on them and chose one.

"Let's see if you're color blind . . . You see this green one? What color is it?"

"It's green."

"How about this orange one?"

"Orange,"

Apa continued testing the man, calling out all the colors. "Okay, no problems here." The man passed with flying colors and Apa signed the forms and turned him loose.

Besides his family, Dr. Gates has two passionate pastimes: Polo (in his youth) and hunting. He's never killed a deer in his life, or a duck, or a quail; "but he sure has given wildcats who prey on cattle and sheep a lot of trouble." He goes after mountain lions with big dogs at the Azulejo Ranch, sixty miles into Mexico. He's worn out several hunting partners, but his most steadfast buddy has been Jimmy Scrivener. Even though the hunters are welcome at the ranch house (having been called by the ranchers to get rid of a bothersome cat), the men prefer to camp out with their horses. Apa has been known to go off for three days by himself "where you can see for fifty miles and it's all blue." In 54 years he has killed five mountain lions and hundreds of smaller wildcats. A few of the cats have been made into rugs, a parody of store-bought big-game skins. The raggedness of the chase is still left in them.

As a young man, Dr. Gates was a fine and much respected polo player and is remembered as being "debonair, dashing and daring." The tougher the game got, the more he laughed and sang. He and his friends were good enough to take on the Mexican Army teams and the U.S. Cavalry teams. Once he locked horses with General Quinones, who had the biggest polo pony going. The General enjoyed chickening out other players by barrelling down on them with his oversized horse.

Apa disapproved of this strategy and set out to teach the General and his horse some manners. When the General began his head-on rampage, Apa and his horse, whose size matched his rider's, kept on their course. At the point of impact, Apa's horse reeled and fell. The second time, the General again set a collision course and again Apa and his horse were thrown to the ground. And so a third time. But this time the General's horse fell, too. There was never a fourth time, and never again did the General and his horse charge players—at least not while Apa was on the opposing team.

The Doctor has one other weakness besides babies, lions and polo. He is a fool for driving, and the town respectfully gives him a wide berth. Every time he'd buy a new car, the word would spread, "Watch out for a tan one now." On one of his cars, he took all the doors off saying it was cooler that way.

Now the doctor drives a well-known blue pickup—his first vehicle with power steering and air-conditioning, both of which he disapproved of as making a man too soft. The city, in deference to Dr. Gates, has taken out the two parking meters in front of his office so he can park at will in his inimitable style.

A few years ago his car almost did him in. He had a ruined parking gear and had gotten in the habit of parking it by heading into the curb with the emergency brake on. This time, when he stopped to open the gate at the ranch, the car jumped out of park and into reverse. When the car lurched backward, Dr. Gates had one foot in the car and one foot on the road. As he fell, he pulled the steering wheel toward him and the car ran over him, then started traveling in circles. As it came around he made a flying leap toward it only to be knocked down, so he crawled off to one side and watched it. As it backed around in its sinister circles, he noticed it went slower at one point in the circle. He was able to jump into it and drive home. He then went to the hospital to make his rounds, and later showed up for Sunday dinner, limping and bruised, wearing one boot and one shoe.

"What happened? You kick someone?" his grandson asked. "No, the car ran over me."

His children sent him back to the hospital, where his broken ankle was put in a cast. That slowed him down a little. For a while he practiced medicine out of a wheel chair while his leg was healing, and enjoyed it so much that he still uses the wheel chair in his office. His recovery is almost complete. Since the accident, his only complaint is that he still can't run.

The Doctor is no stranger to pain but his stoic policy, at least for himself, is to go on. In his first hospital, he installed the first x-ray, fluroscope and radium equipment in that part of the State. He did much work with these dangerous elements. The doctor would set patients' bones while under x-ray without using lead-lined gloves because he needed to leave his hands free so he could perfectly manipulate the bones. He would also put radium pins in areas where he had cut out cancerous growths. At that time, the insidiously destructive effects of unprotected exposure to radiation were not fully understood.

Over the years he became overexposed and a slow, relentless growth of cancer cells began, which could only be dealt with by amputation of his fingers over a period of years. The series of amputations began in his early 40's, and the last was performed in his late 50's. He was no longer a young man, chronologically speaking, and a lesser man might well have retired under such circumstances. If anyone ever heard him express his deep disappointment at having to give up surgery, or heard him complain of the terrible pain in his hands, it would only have been his wife, to whom he was so very close.

Performing surgery was now impossible for him, so at the age of 58, Dr. Gates started a new life. He went back to school and learned anesthesiology so that he could still be close to surgery. Throughout his career the Doctor has never stopped learning. In years past he made it a practice to go to the Mayo Clinic for teaching seminars. When he'd visit his daughter at school in New Orleans, he'd slip off to the City

Charity Hospital every chance he got. He was like a boy in a toy shop, and explained it this way, "But, Lizzy, every disease known to man is in that building."

Despite the fact that he no longer performed surgery, some people wouldn't take no for an answer. One woman whose whole family—sister and brothers and all of her husband's family—had come into this world with Dr. Gates, pleaded with him to at least deliver her first child so the chain would be unbroken. He explained that he couldn't do it without his fingers, but he finaly agreed on a compromise. The Doctor was there instructing a nurse at the birth.

Losing eight fingers would be an insurmountable handicap to some people. But Doctor Gates never gave in to the pain or to his loss. As one patient says, "He has more ability in his two fingers than most doctors have in ten." His colleagues agree. Once, while he was still performing surgery, a patient went to a top surgeon in a big city. The specialist was amazed: "But why do you come to me when you've got one of the ablest surgeons in the U.S. right there in Eagle Pass?"

Although he can no longer perform surgery, the Doctor is still a brilliant diagnostician. Though frequently he will refer his patients to bigger hospitals where a more thorough battery of tests can be run, his diagnosis is invariably upheld.

His colleagues in larger cities have asked him, "Dr. Gates, why do you waste all that medical knowledge in that little town when you could be of so much use in a big city?" Apa shrugs, "Oh no, I could never leave this place." And the Doctor's work is not done. His life and the life of Eagle Pass are one.

That is why on his 90th birthday, on February 6, 1976, there was a great public manifestation of the community's love. The Doctor arrived late to his birthday party, since his office hours were not over until five. His family was there—daughters, grandchildren, great-grandchildren, plus the large "extended family" of his friends from both sides of the Rio Grande—about 600 people in all. Those who could not be there bought radio time and throughout the day regular programs were interrupted so that people could congratulate the Doctor on his 90th birthday.

There were 70 birthday cakes, many with elaborate icings spelling out "We love you, Apa." It was an occasion for rejoicing, and not all the 'whereases,' or plaques, or stiff speeches could disguise or suppress the outpouring of love the people of Eagle Pass showed for their doctor. The American Legion Post saluted him. Maverick County Senior Citizens made him an honorary member. The County Judge declared the week "Doctor Gates Week." Junior Historians made him an honorary member. The Hospital Board congratulated him. He was called "Padre de la Medicina de Eagle Pass." But as one speaker lamely said, "There are too many words and not enough words to express our feelings for Doctor Gates."

Gifts were given. On his 80th birthday, he'd gotten a new saddle which he appreciated, "I really needed this, my other one is just about gone." (Most people at 80 might think a good firm mattress more appropriate.) This time, for his 90th birthday, Dr. Gates got a new

Dr. Gates has leanings toward being a saint, but saints don't drive pick-up trucks.
(photo by Mary Sherwood)

Stetson. It had a wider brim than he was used to, but he thought it was great. "Keeps the sun off. Keeps the rain off." Some remarked that it was almost like an umbrella on his head. "Yah," said Apa, "and you don't have to hold the stick."

One woman rushed up to him, "Oh, Dr. Gates! You just get younger and better looking every birthday," to which Dr. Gates replied soundly, "I can see no reason in getting older and uglier."

In spite of all this love and unabashed admiration, Apa is an unspoiled man. Neither self-effacing nor self-congratulating, he simply goes about his business, conscientiously and joyously. "So many things have happened to me that I have to forget them," he says simply.

The day after his birthday was Saturday and Apa was at his office early. (Neither age nor testimonials can slow him.) At 4:30 he called up his daughter. Did anyone want to go for a ride in his pickup? A flurry of yeses. So with two grandchildren and the windows rolled down to let in the South Texas wind, they drove off.

Dr. Gates is not conspicuously religious, but he always gives God credit for healing. He rarely goes to church; he doesn't go to funerals. He keeps people alive and when they are dying, he holds them in his arms as he did one doctor whose last wish was—"Gringo, I feel so bad. Hold me."

Dr. Gates has leanings toward being a saint. But saints don't drive pick-up trucks. They don't get up at five in the morning and go to the ranch to let the dogs run loose in the dark wind before dawn.

One old friend, Mike Wipf, who has weathered the years with him, said quietly, "He loves horses and cattle and people, most of all people." Happily, for all of Apa's friends, he is well and practicing medicine in Eagle Pass, just as he has done for 57 years.

"Miss Shoes"

by Jamie Frucht

"Fred, I cannot put a plaque up in my garden that does not have an apostrophe in 'God's heart.' "

That seemingly absurd statement makes all the sense in the world if you are lucky enough to know the woman who said it, Inez Hatley Hughes. The poem she was referring to is often committed to cast iron.

> The Kiss of the Sun
> for Pardon
> The Song of the Birds
> for Mirth
> One is nearer Gods heart
> in a Garden
> Than anywhere else on Earth.

Having been an English teacher for 42 years, it went against her grain to leave the apostrophe out. So Fred, the cabinetmaker and former student, obliged his "teacher," improvising with a bolt for an apostrophe.

Mrs. Hughes' life is all of a pattern—the pattern of a crazy quilt. Everything fits together yet everything is surprising, just like a crazy quilt. Now this corner of velvet joins with this piece of gingham, and this silk square overlaps this taffeta diamond. And if we can take the analogy a little farther, you feel warm, you feel good with Mrs. Hughes, just like you do with a quilt. English teachers wouldn't let you drag an analogy too far along a paragraph knowing you will trip on it, sooner or later. And Mrs. Hughes is an English teacher, and is a director of a museum, and is a widely educated and traveled woman.

Inez Hatley Hughes, or "Miss Shoes" as 25 years worth of schoolchildren have called her, is a grand woman who combines style and substance. (Though in her indomitable style, she would laud substance over style.) She is a striking woman whose handsome face with its clear complexion eludes photographs. Her smile is crooked, so no amount of cheese will make her smile on camera. But in real life she smiles and laughs often. She wears a hair-pin chignon and quotes Browning fluidly. Standing on a dock as Caddo Lake slips into the dusk, she reaches for her favorite poet. ". . .the quiet colored end of evening smiles miles on miles."

She favors the color blue which she wears often in all its hues. She has the aura of a crystal clear spring day, when the sky stares down blue with a few white clouds passing through. Every once in a while she will cloud up, responding to some frustrating circumstance.

Her idiosyncracies are lightened by her wit. For instance, she is addicted to ear clips. After resting her ears on a drive, she rummages in her bag for the earrings. "I have to get my ear clips. I feel a bit nude."

Mrs. Hughes has a resonant voice that speaks words phonetically, giving each syllable its due. That word that is alongside the word in the dictionary is the one she pronounces. So the word creation becomes kre-a-shen. For years she has been speaking distinctly with her beautifully modulated voice that can reach unexpected notes, and for years schoolchildren have listened and slurred her into "Miss Shoes."

Her "pedigree" supplies a partial explanation of her voice. She had five sets of great-great-grandparents here before Texas became a state. The names of her ancestors sound like ingredients for an Anglo-Saxon novel. Kinberlings married Pooles; Etheridges married Hatleys; from Wales she got ancestors of her great-great-grandmother Prothro. A great-grandfather, with the rhythmic name of Tapley Bynum Hatley the First, died at 31, looking even too young to be a father; a grandfather died at 26. Though Inez Hughes is several generations removed from her ancestor McPherson who fought in the Bonnie Prince Charles War, occasionally she will roll an R like a skilled Scotswoman.

All that Anglo-Saxon heritage was tempered in the Southern states her ancestors passed through. One family arrived in North Carolina and prepared for the great adventure of moving way out west. They picked up and moved all the way from North Carolina to Alabama. Eventually, however, all sides of the family came to Texas, converging on Harrison County where six generations are buried in one graveyard. (One great-great-great, eight great-greats, six greats, three grands, and two parents.)

Her voice is a mixture of Scotch, Southern charm (not the lazy lip variety) and standard English training. The standard English training was necessary because, as a young girl, she had a deep timidity that held her voice and person captive.

January 29, 1903 Inez Hatley was born in Reelfoot, 11 miles southwest of Marshall. Large families ran in her family. Her maternal great-grandparents had 13 children. Her maternal grandparents had 12 children, and she had seven brothers and four sisters.

Inez was growing up when Hoover was Chairman of the Food Administration. Everyone was "hooverizing." It was unpatriotic to waste food, especially in such a large family. Her Scottish background reinforced this waste-not attitude. As a result, she was and is a charter member of the "clean plate club." Despite the discipline, she enjoys food and doesn't rush a meal. In fact, she eats with the thoroughness of dissection.

While she was growing up, her family lived on a large farm. Her father also owned a sawmill and country store. Inez's mother was a straight-laced person whose conversion at 14 to the Baptist faith left her admonishing her daughter not to read books such as **Inez, A Tale of the Alamo.** Since she was named after that Inez, via her Aunt Inez, this created problems.

Her mother's warnings were too late. Inez was already a convert to the joys of reading. Her mother also tried to influence her daughter's hair, which she thought was taking a turn for the worse. It had started out as a spun gold color but with the years deepened into a lasting brown. (Mrs. Hughes still has brown hair.) "When it first started turning brown she thought I had gotten soot in it and kept scrubbing it."

Inez's father died when she was just 16, the same year she graduated from high school. Her reading ability outdistanced her maturity, and put her two years ahead of other children. She went to the College of Marshall where she received an associate of arts degree at the age of 18.

In 1921 Miss Hatley went off to her first teaching job at the little one-room red schoolhouse on the hill in Terlingua. Her uncle, in whose home she had spent her senior year in high school, was an attorney in Alpine, and she loved the area, willfully choosing that environment over more civilized locations.

She was only 18, almost a child herself. There were 35 beginners in her class, 65 students in all, in a room that was full with 25 students. "I knew two words of Spanish—**adios, mañana** and the students didn't know one word of English. But at 18 the world is your oyster." One of her students in Terlingua was 21 years old. Miss Hatley enlisted her aid in helping the students form letters and do figures. In recess, this "teacher's aid" taught the teacher Spanish.

With the help of her uncle, she drilled herself at home before going to Terlingua on the pronunciation of the children's names. (Later when she taught for three years in Karnes City, she had to master the pronunciation of Polish, Bohemian and German names.)

One day she asked the students about their families and they asked about hers. "I told them my father was dead, and this big 16 year old boy came up and just threw his arms about me and, with tears rolling down his face, said in Spanish, 'You can come live with us, Miss Hatley.' "

She loved the Mexican children who were warm, emotional and responsive. She also loved Terlingua which was the rugged head-quarters of the mining camp. She lived in the company hotel where she soon developed "a boarding house reach" in order to survive and feed herself in competition with the men.

At Terlingua she met a young man who had come down from Maine with the mine owner to be his secretary and run the commissary. Inez and the young man were both strangers to the arid land which they explored on horseback every moonlit night. One formation of big flat rock was especially pleasing. It made the horses hooves sound like they were clopping on concrete streets. "We thought we were back in civilization when we rode that little 30 foot section."

Miss Hatley might have been persuaded by the moonlight and her gentleman friend to settle in Terlingua, but it was not in the stars. "I had an inner urge for travel and education that just exceeded romance." In 1923, when she left, it took four teachers to take her place.

That "inner urge for education and travel" has lasted a lifetime. To satisfy it, she sampled a lot of colleges. She attended Sul Ross College in Alpine, and received her B.A. from Baylor University in 1924. Thinking that eventually she would go north for her graduate degree, she sampled courses at the University of Texas for several summers. While in Austin she took Spanish courses to remedy her self-taught Spanish. She also took speech courses, for in spite of her teaching experience, her timidity was still with her.

"I realized that in order to be a forceful teacher I had to control my timidity and my voice. You couldn't go in a classroom apologetically." Her speech teacher taught standard English by a route that Inez remembers as "torturous." "I was so self-conscious. We had the course in the old law building and he had me walk the length of that building, back and forth in front of the class. I've never been so **tortured.**"

Always pursuing happiness via education, Inez Hatley studied at Oxford and Cambridge as part of a summer seminar for American university women. At Oxford she studied Eighteenth Century England and can still remember the arresting introduction of her professor as he addressed his class of American university women. "Today, I shall talk with you about your last King, King George III."

After several such summers sampling her mind's desire in far off places, she decided to settle down and get her degree. With that resolve, she studied for three summers at the University of Texas at Austin.

Not abandoning travel, just experiencing it vicariously through images, she wrote her thesis on Amy Lowell and the Far East. Her choice was precipitated by an incident preceding her undergraduate years at Baylor. During a poet's symposium in 1921, Amy Lowell had walked down the aisle of Baylor chapel with President Brooks on her arm and a big black cigar in her mouth. Smoking was prohibited on campus. "It intrigued me, her daring."

In the introduction to the thesis there is a short paragraph that illuminates Mrs. Hughes as much as Amy Lowell. "Miss Lowell's form of punctuation and spelling has been closely adhered to in all the quotations from her, though I do not approve of her irregularities in many instances."

Inez Hatley received her master's degree in 1936. Her education was not over, however, as the Marshall school system in which she taught required that every four years teachers go back to school to keep their jobs. She made the most of it, going to the University of London, Columbia University, as well as the closer Texas State College for Women at Denton.

Though she now had her credentials, her timidity was still intact, even after the training and experiences she had been exposed to. What speech courses and discipline could not accomplish, love did, conquering all, just as the cliche says.

As a young woman Inez Hatley was on the verge of being beautiful. A wit protected her beauty and made her more than just a pretty face. In Terlingua, in Karnes City, wherever she went, proposals and promises followed her. Men said, "I'll be whatever you want me to be," to which she'd reply, "I have to have one that's already **it.**"

She wasn't searching for money or even adventure, as she could find adventure and travel and income on her own. She wanted a husband whom she could talk to, as well as love; read with, sit beside the fire and discuss ideas with. So she held out against the ensnarement of proposals, and while she waited, she developed herself.

She met her future husband when she was a student in the College of Marshall in her home town. Solon Hughes was a professor, registrar and business manager at the college (later renamed East Texas Baptist College). They renewed their acquaintance when she came back to teach in 1927.

They were such good friends that it wasn't for several months that she realized he was courting her. During the courtship she went to England and the Continent, pursuing her education. When she arrived in Oxford from the Continent she asked innocently if there were any letters for her. The matron of the college responded by handing over a bulky stack, "Oh my dear Inez Hatley, someone must love you very much." Her husband-to-be was an ardent lover and writer of voluminous letters. They were married in 1939.

"I hope I'm not opinionated in the obnoxious sense, but I do have definite ideas." Many of Mrs. Hughes' ideas center around love's powers. "Love matures a person, being the key that unlocks life's mysteries." With her husband's love, she gained the assurance and confidence to overcome her timidity. From her husband she learned many things.

His father had been a Latin and Greek scholar who had tutored his son in world history. By the age of five, Solon had read all of **Ridpath's History of the World.** Later, his father had him chart the battles of the world on a blackboard. Mrs. Hughes recalls, "I never knew whether Mr. Hughes was going to come home with a philosophy book or a cookbook. He had such range, such versatility. He could do anything."

During their marriage, she continued to teach, but she also developed new domestic powers. In the first year of married life, in 1940, "The day school was out, I thought I would pick a mess of English peas for supper." Finding the peas ready for preserving, she picked them until dark. And the next morning she and Mr. Hughes got up at 4 a.m. and picked peas and picked peas. It was a marathon of pea picking. Eighty cans were processed that day. Conserving every available fruit and vegetable, she put up 1800 containers of food that summer.

In 1948, nine years after they were married, her husband died. Her love and admiration of him were shared by many. Dean Smith of the College delivered the eulogy. "This man came nearer following the footsteps of the Nazarene than any man I've ever been associated with in my life, and I have sat at the feet of some of the great teachers."

After his death, she continued to teach, as she had always done. Mrs. Hughes had come a long way from the "green" girl in the one-room schoolhouse in Terlingua. Years of educating herself had taught her how to help others toward self-knowledge and attainment.

There had been a time when, tired of her total immersion in English—with courses in the summer at universities, and teaching it the remainder of the year in high school, she had decided to study something new. Not quite out of the blue, she chose to go to Harvard and take some landscape architecture courses. This reflected the influence of Mr. Hughes, whose hobby (one of many) was landscaping.

He had landscaped the College of Marshall campus.

She caught the boat in New Orleans for New York. Once at Harvard she discovered a fascinating correlation existed between architecture and literature. The landscape architecture classes took field trips to the homes and gardens of famous writers and publishers, Longfellow's Garden among them. That summer confirmed what Alfred North Whitehead had once said that "all knowledge is a seamless garment," or as Inez Hatley adapted it, "everything is grist for the English teacher's mill."

Mrs. Hughes' English "mill" at Marshall High School turned out some fine students who have become fine adults. They often return and talk to her as a friend. One older man who had been away from Marshall for years wandered into the museum of Marshall recently and was amazed to hear the distinct voice that could only belong to Mrs. Hughes. "What brought me in here today?" he marvelled. After a long talk he said, "I have unburdened myself more in this afternoon than in all the 35 years since I saw you."

"They've changed so much from being little boys to men," says Mrs. Hughes. Having lived in the same area most of her life, she is aware of the changes and also the continuity of life. Her roots are very reassuring.

On the streets, in restaurants, wherever she goes, she sees and talks to many generations of her former students. "Most times it's very gratifying to see how many of my students have done wonderful things." They are at the top of their professions and include writers, ministers, medical specialists, State government officials, and news-casters.

In Marshall she taught English in the junior year. "That age is most in need of counseling. It's just on the brink of adulthood. They have so many problems. Everything is a problem to them because they don't know how to cope. They haven't evolved a philosophy for acceptance of life or a solution to problems."

Mrs. Hughes has never shied away from students' problems. "I always felt the highest compliment a student could pay me was to confide in me, to come to me for counseling." She cites O'Henry's story, **The Third Ingredient** to find her most salient trait as a teacher. In this world some people are Hands, some are Heads, some are Muscles, . . .some are Backs for burdens, and some people are Shoulders. "I've always felt that was my role, just a shoulder to be wept on."

But shoulders don't get inscriptions in books written to them, as Mrs. Hughes has, countless times.

"You steered me to words as both a livelihood and a life," writes one student.

"Your insistence on an intelligible use of English language. . ." begins another.

". . .who as a historian cares about the truth and who as a teacher taught me to write it."

". . .super teacher and friend. . ."

". . .in one year marked indelibly the desire to know."

". . .who taught me that what a man is counts more than what he does, but that the two are inseparable in a full and balanced life."

How could the teacher of a semester of grammar and a semester of American literature inspire such inscriptions? Mrs. Hughes evolved a totally individual course of study. She began the school year with a question.

"Students, this year we are going to study the most important thing in the world to you. What do you think it is?"

"English?"

"No, it's **you**. Yourselves. Everything in this world either comes in to you or goes out from you."

And with that her students began an adventure of self-exploration that they would pursue their whole lives.

She was not teaching selfishness, but self-reliance. In this, Emerson was one of her great allies. "The power which resides in him (you) is new in nature, and none but he (you) knows what he (you) can do, nor does he know until he has tried." (**Self-Reliance**, Emerson) She often quoted Emerson, till some students later, hearing a quote: "Nothing great in the world was ever achieved without enthusiasm," said "We thought that was 'Miss Shoes.' "

She had her students prepare self inventories and here she enlisted the aid of Schopenhauer whose essay, **Personality**, lists the eight most important ingredients in a personality, beginning with Health, basic to all others.

The students wrote self-evaluations, stressing what they were proudest of up to that day in their lives. Mrs. Hughes remembers one little girl's paper. "The thing I'm proudest of in all my life is the **mital** I won for being the best speller in junior high school."

In addition to writing in their autobiographies, during the semester the students had to do genealogical charts. "I always had my students do their genealogies. It's just a phobia of mine. I think people should know their backgrounds, who they are, what they were." The children got excited when they learned about the accomplishments of their ancestors. It helped their self-esteem. Of course, not all children had a pedigree; some family trees were barely shrubs, but they all had grandmas and grandpas and private histories.

Since Mrs. Hughes had had to struggle in her own growth, she tried to help the children in theirs. "I just thought it was my duty and responsibility to help them in every way I could to improve themselves." She taught them speech, and had them demonstrate the proper way to sit, to rise and to walk. "Of course most of them just slouched."

Most of all Mrs. Hughes asked her students to think of themselves as people in the world. To do that, she asked them to think about what they wanted to make of themselves, what profession they would choose.

When they had chosen an area, they had to read a biography of someone in the chosen field, two books about their career, and a personality book.

Her students came up with fascinating fields—scuba diving,

medicine, journalism, barbering. "One boy wanted to work out the formula for the payload trajectories, which demanded a word for that specialist. So we coined the word, 'trajectionist.'"

The students made reports on the books they read and took notes to be used for a paper. At the same time the entire class was reading Franklin's **Autobiography**. From the autobiography, each student would have to take a phase of Franklin's life applicable to his chosen field. Mrs. Hughes counted it—Franklin had 105 firsts. She always emphasized to her students that in life they had to choose a specific phase—not just be a philosopher, but a certain kind of philosopher, doctor, lawyer, writer.

Students interviewed someone in their chosen field. To do this there was a lesson on how to have a telephone conversation for setting up an interview, and how to have an interview. After the interview students wrote thank you notes. Mrs. Hughes remembers some of the wonderful experiences her students had. One of her children, who had had some psychiatric problems, got an appointment interviewing her psychiatrist in Shreveport. She was able to go on rounds with him. Another student who wanted to be a meteorologist, actually got to sit in with the weatherman and help broadcast the weather.

Then the students would give oral reports to the class, so every student would have the benefit of the others' "job experiences." Finally the students prepared outlines for their final theme. In tutorials, she went over the outlines. Mrs. Hughes stressed that they didn't have to follow the career they chose at the age of 16 or 17. They could change their minds.

Throughout the semester the students were preparing themselves for life after their junior years. First she summoned their interest and energy and then, integrated grammar into the larger picture. From her own life experience she knew that everything is connected in life, that knowledge cannot be neatly folded into piles of subjects to be worn a semester, then put back in the drawer.

When her students turned in a report or gave an oral presentation, she listened for content, organization and style. She stressed grammar. "When it was very popular not to teach grammar I just went right on hoeing down the row because I knew they needed it. One cannot be explicit without a knowledge of grammar. It's basic to clarity, coherence and forcefulness. You must learn to say what you mean and mean what you say."

The second half of the year was American literature. Each child chose an author, reading three books by him and a biography of the writer. "It's fantastic what children get out of the printed page." One child discovered Hemingway for Mrs. Hughes who, up to that time, had always considered only the uncouth and rough side of that writer's vision and style.

What Mrs. Hughes demanded of herself, she also demanded of her students: high quality work, integrity, enthusiasm. Here again she used Emerson to rally their energies. "Nothing great was ever achieved without enthusiasm." She turns on her listeners with a teacher's question. "Do you know the derivative meaning of the word enthusiasm?'' Silence. "**En**—within, **asm**—the quality or state of, **thus**—from **theos**, God, the quality of having God within." That is one reason why she loved teaching English. "It gave me a chance for preaching." She preached optimism and courage.

When her students held back or did sloppy work, she had a withering glance that said more than a thousand words. Those students pierced by the withering glance, years later said, "She only gave us what we deserved."

After 37 years in the Marshall school system, her energy had not faltered. But the schools were changing around her, becoming administrative-oriented and less student-oriented. There was a teacher's meeting here and a teacher's meeting there with no time for students. Then too, the children had so much on their minds. She felt her energies were dissipated in meetings.

The culmination came one fateful day in her sixth period class. A student said, "Miss Hughes don't you feel good today? You haven't smiled a single time." Remembering Emerson's dictum about enthusiasm, she thought, "Oh my, it's time to quit."

In 1964 she left the school system. (This time, no amount of teachers could replace her.) Though she retired, a leopard might just as well decide to retire his spots, as Mrs. Hughes to give up being a teacher. As it turned out, she stayed a teacher but just changed her setting.

To celebrate her short-lived retirement, she took a grand tour. "I had liberated myself from the classroom."

Mrs. Hughes has always been strong for travel, taking advantage of a teacher's summer vacations to change her location and explore some fantasy or favorite writer's haunts. She's traveled so widely, if not wildly, that she's developed traveler's luck (read as persistence).

From the very beginning, teaching and traveling have been intricately related. Travel, like poetry, sustains itself by striking images. She still remembers the man at Guadalupe Peak who stood hunched against the sunset. As her uncle asked to take his picture, the stranger said, "If you take me, you'll have to take my mountain."

On her travels she has been in the homes of many famous writers. Of course, they were dead, but her imagination and total immersion in her subject made the visits invigorating. She had a delightful visit at Washington Irving's house, and a lovely stay in Longfellow's garden. During a Columbia University session in 1954, she battled New York traffic to arrive at the Edgar Allan Poe Fordham cottage. The cottage was indefinitely closed, undergoing repairs. The yard man thought that was explanation enough. He didn't realize it was no ordinary tourist with idle curiosity he was speaking to. Mrs. Hughes has a determination that is overwhelming. She uses a line that has served her well. "Oh, I'm so disappointed. I came all the way from Texas to see this." She confesses, "That line does open doors and gates."

Upon hearing it, the caretaker of the cottage poked his head out and invited her in. Not only did she see the setting of Poe and his Annabelle Lee, but she also learned all about the caretaker and his wife who lived in the cottage. The wife had recently died. Now it was up to the old man to keep the cottage alive, as one of three surviving members of the Poe Society. He was puttering about, hanging curtains. Mrs. Hughes helped him with the curtains, and was so helpful and sympathetic that before she left, she got a proposal.

On another occasion she visited the Trappist Kentucky Monastery in search of Thomas Merton, the monk and writer of the **Seven Storey Mountain.** No outsiders were allowed in the monastery during the retreat. However, after the Brothers learned that Mrs. Hughes had come "all the way from Texas and was so disappointed," once more doors and gates were opened. The Brothers let her in the chapel where the monks were chanting Vespers. "Thomas Merton was there. I got to see him. He was one of 176 heads all shaven. I really studied their faces. I'm sure I saw him, I'm just not sure which face was his."

In England in 1960, she arrived early for a lecture to be given by Sir Charles Snow. "I usually try to arrive early, and I saw this man bouncing in and bouncing out." Feeling sure it was Sir Charles, she went to him, introduced herself, and had a good twenty-minute conversation with the writer.

In the course of the conversation, she found that Sir Charles had just returned from Russia. Upon her inquiry about his observations of Pasternak's position in Russia, he told her that the Russians anthologize his poetry while ignoring his fiction. This reminded her of an American author who was ignominious in his own home town. She related a parallel story that very much interested Sir Charles about "our own writer from Oxford, Mississippi, William Faulkner."

She had been in his home town and tried to buy a picture postcard of his home. "I asked at one place and they seemed almost incensed, telling me to check over at the drugstore. When I asked at the drugstore for a postcard, the woman said, 'No, why should we have it?'

"I think you people are missing a bet. For non-natives one of Oxford's chief attractions is William Faulkner."

"We have a lot of writers other than Faulkner," the woman retorted indignantly.

"Name them: for instance?"

"Well," said the woman in a belligerent drawl, "you see that woman that just walked out of here? Her son is a writer."

"Well," said Mrs. Hughes triumphanly, "after all, Faulkner is your only Nobel Prize Winner!"

The "Grand Tour" on the occasion of her retirement was the most spectacular of her travels. It lasted from June to November and included a course in the University of Madrid, every bit in Spanish; touring around England and Ireland with a retired Barnard professor friend in a little car and no commitments; visiting Majorca, Sicily, Egypt, Lebanon, Syria, Jordan and Israel. On the Nile she dined on a boat, **The Rubaiyat,** with a former student who was in charge of the Middle East International News Service. (Even in foreign lands Mrs. Hughes is not immune from her former students who always heighten her enjoyment of travel.) Another student, proprietor of **Estudios Technicas,** sent flowers to her room in Rio de Janeiro when she spent one week of nine in South America on a post liberation vacation in 1966.

The "Grand Tour" was climaxed with a week's seminar in Athens, Greece, for members of the Greek Heritage Society, followed with a week's cruise to Crete, Rhodes, Ephesus and Istanbul in Turkey and three small islands.

In 1971 she went on a "behind the Iron Curtain tour" which included visits to Berlin, Germany; Warsaw, Poland; Leningrad and Moscow, Russia; Bucharest, Rumania; Budapest, Hungary; Bratislava, Czechoslovakia.

From her travels, she has accumulated a hoard of international good luck charms. Figa from Brazil; Mennehuni, the Polynesian charm bought in Hawaii; leprechauns and lucky star glass from Ireland; good luck charms from the Thunderbird, American Indian; glacier boy, Alaska; Ki, Bolivia; and blind musician, Ecuador.

On her return from her 1974 world travels, Mrs. Hughes had to figure out what to do with her time. What does someone with a vibrant voice, an alive mind broadened by traveling and reading, umpteen years teaching experience and a compulsive interest in genealogy and history of her surroundings, do with herself in "retirement?" The turn of events in Marshall gave Mrs. Hughes a solution to the course of her life. On October 3, 1975 two rooms of the Old County Courthouse were converted into a museum.

Mrs. Hughes always loved museums. In fact, she had preached museums to her students. "All the years I taught, I tried to get my students to get their parents aroused to the need for a museum in Marshall." And so, when the curator became ill, Mrs. Hughes was the natural replacement.

When she took over in 1976 there were still only two rooms of museum. "Such a hodge-podge of history—a cane sword, and the key to the first jail; an old folding umbrella, Bristol vases, a handsome Syllabub set—all in one case. It just grieved my sense of correlation. We were so severely limited on space."

She considered it her responsibility to make the museum respectable and worthy of being Marshall's museum; after all, Marshall is "the Athens of Texas." She is fond of enumerating Harrison County's "firsts." It had the first people in the area, the Caddo Indians who supplied the word Tayshas, origin of **Texas**, "friendly." It had the first funeral home in Texas; the first telegraph office in Texas; the first natural gas; the first and **only** "First **Lady** of the Land"—Lady Bird Johnson.

Thirteen Texas counties were named from sometime citizens of Harrison County. She says of Marshall, with much pride and poetic license, "We encircle the globe and the moon." She refers not only to her many students but innumerable other Marshallites who have taken their places in the world, contributing to its human resources. The allusion to the moon is based on her student who was one of the frogmen that retrieved the landing module after the first Lunar walk.

One of the first things she did as curator was get rid of the title "curator." "I don't let them call me that if I can help it. In the first place I don't like that word, and in the second place the word curator implies a specific knowledge of a specific field." Mrs. Hughes needed a catch-all word to more adequately describe her work—which included begging and acquisition, research, editing, touring, janitorial duties. She chose the word "Director." When she told a friend of her decision, the friend was horrified that she would use the title without authorization. "Is that what they call you, Inez?" "That's what they're going to call me."

And that's what they do call her. With Inez Hughes as director, the museum has swelled from two rooms to twelve, thanks to her boundless energies. Mrs. Hughes, who acquired her love of history from her husband, doesn't claim to have the thoroughness or discipline of an historian. But what she lacks in scholarship, she makes up for in enthusiasm and hard work.

The fact that she was a teacher in Marshall for 37 years worked to her advantage. As a result of her students' genealogy charts, she was well-acquainted with family backgrounds. "I knew the people that had things or should have things." Armed with that knowledge, she knocked at the doors of attics. "It just takes someone to walk, talk, eat, sleep, dream, breathe museum." (You could not pay someone to do this. There wouldn't be enough money.)

She felt a responsibility to display the town's heirlooms to their best advantage. So while there is still an odd assortment of history's remnants, it is no longer in hodge-podge arrangements. Mrs. Hughes is a firm believer in the continuity of history. Each room has its own pace and chronology and builds toward the future.

Despite the shoestring budget, Mrs. Hughes had displayed all the objects with great style. "I can't stand flatness," says Mrs. Hughes. "I like to present softness." When velvet is used in the glass cases, it is a hilly velvet, arranged in topographical folds by Mrs. Hughes. Objects are on many levels. And any visual monotony inherent in museums is further relieved by the expanse and range of Mrs. Hughes voice and knowledge.

Tourists expecting the usual remote glasscase-haze of history with exciting events condensed onto 3 x 5 cards, are happily surprised. Going through the museum with Mrs. Hughes as guide is like sharing an intimate afternoon with someone's heirlooms. "I have begged and I have accessioned practically everything and I always have asked everything about everything—who owned it and when and where it was used." She reveals this information on the lively tour. Unlike most museum tours, which seem like history put to Muzak, hers is fresh and exhilarating.

Unfortunately, Mrs. Hughes and her exhibits have been mildly victimized by the capriciousness of the neon lights at the museum. Some have been out for seven years. She gives the neon the withering glances she had formerly reserved for unmanageable students.

The Old Courthouse on Peter Whetstone Square is a magnificent setting for a museum. Included in the exhibits are artifacts of the Caddo Indians. The transportation room spans the steamboat era all the way up to the moon landing. A full size plexiglas horse pulls a courting buggy. Three sketches of the early Texas and Pacific locomotives have been made free hand by an 86-year-old man. Along with the old memorabilia is the latest "transportation," a picture of her frogman in his scuba suit recovering the capsule from the lunar walk. There is a music suite with one of the first recording machines. Early radios of the Twentieth Century with earphones remind Mrs. Hughes that when radios first came out, the fun was seeing how many stations you could get. There is a room of pioneer implements that look like Mrs. Hughes went through the debris of an old garage or barn to collect them. There is a needlecraft room which she calls "Milady's Bailiwick." In that room are linen cloth samples from her own great-great-grandmother. Another great-great-grandmother, Mrs. Prothro raised her own silk worms, spun her own thread and wove her own cloth to make a silk dress. She combined the silk with mohair and made a tailored suit of broadcloth for her husband.

There are many miscellaneous items, not displayed miscellaneously. Publicity for an old beauty shop with croquignole, spiral and special oil wave advertised. There is a fraulein doll with two braids, dolls with porcelain faces, rag dolls, character dolls, dolls of all eras. In the clock room, history's time pieces are displayed, starting from an arabic clock that predates Christ. There are carriage clocks, key wind watches, a Topsey clock, little Bens and big Bens.

There is a room of religious memorabilia which has the ark and Torah from the old Moses Montefiore Jewish Temple in Marshall. There are mementos of lodges and political campaigns, two rooms of military memorabilia. There is to be a local industries exhibit, dealing with Marshall in the age of machines and factories.

One of the outstanding rooms is the celebrities exhibit. It is kind of like parents night at the school for Mrs. Hughes. Many of the people are former students. Bill Moyers, Joseph Goulden, Y. A. Tittle. All have their own cases. In that room the candy case from Lady Bird Johnson's father's store is used for displaying glassware. A specially designed case, containing the First Lady's gown, is flanked by flats filled with pictures and other mementos of the Johnsons.

When the busloads of children surge into her museum, once more Mrs. Hughes is in her element. Instead of one classroom she has twelve rooms that spiral upwards and hundreds of years of history to cover. Unfortunately she no longer has the year to play with, sometimes she has the children a mere hour, which is only enough time to raise her blood pressure.

The children drag from room to room. Mrs. Hughes' voice tries to rally them. "Step briskly, children. If you spend half your time going from room to room, you miss half the museum." As the children wander and fidget, overwhelmed by the many objects of the museum, she says dramatically, "Children, I like to look in your eyes when I'm talking to you. They are the windows to your soul." If the children murmur among themselves, she reprimands them with her philosophy. "Children, you never learn anything so long as you're doing the talking. You learn by listening and reading."

Just as a dancer cannot disguise her calves, so too a teacher has certain markings that don't go away. A joy in the acquisition of knowledge; but also a teacher's exasperation, patience worn paper thin.

As a teacher, Mrs. Hughes was adroit using the red pencil in the margins to mark down ignored rules. She still has a red pencil reaction to improper usage, ill-manners, stupidity. "I have such intolerance for dishonesty, lack of integrity." The withering glance is still in her arsenal, but her smile and optimism are in command.

The bane of her existence as a museum director is discovering objects with "not a sign of a date, not a sign of identification." In the museum office is an old clock that someone very nicely dated "December 1, 1887, 1 a.m.," when it was first set. She encourages the children to "always put a date on everything you do."

Mrs. Hughes is a volunteer without any 9 to 5 to define her days. Her hours are her own, to give away. Her life is joyously given up to the unexpected. The phone rings. "Hello?" A new name. She takes hold of the name learning to pronounce it, discovering its origins, as if it were a rare vase. The woman with the strange name asks if she might come in and discuss genealogy. Mrs. Hughes says "Certainly. The afternoon looks free so far. But that's my life. Always something unexpected." Her freedom means that when the museum closes at 4:30, if a couple comes and expresses interest in the museum at 4:15, she will take them around.

Mrs. Hughes is just as busy as she always was. "Before I was too busy grading themes, and now I'm too busy with the museum." Besides spending days touring classes in the museum and doing research, helping people to shake their family trees, and creating displays, her nights are equally occupied. Like Robert Frost's traveler she has miles to go before she sleeps. A stack of newspapers stands a yard high in the center of her much lived-in library. It's gerbil paradise. She has miles of newsprint to scan every night and clip to fill the scrapbooks and folders that Marshall's history is divided into. She has magazines to read and letters to answer. Usually as the birds begin their pre-dawn shift, Mrs Hughes is just retiring.

If there would be rooms enough and time enough, there is certainly history enough in Harrison County to fill the Old Courthouse. And Inez Hughes is the woman with energy enough to do it. Not only has she generously preserved the history of her town, but she helped shape the lives of the children who will make new history.

As a teacher Mrs. Hughes tried to instill in her children a sense of the world and a sense of themselves in the world. The lesson à la Emerson that she taught most thoroughly is the lesson that her existence exemplifies: "The only true gift is a portion of thyself. . ."

In her life, Inez Hatley Hughes has given a portion of herself, again and again and again.

A Self-Contained Man

by Donna Darling and Jamie Frucht

Edward Bertram Evans, like Will Rogers, never met a man he didn't like. The conversation and memoirs of the man who came to Praire View A&M College in 1918 and served as its president from 1946 until his retirement in 1966 are filled with complimentary adjectives about those he has known. Relatives, friends, and fellow educators are described with words like "kindly," "Christian," "pleasant," "sympathetic," "understanding," "frugal," "fine," "brilliant," "dedicated," and "conscientious" to name only a few.

"Whatever I have acomplished, if anything," says Evans, "has been done with the help of all the fine people that I have met along the way. They are the ones who deserve the credit."

However, a closer look at the impact this capable educator and administrator has had on the development of Prairie View A&M College would tend to indicate that many of the kind words and much of the credit he assigns to others must at some point come full circle.

Edward Bertram Evans was born in Kansas City, Missouri on May 10, 1894. Dr. Evans describes his ancestors as average, God-fearing Americans and ascribes his later success to the loving care, interest and home training given him by his parents during his formative years.

They lived in the home his father, a carpenter, had built. His father was a man of many talents and many jobs. He worked for the railroads as a porter and liked to take his son with him. "Wherever he went he managed to take me with him, saying, 'You want to go to Denver with me tonight? (or Chicago, or wherever).' " His father also had a moving business, and in his later years became one of the best embalmers in Kansas City.

The young Edward was to grow up and become a veterinarian. As a boy, thanks to his father, he was surrounded by an assortment of animals. There was a string of also-ran racehorses. And eight hounds that got the benefit of his mama's home-cooking—great pans of corn bread. Edward used to raise rabbits and pigeons and always had a pet dog at heel.

There was also a little stream that ran through the farm. Edward watched over the stream, pursuing wayward wildlife. "When I was a boy, I used to go down there and catch the little crayfish, and we had ducks. When those ducklings would get in the water they didn't have sense enough to come back home. They'd get started down the creek and never look back. I'd have to go down the creek about half a mile and get them. The little creek looked like the Mississippi River to me, but when I went back home and looked at that thing, you could spit across it. It was a big disappointment."

It was one of the few disappointments in Edward's early life, and that only in retrospect. "No boy has ever had a happier life than was mine during childhood days. My mother always saw to it that I was properly dressed, polite, respectful to my elders, and attended school regularly and promptly. From the very beginning I always enjoyed going to school and quite often endured severe, cold weather to attend.''

Of all his early attributes, which Evans still displays, and which were to stand him in good stead on the road to success, politeness is valued above all. Politeness, however, the way Dr. Evans practiced it in life, does not have the contained connotation of manners. Politeness was a philosophy of respect and caring for others.

Dr. Evans recalls that in the third grade, he would go home after school and sit on the high fence around the lumberyard next to his home. This was on the route that the principal of his school, Mr. J. Dallas Bowser, often took, and Edward always tipped his hat and spoke to the principal as he passed. During the closing exercises at school that year, Edward was called to the platform and awarded a prize for being the most polite student in the school.

This prize was to be the first in a long line of honors Dr. Evans would ultimately receive. Politeness coupled with good common sense would prove valuable during his adult life as a Negro in the south, where segregation and discrimination were the rule rather than the exception.

While working in a Kansas City drugstore, Edward became acquainted with a Negro veterinarian, C. V. Lowe, who encouraged him to study veterinary medicine. It's hard to tell which convinced Edward, Lowe's pleasing personality or the gold coins he so freely flashed around in public.

At any rate, Edward saved up $80 and set out for Iowa State University. It was a September day in 1914 and the first time he had ever been away from home alone.

When he arrived in Ames, he asked the first man he saw where the Negroes lived in the town. ''He appeared puzzled, looked up and down the street, and said that he did not know.'' A second person directed him to a barber shop where he met a Negro porter. Again, he asked where the Negroes lived. The porter pointed to a shoe shine parlor across the street and said, ''That fellow and his family are the only other Negroes in town, and we don't speak.''

''That other fellow,'' George Gaiter, took Edward in for the night.

While searching for a room near campus, Edward met a young Negro from South Carolina who was also enrolling in the School of Verterinary Medicine. He had been an aprentice to a Spanish shoemaker and was running a small shoe shop in the basement of a building just off campus. The two young men found a room over a corner barber shop and Edward went to work as a porter in the shop. They put in long hours at work and studied late at night. ''We frequently closed our books and raised the shades to find that it was morning and we had studied all night.'' They prepared their meals in the shoe shop and often existed on one meal a day.

The second year was even worse. The winter was intensely cold and they frequently had to study in caps and overcoats. In the middle of the winter, Edward ran out of money and had just about decided to call it quits. He told one of his professors, Dr. H. S. Murphy, about his decision and Dr. Murphy urged him to stay, saying he would try to help find Edward a job and a decent place to live. Dr. Murphy arranged for the two students to live in one of his own bedrooms if they would tend the furnace and remove the ashes from the basement once a day.

"The bedroom that we occupied was heated from the furnace and was so comfortable that it took us about two months to become adjusted to the warmth and stay awake while studying at night."

At the close of his sophomore year, Edward was employed as a laboratory technician by Dr. Hans Jensen, President of the Jensen Salsbery Laboratories, a Veterinary Biological Manufacturing Company which at that time was the largest in the country.

"At the close of my first day's work in that laboratory, a committee representing the employees informed Dr. Jensen, my boss, that if I continued to work in the laboratory, they would all quit. He informed them that I was going to work and that if they were not willing to work with me, then they need not return the next morning. All of the employees reported for work the following morning, and when I resigned at the close of the summer to return to college, they had a party for me and presented me with a gift." Experience has taught him, Dr. Evans says, that "regardless of the prejudices people have, if you can establish a good relationship where one man can see the good in the other, that's the best way I know of to establish good will."

The urgency of World War I was so acute that the Veterinary Medicine program was accelerated. At the completion of the program in January 1918, most of the members of Edward's class were called to Officers' Training School in Fort Snelling, Minnesota. At that time the Army was not accepting Negro veterinarians for active service as commissioned officers in the Medical Corps. Before leaving college, however, Edward did enroll as a private in the reserve of the Veterinary Medicine section of the Medical Corps.

About two weeks after he graduated and returned home, he received a job offer from I. M. Terrell, principal of Prairie View Normal and Industrial College, Prairie View, Texas. The position was Veterinarian for the college and professor of Veterinary Science and Animal husbandry. It paid $75 per month. He accepted the position with the intention of leaving after that year and opening up his own private practice. But Prairie View won him over, and the one year turned into 58. Prairie View, a livestock community, was an ideal location and atmosphere for Dr. Evans to pursue his career, which was to include service to the school, the community and eventually the world.

Before he retired, he would serve as director of athletics, acting registrar, acting director of the School of Arts and Sciences, state leader for Negro Extension Service and finally principal. In 1948, with the organization of the A&M College system, he would become president of Prairie View A&M College. He would also help establish a school of Veterinary Medicine at Tuskegee Institute in Alabama.

Dr. Evans mustered the $18 one-way railway fare from Kansas City to Hempstead, the closest stop to Prairie View and was ushered into the dining hall upon his arrival at the college. "I shall never forget my amezement and astonishment when I walked into the dining hall and saw 700 Negro students—it just took my breath away. I had been raised among my own people, but I had never seen that many young Negro men and women assembled in a dining facility."

Later, Dr. Evans described his elation. "It was just like throwing Brer Rabbit in the Briar Patch, me going there. I never looked back. I've had a mighty lot of fun."

Soon after coming to Texas, Dr. Evans had the distinction of being the first Negro ever to take the State Board veterinary examination. There was speculation about whether or not he would pass; and on his part, about whether or not he would be licensed. He passed the test and received license number 237, indicating that only 236 persons had been licensed as veterinarians in Texas to that time.

When he first came to Prairie View, the classroom facilities were rather crude. "I had no equipment, no funds for a laboratory or teaching materials. Consequently, I set about immediately, with the assistance of my students, to prepare teaching specimens from material coming from the slaughterhouse and any other sources from which they could be gathered. Our ingenuity plus hard work resulted in an effective teaching program despite the absence of a laboratory and teaching specimens."

It was not long before farmers and ranchmen began to come to the campus seeking information and assistance. "I had no means of transportation, so it was provided by those who needed my services. Often I would leave the campus in a buggy to travel to points that required a full day to acomplish my mission. I was so interested in serving people that I never thought of money, and I gave the best service that I knew how to give to the rich and poor, black and white alike."

Dr. Evans' "house calls" did more than cure animals. By his example, he helped lessen the prejudice that was endemic in the area. Later he was told the Klan had discussed him but took the position that he was helping the community.

Dr. Evans took risks that paid off. For example, he was once summoned to the little town of Field Store about three miles from Prairie View. Previously, Negroes had had to make a big detour around the town. Evans was the first of his race to go there. Dr. Evans skill was needed. The hogs had to be inoculated. People from miles around had come to see the spectacle of a Negro in Field Store. Dr. Evans recalls the scene.

"They had the hogs all penned up—a couple hundred head. I took two students to help with the vaccinations. An old man with a cane walked up to the farmer whose hogs were being vaccinated, and said, 'I wouldn't give you 10 cents apiece for these hogs tomorrow.' Six months later I went back and vaccinated **his** hogs."

The white farmers and ranchmen who had profited from Evans' advice and assistance sent a petition to the principal of Prairie View, stating the valuable service Dr. Evans had rendered the community and expressing the hope that school officials would do all they could to furnish him with the necessary facilities and equipment to expand his services. Eventually the people from Field Store, thanks to Dr. Evans, came down to Prairie View and used the resources of the college. The incident reconfirmed Evans' conviction about the importance of giving conscientious and dedicated service to the public under all circumstances—a lesson he feels mankind today should remember.

Dr. Evans puts great stock in teachers as motivators. He can call by name the teachers who greatly influenced his life. He is firm in his belief that if a teacher is to inspire anyone else, he should know his subject matter thoroughly and believe in what he is teaching with all his heart. The teachers at Prairie View, though they didn't have a string of degrees, did have the dedication.

The atmosphere at Prairie View was examplary, "Students sat at the feet of educators, almost worshipped them," he recalls. In 1918, the 700 students were a captive but appreciative audience. Since they had to stay on the campus from September to May, it was up to the college to furnish recreation, culture and religion. Because of this necessity, a community developed that went beyond just studies. It was a closely knit faculty and student body that functioned more as a family than as an institution.

All 700 students ate at the dining hall at one time (the amazing scene Dr. Evans had seen upon his arrival) with a faculty member at each table. And all the students sang grace at one time. People would come just to hear them sing. Manners were practiced at the table. Dr. Evans looks back at those times with longing. "Today students grab a sandwich and run with it."

Clothing was also of a pattern, not haphazard. The dress requirements are reflected in the Board minutes dated May 22, 1911:

"That the uniforms for girl students shall be dark blue made into a coat suit and that each girl provide herself with two suits; that the uniform for boys be of some serviceable blue material at a price not to exceed ten dollars per suit with a brown campaign hat similar to that worn by the United States Army; that all girls be required to deposit on entrance $7.50 to cover the cost of two uniforms and a hat to be selected, and that all boys be required to deposit $12.00 on entrance to cover the cost of uniform and hat; that the principal be authorized to select and purchase the material for making the uniforms for the girls and employ necessary assistance for a teacher in the sewing department for making of these uniforms during the first three weeks of the session of 1911-12; that the principal secure bids from the manufacturers of uniforms for boys, such bids to be opened at a special meeting of the Prairie View Committee of the Board."

The students' dormitory rooms had wood burning stoves and the students had to go to the wood yard and get wood to keep their rooms warm.

In the Chapel, girls sat on one side, boys on the other. The Gospel singing was inspiring and earned the choir the opportunity to make annual tours to various sections of the country. Dr. Evans recalls some of the difficulties of traveling with a large group of Negro singers during the earlier days. "The choir was invited to sing at the general session of the annual meeting of the Association of Land Grant Colleges, which was held at the Rice Hotel in Houston. When the choir arrived at the hotel, they were refused entrance through the front door and had to go to the back of the hotel and go up to the conference on the second floor on a freight elevator."

Among other entertainments at Prairie View, there were debates and silent movies. Dr. Evans remembers Miss Vigie Carrington, a student from Austin, who accompanied the silent pictures as a pianist and vocalist. He remembers the beautiful spring garden, which students would stroll through on Sunday afternoons after "quiet hour." Dr. Evans has many memories of those good times and sums them up in the words, "The students were so fine."

At one time, 90 percent of all the Negro public school teachers in Texas were graduates or ex-students of Prairie View. One of Dr. Evans' concerns has been the small number of agricultural graduates from Prairie View who have taken advantage of the opportunities to become managers of large ranches and farms owned by wealthy citizens, and the small number of graduates in agriculture who go back to the farm or become interested in dirt farming.

Dr. Evans' concern for people dominated his presidency at the college. "When there was a family on the campus in trouble, I was never happy." He was influential in developing the Alta Vista Community which made it possible for Negroes to live in an area that was first-class and affordable. Dr. Evans told the architects not to build any house more than $17,000. The development was a success.

Dr. Evans was a man of action who followed the tortoise's strategy, not the rabbit's. Prairie View was a campus with few real streets, only trails of dust or mud, depending on the weather. Dr. Evans, through his friendship with the county commissioner, was able to prevail on the county to build some roads. "I just took it in bites; I'd ask them to pave five or six blocks at a time."

Dr. Evans helped encourage athletics at the college. "One of the most sensible moves that I made in my early days on the campus was to associate myself with the more mature, solid citizens at the institution, most of whom were interested in and closely associated with athletics." Prairie View has dominated the athletic field among the Negro colleges of the Southwest since the beginning of intercollegiate athletics.

For many years, Prairie View promoted the second oldest football bowl game in the country—the New Year's Day Classic, played in Houston. The Cotton Bowl Game, played at the State Fair, was held for 33 years and was played on "Negro Day," a day set aside by park officials to permit Negroes the use of all facilities. It was an occasion for a statewide holiday for all of the Negro public schools.

In 1922, basketball was recognized as an official sport in the Southwestern Athletic Conference, of which Prairie View was a part. The colleges had no gymnasiums or field houses; consequently, the games were played out-of-doors on dirt courts when the weather was good. In extremely cold weather, some resourcefulness was necessary:

the games were played in the college dining halls. Tables and chairs were removed, and players learned to manuever around the posts on the playing floor.

Being black during the early 1900's provided Dr. Evans with some "interesting" experiences, all of which he handled with common sense and reason. For example, most of the transportation of football teams and fans at that time was by train. "I shall not forget a trip that the team made to St. Louis to play Lincoln University of Missouri. The Missouri Pacific Railroad furnished the transportation, and we departed from Houston around 4 p.m. When the dinner hour arrived, we were permitted to go into the dining car to eat only after all of the other passengers had been served.

"The next morning before breakfast, a waiter came into our "Jim Crow" car and began taking orders for breakfast. Coach Taylor asked him why he did not wait until the men were in the dining car. His reply was that they intended to bring breakfast to our car and serve it on trays to be held on our laps. This so infuriated the coach that he announced to the waiter that if we could not eat in the dining car, we would not eat at all.

"The dining car steward and the conductor came to persuade us to change our minds, but we would not yield. When the train reached a station about two hours later, a small dining car was attached to the train next to our coach and we were served in that facility for the remainder of the trip."

Discrimination created severe inequalities in education. Dr. Evans describes the inequities in the separate but unequal Negro agricultural college. "For many years Negro agricultural colleges had wanted to conduct research programs just as the white land grant colleges were doing. They were always told that there was no need for them to carry on a research program because the white institutions were already engaged in research and their findings were available to all of the colleges and citizens of the U. S. There was one thing that they forgot to recognize, probably on purpose, and it was that Negroes were not being given a chance to engage in the scientific laboratory experience associated with research work." In 1948, the situation changed. The Nation's first bona fide experiment substation at a Negro college, under the auspices of the U. S. Department of Agriculture and a state land grant college, was established at Prairie View.

Dr. Evans, in the opinion of an associate, was "the best public relations man that has ever been on the Prairie View scene. As an administrator he could get along with anybody." This ties in with his concern for people. His philosophy is elementary. "The golden rule. It's just that simple. I never let anybody treat me better than I treat them."

This ability to get along proved invaluable in his global work in 1953 for the Food and Agricultural Organization of the United Nations and Department of State. He was involved in Point Four Evaluations and in studies in Ethiopia, Egypt and Pakistan to determine the progress being made in Rinderpest eradication. Rinderpest, a disease of cattle and other animals, was responsible for half the livestock deaths in

African countries. If it could be controlled, there would be more protein available for the people in Africa.

During his stay in Pakistan he was continually warned about a certain ferocious doctor "This man he is the very devil to get along with, a tough nut to crack." With those advance warnings, Dr. Evans set out to meet the doctor. "We were out there in the country, sitting on a well top, just about dark. I had tried to avoid mentioning the purpose of my visit to the doctor, but finally I told him I was checking on Rinderpest eradication. The doctor said, 'Well now, Dr. Evans, I guess people have told you I'm the very devil to get along with.' " Dr. Evans parried words with him, and in the end the Pakistani doctor was receptive and they became working friends. The moral was not lost on Dr. Evans, "I never would have known him as a man if we hadn't gotten together. You never know people until you get with them."

Along with this lesson in fellowship, Dr. Evans made other important observations based on his travel in Third-world countries.

"I observed, first, that men are basically the same all over the world. Environment and climate may be responsible for some variations in their ways of life, but men are basically the same.

"My second observation was that brilliant minds and ideas are not confined to America. They are found in the underdeveloped countries as well.

"My third observation led me to conclude that the two most important needs in the underdeveloped countries are technical education and unselfish leadership. The leaders must be persons with a spirit to serve humanity and with a sympathetic understanding of the needs of people." (This description fits Dr. Evans himself quite well.)

"My fourth observation of the people of the countries that I visited revealed that they have learned that there is a better way of life and that they are determined to have it. The extent to which land reform is being carried out is one of the first steps in that direction."

In 1958, Dr. Evans was given the Texas State Teachers Association Award as an Educational Pioneer in Africa and for rendering distinguished service to mankind.

In 1963, Dr. Evans participated in the World Food Forum and rates it as "the most thrilling experience in public appearances that I had as a public servant. I was selected to serve as chairman of the Third Plenary Session of the World Food Forum. There were more than 2,000 scientists present from all parts of the world—men and women trained in agriculture, nutrition and other sciences, along with experts on the world population and the world food supply."

Dr. Evans' dedication, ability as an educator and administrator, and devotion to the betterment of mankind in general have brought him such recognition as the Silver Beaver and Silver Antelope Awards, presented by the Boy Scouts of America; the $5,000 and a gold medallion which go with the Hoblitzelle Award for contribution in the field of Rural Development; the National 4-H Club award; the Good Neighbor Distinguished Alumnus Award from Iowa State University; and an honorary Doctor of Science degree from that same institution.

Dr. Evans' basic concern for people and his even greater concern for the future of mankind and the world, he says, is best expressed by the passage in the Bible which says, "For what does a man profit if he should gain the whole world but lose his soul?"

He sermonizes on his concern: "We have mastered the land, the oceans, and the skies and are in the midst of conquering space. We have exploited the earth of its minerals and the forests of their timber. We have polluted streams and poisoned the animal life therein and have long taken from the land its fertility.

"Unless we give dedicated efforts to conserving human resources, our efforts to conserve nature will go for naught. People, not green fields and skyscrapers, will remain the cornerstone of a great civilization.

"When we think of man in relationship to society, we can but think of the unit of its structure, which is the family. The family is man's basic social institution, for it is in the family that one receives his basic and long-lasting values, attitudes, hopes and aspirations, or conversely, dependency, futility and despair.

"Thus our efforts to improve the lot of the individual should be aimed at building and conserving healthy family living, the basis of which are education, good health, and economic stability.

"Much greater impetus should be given to adult education, which is the most neglected of all educational programs, and a more realistic and practical approach should be given to study and education in the area of family life and living. We have just scratched the surface in our practical approach to bringing about an improvement in our human resources."

In his retirement, Dr. Evans still looks to education to provide solutions to a mode of life that is becoming increasingly complicated as the century progresses. Having contributed to some of the world's solutions, he now sits sequestered in the knowledge of his active and rewarding past, and prays that Man will choose the right paths, those that lead to more than survival—that lead in fact, to renewed quality and meaning in life.

In retrospect, Dr. Evans expresses no regrets about his life.

"If I had my life to live over, I would like to chart the same course that I have traveled in the past. Life has been sweet; it has been exciting and challenging all along the way. Shakespeare said, 'There is a tide in the affairs of man, which, taken at the flood, leads on to fortune; omitted, all the voyage of their life is bound in shallows and in miseries.' Through divine guidance, I suppose, I have been successful in taking the tide at just the right time."

THE PLAYBILL

Works in Progress

by Jamie Frucht

Scene: Broadway

Ada Elliot, second lead, is standing in the wings of the Empire Theater waiting to go on. Jovena Howland, big Hollywod star stands with her. The play is a real turkey about the life of Marie Dressler. Jovena suddenly looks down at her feet and realizes she's forgotten to change her shoes for the next scene.

JOVENA: *(to Ada)* Oh, dear, go back to the dressing room and get my shoes.

ADA: You go back to the dressing room and get your own shoes. *(Just then their cue comes and both women sweep on to the stage in character. But after the final act, Jovena sends her maid, Germaine, up to Ada's dressing room with an ultimatum.)*

GERMAINE: Jovena wants you to come down to her dressing room.

ADA: *(removing make-up lines that turned her into an older woman)* It's no further for her to come up here than for me to go down there. If she wants to see me, tell her to come up here.

(Jovena comes up, stands glaring in the doorway, eyeing Ada. After several silent seconds)—

JOVENA: Kid, where you from?

ADA: Texas.

JOVENA: By God, that explains it!

But does it?

THE EMPIRE THEATRE

Forty years have gone by. It's now 1975. Ada Elliot is at the Capitol in Austin. It's early in the morning but a group of women in pink are swarming about the lobby. It's Ada's turn to stare; she thoroughly enjoys herself. "Long pink velvet formals at 9 in the morning?" Rather than retreat, she gamely sits down stage center at a table. A preacher, petition in hand, approaches her—a sure bet.

PREACHER: Would you like to sign it now?

ADA: *(relishes the moment, keeps her trained voice level)* What is it? *(Of course she knows what it is.)*

PREACHER: *(leads with his pen)* A petition against this terrible Equal Rights Amendment. Would you like to sign it now?

ADA: No, I would not like to sign it now or any other time.

PREACHER: *(confused)* Well why not?

(By now several women, hearing the sweeping voice, have come over to find out what the trouble is. Ada is engulfed in a pink sea. Later, in retelling the incident, she uses falsetto to capture the pink ladies' plea.)

TWO LADIES: It will ruin our homes. It will ruin our homes!

ADA: What's the **matter** with your **homes?** How is giving you the same rights as a man has going to ruin your homes?

TWO LADIES: *(frightened, cling to each other)* Well, we'll be drafted.

ADA: If an occasion arose where they needed to draft women to defend the country, wouldn't you be **willing** to be drafted?

TWO LADIES: Well yes—I guess so.

Ada is still a force to be reckoned with. She played that scene so well because she's had ample practice. The last time Ada had to say those lines was in 1918 when she was working to get the vote for women in Texas. History is a terrible repetition. "I hear the same argument used today against ERA as I've heard against women's having the vote. Same identical thing. 'It will destroy our femininity: It will destroy our homes.' "

Then as now, Ada uses the power of speech and intelligence to get her point across, to change minds and counteract the flimsy pink arguments. "I never did break up any furniture or go into violence of any kind; I just made speeches around the State."

The leading lady who asked her to fetch her shoes, the preacher who asked her to sign up against ERA, they couldn't have been more amazed than the creative writing teacher who assigned a short story to her class and received a shocker from that older woman in the back row. The story entitled "Sex and the Senior Citizen" is about an older woman who decides to research first hand that intriguing subject. "I wanted to find out when the sex impulse stopped impulsing, if ever. . . I got no encouragement from any of the various foundations, though many of them are headed by men who are in the senior citizen bracket. So I started out to do a 'Kinsey' on my own." After a few dates and beers and many entertaining pages later, the story is resolved. Yes, there is sex after Medicaid.

The actress, the preacher, the creative writing teacher, all were confused and surprised—some pleasantly, some otherwise. The contralto of her voice does not explain it. When someone who doesn't know Ada speaks to her on the phone, he will invariably say, "Yes, Sir." The voice defies categorization, but Ada has more than a deep, full voice. Faces are mere facades which age can harm. But age can't touch Ada's voice. Her's is a three-dimensional voice. It can whisper into the past, analyze the present and command the future. Ada can be anything she wants, and has been—writer, raconteur, newspaper reporter, stage actress, singer, suffragist. But it is Ada's energy and interest that define her, more than any role. Force, conviction and sureness come through that voice and convince others, impel others, to say "Yes, Sir."

Yes sir, Ada Elliot is quite a woman. But how to explain her. The Past?

Her papa was a villain. One afternoon he grabbed a crying baby out of the arms of an abandoned mother and in a moustached aside bragged, "Little does she know I already have a wife. Ha Ha Ha." Ada's papa, whom she describes in one of her stories as a "mature man with a wealth of dark brown hair and a well waxed handle-bar moustache," was the director and chief actor on the showboat "Mississippi." He was very good at his profession. Too good. One day in the child-snatching scene, an incensed patron, unable to withstand the mother's tears, stood up, pointed a pistol, and in a dead serious voice said, "Give her back her kid. I said, 'Give her back her kid!'" He did.

Ada's grandfather had preached from the pulpit; her father had fulminated from the stage. Ada was a natural. When she was eight, her family moved from a resort town in Arkansas to Waco, where she grew up. She and two sisters sang with a local group called the "Forty Singers." They were the only girls among 40 boys, and caught the eyes and ears of a visiting talent scout who booked them for vaudeville in 1905-1906. Traveling the Southern route, the three girls performed in a sister act similar to the McGuire Sisters, and also sang a medley of Stephen Foster songs in black face. Ada was a real trouper.

Many years later in 1935-40, the theater bug still in her system, Ada took on Broadway which was then experiencing an era of good shows. She went around to casting calls but was told she wasn't old enough or heavy enough for the character parts she was reading for. Ingenuity and perseverance saved the day. She returned to her little hotel room behind the Palace Theater, padded herself with towels, powdered her hair white and drew lines on her face to make the transition. Then she marched back to the audition and captured the part.

On Broadway she appeared in **Personal Appearance; Three Men on a Horse; Blind Alley;** and **Evening Star,** to name a few of her choice roles.

Ada Elliot has the kind of past that thrives in scrapbooks. She could sail by on that past if she wanted to, which she doesn't. All that remains from her era of vaudeville and acting is the trained rich voice. The mementos—playbills, photos, reviews, she relegated to the basement of her big house in Dallas where she lived upon returning from New York. When the basement was flooded, it took all her photos as souvenirs. Even if the mementos were still around, Ada would not be fingering those old photos and memories.

She does not dwell in the past. She occasionally borrows its episodes for her stories as she does in "Rescue at Bugscuffle." With a little prodding, she can backtrack 68 years to the time when she was 19 and only one year out of college. Ada went to Bugscuffle (20 miles northwest of Waco) to a one room schoolhouse that had no inner walls and no desks. Thirty-seven boys and girls called her Teacher as they sat attentively on their crude benches learning "readin', ritin', and rithmetic.' Then the 38th child entered. He didn't want to learn; he was only interested in rocking the bench to everyone's distraction. "NO" wouldn't stop him. Writing a letter home to his parents didn't work since they could not read. As a last resort, Teacher gave his legs a good switching. The kid vowed that his grandma would hang the Teacher for that, but Ada pushed the suggestion out of her mind as being ridiculous and illegal. Later that day the kid showed up with the whole clan in a wagon. Grandma had a hanging rope and meant business. Then in a spectacular Hollywood ending, the son of the family Ada was boarding with came to her rescue. It was rumored he was a horse thief, but he was a handsome horse thief. He galloped up and, pointing a gun at Granny, said, "Hol' it." Granny protested, "She whooped Jimmy, an' I'm goin' to hang'er fer it." The episode has a happy ending. The clan was persuaded that Jimmy was really unhurt and a pest, and Teacher got to teach in peace.

Ada's repertoire is full of adventures. She enjoyed gambling in the fiesta halls in Mexico in the State of Nogales. One night, sitting right next to Ada was one of life's great gamblers—Pancho Villa. Ada and the rest were gambling with real silver dollars.

When Pancho lost his last silver dollar, he pulled out a new crisp bill of his own printing and put it neatly on number 13. (His currency was accepted in Northern Mexico.) The croupier pushed it back to him with his rake. Villa leaned over and whispered something to one of the two soldiers who were standing gargoyle-like at his side. The soldiers left. Pancho sat with folded arms, powerfully silent. All eyes in the Fiesta Hall were riveted on the roulette table as a column of twenty soldiers, rifles ready, moved in behind Villa. The clink of the dice and the whir of the roulette wheel stopped. The croupier stared as Villa calmly brought out another of his bills and laid it on number 13. The croupier nodded nervously and spun the wheel. Again the dice clinked as ripples of conversation rolled over the tension of the hall. The rest of the evening Ada and company played with silver while Pancho Villa lost with his own printed currency.

Many of the episodes and locations in Ada's life seem more fictional than non-fictional. Bugscuffle, for one. "Hog Town" for another. In the late teens, Ada was first lady of "Hog Town" by virtue of being the wife of the mayor. The town of Desdemona in Eastland County was aptly nicknamed after the hogs that ran wild, wallowing in the little creek at the edge of town and dining on the bounty of fallen acorns. Discovery of the Duke Oil Well in 1918 transformed the town overnight into the big time for a small time. Within a few weeks the population which had been 100, pushed to the 10,000 mark. The increase created pandemonium. People lived in the streets, in tents, in cars, in whatever covering they could find. Those streets were unpaved and deep in mud. A horse, falling in the thick of it on Main Street, drowned.

Prices skyrocketed. Ada paid $50 a week for a cook and $25 to have the washing sent out. In the evening, the townspeople queued up for the privilege of a dollar's worth of cold water at the Come Clean Bathhouse.

Forty-niner dances in the local dance hall were an occasion for cleaning up and dressing up, but even in the midst of finery, Ada remembers seeing "two men just fighting away to beat the band, while people danced around them not paying them any mind."

In this confusion, Ada and her husband started a newspaper called "Desdemona Oil News." The paper was housed in their new building that also contained living quarters. Across the street was the popular Come Clean Bathhouse, owned by two vaudevillians who played banjo and guitar. After hours, with instruments in tow, they'd come over to Ada's and jam till the wee hours. Chill Wills often sat in.

In that rough town, Ada's head almost intercepted a bullet meant for a gunman who was standing behind her. After two years in "Hog Town," Ada and her husband left for safer ground.

A word that describes Ada is activist. She has a great capacity to enjoy life, not as an onlooker, but as a participant. Politics has never been a deterrant. In 1907, while Ada was a student at Baylor, she organized a protest to allow a socialist to speak. "A socialist then was no better than the devil himself." But this particular socialist happened to be a past president of Baylor University, and Ada assumed that, owing to the man's status and education, the administration would allow him to speak. She was wrong. They wouldn't even allow him to come into the building. Ada, who wanted to learn about socialism, "staged a little rebellion." The administration couldn't stop him from coming on campus. The day he was to speak, the weather was sympathetic. The students left their classes and went outside to hear him deliver a beautiful speech. There were repercussions such as the lowering of grades. Ada, who had been an A student in math, received a B. When she asked her professor why, he answered that he was instructed to lower her grade.

Ada was active in 1907. She's active now as a life-long and charter member of the American Civil Liberties Union. Recently she was interested in a case in the Corpus area. A fellow who had been indicted for a felony was out on appeal when he had a bad car crash. He was taken to the hospital where his leg was being treated. While undergoing treatment, officers from Huntsville came and took him back to prison where he was given no special consideration and was in danger of losing his leg. The case was given to the ACLU. Ada interceded with the prison warden, explaining the circumstances and the man's rights. The prisoner was promptly removed to a hospital for care.

Prison reform has been one of Ada's concerns. Eugene C. Debbs was a friend of her father's and a guest at their house several times. He often spoke about the injustices of prison life that he had witnessed during his imprisonment for his pacifist beliefs during World War I. Ada listened and the stories must have taken root, though it was not till years later that she became active in prison reform. In Corpus Christi where she's lived for the past six years, she's fought for a modern prison for the new courthouse. She fears that the planned prison will be obsolete before it's built.

Ada had a modern education even in 1907 because her outlook and goals were advanced. She took courses because of interest, not because they headed toward a degree. "I took the subjects I was interested in. If they happened to build toward a degree, that was fine."

She was no Hedda Dabler, however, learning superficially. She was able to put her studies to effective use. Psychology is one of the subjects she pursued. Ada became engrossed in medical hypnosis and has been practicing it for 20 years with dramatic results. Her sister, who was a soloist with Paul Whiteman, had severe neuritis. The doctors could do nothing to stop the pain and encouraged her to explore hypnosis. Ada, through medical hypnosis, was able to keep her sister free from pain.

In another case, a beautiful young woman who was dying of terminal cancer came to Ada to lessen the emotional pain she was also experiencing. She was "cursing man, God and doctors, alike." Because of what she was doing to her family, she sought help. Ada was able to calm her so that she could return to her religion and face her death. "It didn't make a damn bit of difference whether it was Buddhism, Catholicism or what. I thought she needed her religion."

Ada believes in hypnoanalysis. "The subconscious mind seems under hypnosis **eager** to give up what is causing the trouble." She can understand why some psychoanalysts shy away from it. "When you're getting $50 an hour, who wants to reduce the time?"

Ada has used medical hypnosis to help the people in Corpus Christi. One woman had a fear of flying. A circumstance developed where she had to fly. The woman was sure she would die if she got on a plane. Ada hypnotised her and told her she would take something out of her purse and hold it in her hand when she got on the plane, and that as long as she held it in her hand, she'd feel calm. She got on the plane, took a credit card out of her bag, and didn't have one particle of trouble.

While Ada is not too interested in recounting the last 50 years, she's fascinated by previous lives—what happened in 1600 A.D. or so. Through medical hypnosis she has uncovered memory that is centuries old. Although she does not believe in the supernatural, in several of her short stories she toys with the idea of genetic memory. Some of the plots might make Hitchcock tingle, as people act out the footage of some previous life and guilt. Ada enjoys the possibilities while remaining level-headed with both feet firmly in the Twentieth century.

Ada, however, does not need hypnosis to open up people. She wins friends and influences people on her own steam. Her phone is continuously ringing, with people asking her to do this and that, meet them for dinner, help with one cause or another. Ada is friendly and has a rare ability to make friends of all ages. These friends love the invigorating jam sessions of ideas. Perhaps because Ada never paced her learning to some ultimate and final degree, she has never stopped learning. Ada is still an intense, inquisitive woman. Age has not censored the breadth and grasp of her mind. She has no taboos.

The flood that took away the scrapbooks of fading faces left her free. Ada's room is congested now with the present—typewriter, tape recorder and folders of works in progress. She is eleven chapters into her book **Hypnosis Develops Strange Powers.** She is trying to learn Spanish but has not gotten beyond the slang and bad words. She has been practicing TM (Transcendental Meditation) for three years. She is an active member of the Unitarian Church. She loves fast travel and her son in Corpus often takes her up in his plane. She has another son in Abilene.

Ada's humor has always tempered her ideals and battles. She is 86 and a half years old. "The 86 doesn't bother me too much. It's that last half that really gives me trouble."

On Broadway, Ada padded her figure, powdered age into her hair, lined her face and succeeded as a character actress. The part she never could play is "little old lady." Today, with her hair white in earnest, and one or two real lines on her face (but her figure still not heavy enough), Ada Elliot **is** the leading lady.

Band, Baseball and Best Efforts

by Helen Fischer and Donna Bearden

"I think everybody should do something to make the world a little bit better than it was before he came into it."

That's Hubert "Tack" Wilson's personal philosophy, his golden rule that he lives day by day. At 73, he's somewhat of a natural philosopher with a little preaching mixed in. He readily quotes scripture and it rolls off his tongue easily as he expresses his simple, pure love of his fellow man.

Tack is a very loving man, a big man—6'1", 250 pounds—and a fighter. He has strong convictions and doesn't mind expressing them. You learn to listen carefully to Tack. He talks in poetry and parable, combining words and phrases to get the most from their meaning. And his deep voice takes on the tones of a country preacher as he pauses to let the full impact of his words sink in.

Tack has always been a lover of people, he's always been involved— first as a pro baseball player, then as a musician, and now as a senior dedicated to helping other seniors.

In 1966, two years after his retirement as a professional musician, Wilson became one of 15 senior citizens who canvassed "the alleys behind the alleys" of Houston's poverty-ridden North Side, searching out people 65 and older who needed to apply for Medicare.

At the close of the program, Wilson involved himself in other programs for the aging, and is now employed as Technical Assistant to Senior Citizens by the Harris County Community Action Association (HCCAA).

He works with the Senior Action Senate Groups sponsored by HCCAA. "They organize and decide what needs to be done in their neighborhoods, and then they work on getting it done. It's a wonderful thing to see. Everybody's always hollering, 'Why don't they give us something?'—but most people don't like to get out and try to do things for themselves. These folks get things done.

"One group got the city to clean out the drainage ditches, and one got a big bawdy-house closed down where there used to be a lot of murders. Some of them got programs set up for elderly people, like nutrition sites."

Wilson helps them get organized and sees that they stay within HCCAA's guidelines; and on the other end of the line, when people come into HCCAA who are going to work with senior citizens, he sets up a training program for them. "I know a lot about working with the elderly, because I'm one of them and I've worked with a lot of them. I've been out in the streets and knocked on 40 or 50 doors a day, and found out what it takes to get through to the people.

"Especially when you need to reach people below the poverty line, there are certain techniques you have to use. For instance, they're mostly not educated, so you have to use plain language. If you confuse them with a bunch of big words they don't understand, they get

(photo by Coy Jennings)

suspicious of you and think you're trying to trick them into something. You've got to be down-to-earth and speak their language and put them at ease.

"You need a gracious manner. That's 50 percent of getting anything accomplished—being polite and courteous, respecting the other person. It doesn't cost you one dime, and it'll take you places that money won't take you.

"Of course, I can say things to old people that young people can't tell 'em, but I can tell 'em anything I want to, because I'm old just like they are. And I can say what I want to say to a young person, too, because he's saying to himself, 'He looks just like grandpa!' He may resent what I'm saying, but he won't insult me. You have a lot of freedom, being old.

"A senior citizen is the freest person in the world, for this reason: he doesn't have a job, you can't fire him, so he can tell anybody anything he wants to tell 'em. He can go to meetings all day long. They'll finally have to hear him, see. But I tell 'em, 'When you go, be sure you got something to say. Have your facts right.' "

Tack's "freedom" cannot fully be attributed to his age. It comes from knowing who he is, what he believes in and how to apply that to make the world a bit better.

"I believe that every person in the world has got a certain problem that he will have to be continuously working on all of his life until he overcomes that one particular thing. Everybody's got a problem. Paul said, 'I got a thorn in my side.' And he was a great evangelist. But everybody's got something that he needs to work on. It could be your temper, could be just anything, and you have to just continuously work on it. And some of them's hard and you can't do it overnight. Your brain is made for your thoughts, and nobody else's but yours. OK. But we can get together and discuss intelligently certain issues and we can come up with something that both of us can live by. You got to give and you got to take."

Hubert Wilson was born at Van Alstyne in 1902. He grew up on a farm. "All the things that are to be done on a farm, I did them."

When he was 13 years old and hired out to work in the fields, he drew as much money as a man because he did as much work as a man. Chopping cotton, however, was not what Hubert Wilson wanted to do all his life.

In 1923 he entered Texas College at Tyler, where he played both football and baseball. It was his teammates who dubbed him 'Tack.' "My hair was of such a texture that the boys got to calling me 'Tack Hair,' " he recalled with a grin. "After a while it got to be just 'Tack.' "

His athletic skill did not go unnoticed, and in the summer of 1928 he was hired by the Kansas City Monarchs, an all-black baseball team which barnstormed through several states.

"The Monarchs were one of the all-time greats among the black baseball teams," Wilson reminisced. "In the small towns, the banks, stores, picture shows, everything closed down when we came. I played for the Monarchs in 1928 and 1929, and we won the Negro National League pennant both years.

"We had some wonderful black players back then," he continued, "but they couldn't get into the major leagues. There was no integration then, remember. The teams were either all white or all black. Usually a town's black team named itself after the white team. If the white team was the Bears, the black team was the Black Bears.

"Then finally the major leagues began hiring some black players. Jackie Robinson was the first. Now, there were players that were better players than Robinson, but they didn't have Robinson's overall intelligence and his education and his cool head. So in 1947 Branch Rickey, who had the Brooklyn Dodgers—he hated to see all that talent go to waste. He wanted to get it to where the major leagues could hire any good player, never mind what color he was—so he interviewed Robinson and he said to him, "Now, you're going to have to get used to people calling you names like 'nigger' and 'coon,' maybe even your own teammates, because if you ever lose your temper, even once, you'll set baseball back 50 years." So Robinson took the job, and he broke down the race barrier, because he could keep his head.

"After that there were others, like "Satchel" Paige, the ace pitcher. He was great, really great. You know he had to be, for them to put him in the Hall of Fame."

The great incident of Tack's baseball career was the time he pitched against "Satchel" Paige. It was in his first year with the Monarchs, 1928. "There I was, a country boy from Tyler, never been out of Texas before, and we were playing the Birmingham Barons, and I was pitching against Satchel Paige! He was the ace in those days, but luck was on my side, and we won, 9-5. Bullet Rogan, our manager, pulled me out in the bottom of the ninth inning, with a four-run lead and one out—said he thought I was getting nervous. So he finished pitching the game.

"Something else about baseball back then—you talk about being rough, it was really rough. They'd holler from the dugout, 'Put it in his ear!' and when the second baseman tagged the runner, he'd bring the ball up'side his head fit to knock all his teeth out. And the slider would really cleat him."

When the summer baseball season ended in 1928, Wilson returned to Texas College, where he majored in education, He also courted one of his teachers, and in May, 1929, she became Rae Wilson in Kansas City, where Tack rejoined the Monarchs for the summer.

That fall, the young couple moved to Amarillo, where a cousin of Wilson's lived. The Depression had arrived, but Wilson found work as a chauffeur for a wealthy widower. The following spring, he was offered a job as pitcher with the Houston Black Buffaloes. The Wilsons moved to Houston. For three years Wilson played professional baseball with the Buffaloes, finding whatever work he could during the off season.

"Finally," he said, "it just got to be too much, being on the road all summer, a night here and a couple of nights there, away from Rae so much. And I had financial obligations as a married man, and payday was so irregular.

"Back then, professional athletics wasn't the same as it is now. You couldn't make a living with that as your only profession. You'd play ball all summer, but when the summer baseball season was over, you had to find something else. You can name practically anything, and I've done it, some time or other. I worked on the railroad and on the docks, fired furnaces for heating buildings, worked at oil mills and cotton gins, whatever I could find.''

So when the season was over in 1932, Tack went to work singing. He and three other fellows formed a quartet called the Nightingale Four. They used to broadcast over KPRC and KYYC.

"Well, one night we went out on a job and the drummer quit. And one of the boys said to me, 'Tack, we're gonna make a drummer out of you.' I didn't know anything about drums, but I could keep time, so I took some private lessons from Abner Jones, and I learned what I could from anybody else who could help me, and after a while I got pretty good at it.

"We might eventually have got somewhere," he added, "but one of the fellows loved to play pool so much, that whenever we were supposed to be rehearsing, he'd be off playing pool.''

So in 1933 he got together a little group of his own, four to six pieces. "It was what you'd call a combo nowadays, but we called ourselves 'Tack Wilson and his Orchestra.' ''

Besides Tack on the drums, there'd be maybe a piano, a bass, a trumpet, a sax, and a singer.

He had that little orchestra for over 30 years, playing mostly just in Houston. It wasn't the same people the whole time, they came and went over the years. He played with some good musicians and can still name them all, what instrument they played and probably where they are now.

They played "strictly commercial music, not bop or anything like that." Songs like "Moonglow," "Embraceable You," "Caravan," and "The Desert Song" were among his favorites.

"We played in both black and white establishments, but mostly in white clubs because they could pay us more. We played a good while at the old Cotton Club, and you know, it used to be, when you came to Houston, if you didn't come to the Cotton Club, you hadn't been to Houston.''

Meanwhile, Rae Wilson went into social work. "For over 10 years there'd been just the two of us," Wilson smiled "and then, in 1943, overnight she presented me with my first son! She'd been trying to persuade this 14-year-old boy in our neighborhood to enroll in school. She didn't know he was a habitual 'delinquent'—we didn't know anything about delinquency, as such.

"Anyhow, he got picked up, and when Rae heard his crime record read in court, she was shocked that a youngster living so near us could commit so many misdemeanors and all of the neighbors, including really ourselves, thought it was no concern of ours, that we ought not to meddle in other families' scandals.

"He belonged to a gang that robbed delivery boys and broke into homes. He nor any of his family of 14 worked. After the judge had sentenced him to the Gatesville School for Boys, Rae asked him to parole Lloyd to us. I didn't know anything about it. She said she thought the whole community was partly responsible for the boy's behavior, because we all turned our backs and just let it go on, and she thought the boy ought to be given a chance to redeem himself. So the judge gave her the boy and permission to supervise his entire family.

"So I came home from playing in the band that night, and here was a brand new son in the spare bedroom! Neither Rae nor I knew any of the many theories on how to combat 'juvenile delinquency.' We just knew we had a misdirected kid who needed a lot of loving and a lot of training, and we were going to try to make a useful, respectable citizen out of him."

It was hard work. But they were so successful with Lloyd that from time to time the judge asked them to take another 'delinquent' to straighten out. They had a total of 32, both boys and girls, at various times.

It got to where the police knew the Wilsons and when they picked up some stray youngster who wouldn't tell them where he belonged, they'd call up and say, 'Can you put this boy up until we figure out what to do with him?' Or Tack'd come home at night and there'd be a young girl in the spare bedroom who looked like she was about to give birth, and Rae would tell him the police had found her someplace and they didn't have a bed for her at the jail. Next day they'd take her to the Florence Crittenden home. After a while, Tack never knew who he was going to find in the other room when he came home. "No telling how many youngsters came in and out of our house that way.

"But the ones the judge put in our care, we handled them all about the same way. We never had a child paroled to us unless the judge would give supervision of the family, because we felt the home was mostly responsible for the child's delinquency.

"Whenever possible, we let the child live with his own family, because no foster home can really replace one's own family. Besides, we figured that by changing the home situation from one that encouraged delinquency to one that didn't, we were helping to prevent other children in the family from becoming delinquents."

All the children paroled to the Wilsons came from low-income families, and most of their homes were overcrowded and unsanitary. The Health Department cooperated with them in seeing that the landlords made things sanitary.

"Then we would get the child a bath, a haircut and a whole new set of clothes. If school was in session I took him to the school and talked with the principal and his teacher. None of these children were attending school when we got them; some of them hadn't been to school for two or three years, and nobody was doing anything about it. Sometimes we'd find out there were eight or ten children of school age in the family, and not a one of them in school.

"Sometimes the adults were living on the money the youngsters would steal. We saw to it that every adult member of the family got a job and worked, or got out. Where there still wasn't enough money to get by on, we got the welfare agencies to supplement what there was."

They encouraged the children to take part in school activities, like baseball and football. If they were musically inclined, they were encouraged to join the school band. The children were kept under very close supervision. Two or three times a week, one of the Wilsons would go to the school and talk with the teacher. "I don't believe in punishment much, but if one of the boys got too unruly at school, I'd go over and give him a few licks in front of his gang. Didn't hurt him much physically, but it sure did make a dent in his pride. I never had to do it a second time."

At night the Wilsons' house looked like a study hall. Most of them needed lots of extra help to keep them interested, since they weren't used to attending school and they were behind.

Evenings after school and summers were work time. They had to earn their spending money. "We'd let them get their own jobs. They seemed to take more pride in their work that way, and that was an important thing. But I'd soon visit the employer and let him know I was interested in the child. It was remarkable how well the employers would cooperate. If a boy didn't show up for work, his employer would call me—and I've spent many a day hunting down the culprit and taking him back to work."

On pay-day, the youngster would bring in his pay, sit down with Tack and Rae, and work out a plan for what he'd do with it. He would give a certain amount to his mother for room, board and laundry, and they tried to see that he got his money's worth. A certain amount he could use for recreation, new clothes, and such, and some he was to put in a savings account. "And did they ever love to brag to their friends about their bank accounts! It did a lot for their pride.

"We always made a point of being fair to the children and setting good examples, but we made sure they knew we weren't going to let them get away with anything. The child always knew that day and night we were in touch with those that had him in charge. We never let up on that.

Not a single one of the Wilsons' children had to go back to the Probation Court. None of them ever went back to being delinquent. "Why should they? Their homes were clean, they had food and clothes, a job, and money in their pockets.

"School days they went to school, evenings they worked out with the team or worked at their jobs, nights they studied at our house. Sunday mornings we took them to church and Sunday school, Sunday afternoon they might be at the park swimming pool, the movies, a sandlot baseball game, or the YMCA. Friday and Saturday night they'd be jitterbugging at the teen dance. They didn't have time to rob delivery boys, and besides, why would they want to? They had money in their pockets and pride in themselves. A happy child is usually a good child."

Wilson continued making music professionally until 1964. By then, he said, such changes had taken place in musical styles that "I couldn't get musicians to play my style anymore, so I quit."

His retirement didn't last long. "I've worked all my life," he declared, "no use stopping now. I think as long as a person can work, it's a waste to go home and sit down. I think it prolongs life—working. I believe a person should support himself just as long as he possibly can. That's just my philosophy.'' And so, after a lifetime of working with the young, Hubert Wilson set to work on the old.

He says, "I've done a lot of things in my life, but I never had a chance to really do anything until I went into this poverty program."

"People need something useful to do. Too many people say to us senior citizens, 'You've got a TV set, haven't you?' But you can't talk to a TV. If you do, people think you're crazy.

"There's a lot of people who would do a lot of things if they had the initiative. A lot of folks look at these government programs and say, 'You're just spending a lot of money for nothing!' But they don't know how many people those programs have helped to take a different outlook on life and start really doing something. Some of them have gone on and become self-supporting. Whenever you can take a person and motivate him and help him get a job where he can take care of his family and have pride in himself, it's a wonderful thing, whether he's a teenager or an old man. You just can't measure that kind of thing in dollars and cents. And one of the reasons I like to do it is, so many people have helped me in my life—so many."

Tack lives in the neighborhood he serves. "I do more work by living in this poverty area because I do have the respect of the people. They don't raise too much sand on the street where I live. Most people move out as soon as they can. Anytime somebody gets a little high on the ladder, he says, 'I got to move out here in another area.' " But Tack will stay. He's committed to people.

"When the logs were taken to the mill, they were nothing in the world but a round log just like you seen growed in the woods." Just like the timber, the men were transformed from green inexperienced boys to skillful workers.

(photo courtesy Ouida Grogan)*

Family Trees

by Jamie Frucht

"History is life; it provides the opportunities for and sets the limits to our lives in the present and the future," says Ouida Grogan, third generation of the Grogan lumber family. Her history is like a shadow cast behind her and a vision before her. She is surrounded by her history as East Texas is surrounded by its forests.

Her great grandfather, Richard W. Grogan came to Queen City, Texas from Atlanta, Georgia in 1886. Though he farmed for two years in Texas, the great pine forests with their timber to be harvested seemed like a better idea. He bought a team of horses and began doing contract hauling of lumber from a mill near Springdale to a station on the Texas and Pacific Railroad. Watching the workings of the mill, he decided he wanted to become a lumber mill owner and operator. He bought his own mill near Atlanta in the early 1890's, and opened up other small mills in Texas, Louisiana and Arkansas. One adventure led to another. He bought a block of timber about twenty miles west of Jefferson and organized the R.W. Grogan Lumber Company, and then built a mill to cut the lumber. Later he sold the company and the mill at a profit.

In 1902 standing under an oak tree in Cass County, near Bivins, R.W. Grogan and his sons, and brother-in-law, T.M. Cochran, bowed their heads and prayed for their new business venture—the Grogan Manufacturing Company. After the retirement and death of the senior Grogan and his eldest son John, the running of the business fell to Will R. Grogan, Ouida's father. Through a series of far-sighted maneuvers, Grogan Manufacturing and Grogan-Cochran took hold in East Texas. They extended their holdings, making sure that their log roads connected with railroads. The Grogan lumber industry spread to other parts of Texas. In Liberty County, a mill was built at Gladstell; in Montgomery County, a mill was located at Conroe, and then at Magnolia. At the peak of the Tamina Mill near Conroe, in the 20's, some 200 to 300 people were employed. In 1964 when the Grogan Manufacturing Company sold their holdings of prime timberland in Montgomery, Waller and Liberty Counties, it totalled 45,441.69 acres.

Grogan Industries and the Grogan family kept pace with each other becoming numerous and diverse. It was said that when the large family opened the Tamina Mill near Conroe, they overwhelmed the church congregation. According to gossip following Sunday service, one lady was to have said to another, "Now brace yourself. When the preacher called for new members, 32 people responded."

The other lady was astounded. "Why that's more than we take in in a whole year at our Methodist Church."

"They were the Grogan and Cochran families and filled two rows of pews across the entire church."

Ouida was the fifth child in Will Grogan's large family. Ouida is a French Indian name. Enclosed within her name is the French "oui" meaning yes. Cherokee blood from her mother's side of the family gave her a dark complexion for which she was duly teased. Her family said that she'd stayed in a sawdust heap too long and turned brown. Ouida innocently took the teasing for the truth and shocked her teacher.

"One day teacher asked all of us where we came from and everybody had a town that they moved from. I stood up. 'Well, I don't know who my parents are and I don't know really where I came from.' "

The teacher said, "Why Ouida, you do know."

"No, I don't know. We moved from my daddy's sawmill in Gladstell but that's not really where I came from. My family found me. They were at a sawmill in Cass County and they were in a big horse drawn surrey and they heard a child cry. There was a big sawdust pile there and they found me in the pile of sawdust. I can't study very well 'cause I wake up at night and I wonder who my parents really are."

The teacher said, "Well, Ouida, talk to your Mother. She'll tell you."

That afternoon Ouida asked her mother where she had come from. "Mama thought I really wanted to know where children come from. Of course, I didn't think about **that.** I just wanted to know the name of the town."

Ouida was actually born at the old Rockpile Mill in Cass County in 1907. It was a natural birth in a bed, not in a sawdust pile. She was the baby girl in a family of eight children, split evenly between boys and girls. There were three older sisters and a brother, and three younger brothers—Poindexter, Chessley, and Lester.

Being the baby girl had its hand-me-down drawbacks. Dressmakers would come in before school started to make the older girls dresses. Ouida finally had a dress made for her but didn't like it, and in fact refused to wear it. She was going to meet a school friend, Pearl, and play. Her mother, ignoring Ouida's protests about the despised dress, said, "You're going to leave here in that dress." Ouida did, but as soon as she met Pearl down by the big oak tree, she set about trying to convince her to swap dresses.

"Pearl had on one of her little summer dresses. I said, 'Pearl do you like this dress of mine?' She was raving about it and I said, 'Well you can have it.' She said, 'Ouida, your mother will whip you.' and I said, 'No she wouldn't, my Daddy wouldn't let her.' And I talked Pearl into trading dresses, and I traded shoes with her too. I didn't like my billican button-ups. Pearl was still worried. 'Ouida, my mother will whip me for taking this dress. She'll make me bring it back to your mother.'

"When it was time to go, she pleaded with me to take back my dress. 'Pearl you keep it. I'm more worther than you are.' (Pearl had even more children in her family than I did.) And I didn't get a whipping over it either because I didn't like the dress and my mother knew it." (At an early age Ouida displayed her forceful disposition.)

Even though Ouida was "more worther," in other words wealthier than many children, she did not get sent off to finishing schools. Ouida's father, an ordained Baptist minister, believed firmly that a religious education was the only finishing school a person needed and far preferable to an education of manners. "Besides, I knew how to pour tea."

So at an early age the children were sent to religious boarding schools. Ouida, sharing a suite of rooms with her sisters, Gladys and Christine, attended the San Marcos Baptist Academy when she was just 13. It was like sending an "innocent abroad," sending Ouida to San Marcos. She had only known the woods of East Texas and her family, large though it was. At home she'd been a little rebel, but as Ouida recalls, at San Marcos she was a little fool.

"I had never written a check in my life. With our large commissaries at the mill, I had charged everthing always, actually never realizing my Father had to pay for it. Now away at school we each received an allowance by check individually. Our school post office was the bank. When the checks from home arrived, all students had to deposit their allowances. I didn't know how to deposit my allowance because I had never written or signed a check. I stood in line behind 50 or 60 people. Each time I got to the window, the postmistress, an elderly lady named Miss Fann, would tell me to endorse the check on the back; and each time I'd fade to the back of the line, not knowing what she meant. On my third trip to the window, again handing her the check, she was furious and purely disgusted with me.

"When the line of students had dwindled, I tried it again. Miss Fann said, 'Ouida, turn the check over; write your name on it. It's to let your Daddy know that you received the money, and no one else did.'

"So I went over to the desk where I had seen all the kids go, and I wrote an epistle on the back of the check, upside down, stating, 'Dear

Daddy this is to let you know I got the check and no one else did.'' Ouida remembers that her Father got the best laugh out of that check, cherishing it always. When he died, that check was still in his Bible.

After Baptist Academy, she attended Baylor College in Belton (now called Mary Hardin Baylor). "I didn't like it. I kind of wanted the boys around." She was graduated from Hardin Simmons School in Abilene with sister Gladys in 1927, both receiving B.A. degrees with double majors.

"I get such pleasure now returning some of the good that I got out of going to each school. I like to tithe, and share." Following the example of her Father, Ouida is a living philanthropist. "I intend to give all my money away when I'm alive."

Also, like her father, she always believed in the importance of education to adults. Years later, in 1945, she helped organize an adult education night school in Atlanta. The night school helped a lot of young preachers in the county, who had the calling but no high school education, to attain their diplomas.

As she had demonstrated early in life, Ouida was high-spirited and knew her own mind. College increased the range of her inventiveness. Her father wouldn't let his children dance. "I had to slip around to dance." At college she had an auction of some of her sister's dresses to get enough money to buy a dancing dress for herself. She competed in a Charleston contest. "I could do 142 steps. Ginger Rogers beat me out by one step."

After graduation from college, Ouida became the head of the English department at Conroe. Then she had a fling at going East. In 1928 she went to New York and became a reader at the 42nd Street library. Her job was to read books to see if they should be banned. "The only book I ever banned was a book on abnormal psychology and that was because I didn't know enough about the subject."

Even though Ouida is a small town girl she has done big town things. Ambition and ability were equally salient in her, but she had to create her opportunities. After she married, she moved to Tulsa, Oklahoma, where for 20 years she was a sportswear buyer working for Brown and Dunkin Department Store and Seidenbach's, a speciality shop. In 1942 she launched Renberg's ready-to-wear department for women. Renberg's, an exclusive shop, handled only men's wear; but during the war, Mr. Renberg was afraid they'd go broke with all the men in uniform. Ouida was given part of the second floor where she successfully created the new women's department.

As a buyer, every nine weeks she'd go to New York on buying trips and three times a year to the West Coast. World War II made traveling an ordeal. Trains were filled with soldiers. "You'd have to book a roomette a month in advance to get out of Tulsa. Tulsa's a hard place to get out of anyway. (It's just a terrible place.)"

As a buyer, Ouida once bought $70,000 worth of suits. (Not bad for the girl who didn't know how to endorse a check.) Gabardine was the most popular fabric. Tailored suits and toppers were what a lot of girls got married in, as weddings adapted to soldiers' leaves. A dressy blouse worn with the suit would see them through the wedding, and a few extra blouses would do for the short honeymoon. The eight gored skirt (like an A-line) was also big in those days. "I bet I sold 8,000 skirts of that one number." Ouida believes that every woman must find her own flattering lines. She thinks the mini skirt was a disaster.

In Tulsa, Ouida had her own radio show, "'Slip Into Your Slacks." "Boy, during the war I really sold slacks. A lot of women were working in war plants. Half of my girls quit me to go work for Douglas Aircraft War Plant."

Although Ouida was away from home, first at boarding school and then pursuing her own carreer, she always kept in close contact with her family. "That grey-haired father of mine," as she affectionately referred to Will Grogan, always exerted a strong and loving influence on his daughter. Though he was a small man with a mustache and, not a well man, there was nothing diminutive or weak about his personality and fortitude. He had worked his way through Baylor University firing the boiler in the boy's dormitory. He had created a great lumber industry in East Texas. He helped others to attain their goals in life through education and employment.

All his life he educated his own children, by example and sermon. For 54 years he was a Baptist minister. Ouida recalls his morning regime. "Every morning of my life he'd get up and have a cup of warm water. Then he would walk a mile one way and a mile back. He'd say his prayer was two miles long."

In the Grogan family there was always time set aside for family prayer. To impress upon his children the importance of the enduring family circle, he once sent his older son out to get a stick. Ouida remembers the time vividly. "We were in my daddy's study. He crossed his legs. There was a fire burning in the fireplace." When the stick, a rotting limb, was brought back, the father said, "I want you to notice how easily it breaks." Then he sent the son out to bring back a bundle of sticks tied together. He asked his children to try to break the bundle. They couldn't. The lesson was clear—"if one of you leaves the original family, it will be easy to break you. But if you stick together as a family and always have your family prayers, then you will be strong." Ouida says, "Father wanted us to stay together and be close and that we have done."

It was not surprising then that when Ouida's brother, Chessley, called her in Oklahoma asking for her assistance, she gave it. Large families depend on each other. Chessley said, "Sister, we're going into the department store business." They'd already purchased a building and Chess asked her to start buying stock for the new store. Since it was war time, clothing, like everything else, was rationed. Many factories were turning out clothes for the military, so merchandise was alotted. Chess said, "Use your influence if you have any." To which Ouida replied, "What'll I use for money?" He told her to have them check *Dun and Bradstreet* where the name Grogan had some clout.

Ouida bought for two stores at once, jotting down style numbers that she thought would sell in a small town and having another buyer write her orders. In this way, the opening stock for Grogan Department Store was bought. In 1945, when she could get away, she came back to

"Father wanted us to stay together and be close and that we have done."
(photo courtesy Ouida Grogan)

Atlanta to work with her family.

Even though from an early age Ouida had been absent from home, she'd returned during the summers and for revivals and had gotten to know the men who worked at the mills. She also used to drive her father around a lot and became friends with the workers in that way. So it was like returning to one big family that she'd known over many years.

Her own brothers, Poindexter, Chessley, and Lester worked beside the men as laborers. Her brothers were laborers, and laborers were brothers. When one of the men who was taking care of the stock of mules was fatally kicked by a mule, the Grogans adopted his orphan son and reared him as their own. "Not many of the people who worked at the mill were strangers. Some of my childhood friends worked for my father. It was one big family." As though to emphasize that, Will Grogan was often called Uncle Will, or Mr. Will, if you were being formal.

After the Liberty County Mill had cut out, Will Grogan tried to borrow money from the Federal Government to open a mill at Bivins. He was refused. His secretary recalled how he often translated his fury into letters to Congressmen. He was an active citizen, exercising the rights of the Constitution and the Ten Commandments. "It was nothing for him to come in of an afternoon and say, 'Let's take a letter.' He wrote some pretty sharp letters. By the time you'd got it written, he'd want to send it to all the congressmen."

Sometimes he kept his staff working late, but next day he'd tell them to go into the store and pick out the most expensive dress each. It was his way of compensating. "We would have gladly worked anyway for Mr. Will," says his secretary, Marie Davis.

Years later he visited Washington with a train load of businessmen.

When he presented his card at the Library of Congress, a page said, "We have some pretty bad letters over here from you, Mr. Grogan." To which, Will Grogan replied, "I want those letters to stay on file. I wrote those from my heart so you just leave them here."

He was able to borrow the money from a Shreveport bank, and ground for the Bivins Mill was broken in 1931.

The first task was elementary—clearing the site so a mill could be built.

Chessley, an engineer, designed the rows of mill houses in the Bivins Mill. Some 200 houses accommodated the families. Mr. Will's priorities for his own family—religion, education and health, held for his larger family of workers, as well.

Will Grogan would always have a doctor, a two-room school and a church at the mill sites. The doctor would handle dental work, births, everything but embalming.

Ouida recalls, "My father built the church even before he finished the mill. The laborers, those that could hammer and design, volunteered their services once a week until the church got built."

Mr. Will took the church to the laborers. Morning services were always held each day under a lumber shed so the men would not have to leave work or change clothes to pray. Twice a year there was a revival. The mill would cease running. The planer that finished the lumber would stop and everyone would attend the revival. There'd be children with a spell of fidgeting, but it was all one big family.

Mr. Will and his lumber mills were a salvation to the area in desperate times. During the Depression, Cass County, as everywhere, was hurting. Many of the men who came looking for jobs had cardboard in their shoes. There was plenty to eat, as people raised their own food in East Texas, but no money.

It was more than just a payday . . . Grogan Mills. It was a community of people, a way of life.   *(photo courtesy Ouida Grogan)*

At the mill the men were paid in brozines, a kind of coin imprinted with the Grogan name, that could be turned in at the end of the month for cash. The brozines were good in the commissary which sold everything "from baby clothes to caskets." In those days money went a long way. A dollar and a dime a day looked good and that's what Uncle Will paid.

What was money then (brozines) is souvenirs now. As of 1971, the Grogan Mills have closed in East Texas. The timber land has been sold. The long history of growing and manufacturing lumber has come to an end, yet the relationships that were formed over the years of the Grogan lumber empire endure. It was over sixty years of shared history and locale. Forty years of one man's life, thirty years of another's, fifty-four years of another's and so on. Each man has his own story, but the setting is the same with the Grogans playing leading roles.

Jim McDuff recalls, "I walked up to Mr. Will and said, 'I'd like to go to work.' "

"Do you want a job or do you just want a payday?"

"Well, I need a payday, but I figure I'll have to work to get it."

And work Jim McDuff did—for ten hours a day loading lumber by hand at first. When he started work in 1930 he walked the seven miles from his farm, progressing to horseback, to wagon, to Model T. Jim McDuff, like many of the laborers, was a farmer. "I went to work in the summer and worked in the fall up until it was time to gather my crops. Then I'd quit for a spell, harvest my crops, then go back to work." In all, Jim McDuff worked 22 years for the Grogans.

Judge Crow, 40 years with the Grogans, exemplifies the caliber of worker. He claims, "I've seen 71 Christmases but I ain't but 16 years old." His exuberance backs him up. Starting in 1930, he helped build the business, literally from the ground up, clearing the virgin forests, digging the mill pond with the mules. He'd get up early and go home late. He'd work at least ten hours a day driving mules. He'd walk about six miles round trip.

After he got home and ate, he and his wife would go out back to where Crow was building his own house with lumber from the mill. He'd chop splinters from a stump and light them as a lantern. "She'd hold me a light and I built my house that a way. It took me three months."

The story is the same for the other men. Jim McDuff also bought Grogan lumber at $12 a thousand feet and hauled it himself. He built a four room house for $450.00. "After it was done I went to the bank and borrowed money and Mr. Will went in on the note."

The men who helped clear off the mill site watched the mill take shape, and grew up with the business. When the logs were taken to the mill they were "nothing in the world but a round log just like you seen growed in the woods" remembers Judge Crow. The lumber that was loaded on the trucks to points all over the Southwest, was of a high quality—well manufactured, seasoned, dressed and worked. Just like the timber, the men were transformed from green inexperienced boys to skillful workers. These men became more precious to the Grogans than the Southern Pine Timber reserves.

Boston Kyle, who drove the lumber for Grogan-Cochran and later for Atlanta Lumber, had only one accident in over 30 years as a driver. The policeman who notified the mill of the accident later said, "You must be working for a good company. I call them up, tell them there's been an accident. And they want to know did you get hurt. Usually they want to know if their truck got hurt."

When a mill was cut out and would close, the Grogans rented a train, a mixture of passenger and box cars, and moved the families and their belongings to another mill. Jerome Graham, one of two brothers who worked for the Grogans, recalls that a time or two he quit. "But Poindexter came and got me and moved all my stuff back. They wouldn't let me get away." His brother Cicero says, "I never worked for a better group of people than the Grogan outfit."

Over the years the mill technique and technology changed, but the men were a constant. When John L. Rayomond started work, he was driving a dolly with mules. Later "they bought me a brand new dolly and I wore it out." Jerome Graham recalls sorting lumber by hand, drying logs by air, loading lumber by hand. Before the Grogans bought a debarker and realized that bark and sawdust could be used, a small fortune had been burned. Over the years, the Grogans learned to conserve, until it could be said that at the mill they wasted nothing except the steam it took to blow the whistle three times a day.

As the father had prophesied, if the Grogans stuck together they would prosper. From lumber mills, the family tried other ventures. Poindexter bought trucks to transport lumber and eventually bought his own mill (The Atlanta Lumber Company) in 1946. Lester opened a nursing home, a motel, and the first butane business in the town. (Jim McDuff became one of his drivers.) A Grogan hotel and health resort was started in Sweetwater, Texas, where the Grogan Brothers discovered mineral water, labelled it crazy water, shipped it all over the U.S., and launched the health spa. The brothers went into the dairy business, too. They went into real estate. The Grogan-Cochran mill was sold to the Mitchell Brothers for a development known as the Woodlands complex and called Grogan Mill Village where a replica of the old mill and an old ice house were built. In the center of all the developed acreage a green path was left so children could walk to school in the country.

The Grogan Mercantile Store opened in Atlanta in November 1943 and is still in business. It features dry goods, fashions, hardware, a grocery store and super market, feeds and lumber.

Ouida, with her merchandising background, took over buying and promotion for the store when she returned from Tulsa. Her father later said, "I don't believe the boys would make it without you."

She'd write her own promotions and scripts. "I'd advertise them in the future tense, write them in the present tense and a week later, in the past tense, as they were reported in the paper." (In a small town you were your own reporter.)

For inspiration Ouida watched her calendar and on every occasion would promote something. She'd take something natural like Mother's

Ouida Grogan
(photo by Mary Sherwood)

Day or Father's Day and use that as a starting point. For example, on Mother's Day she'd have a Grandmother's tea in the store. She'd move a piano into the store and have a minister in from the church as her M.C. Ouida was smart and rotated her ministers so that one church was not favored. She'd get the most respected women in town, let them wear evening dresses in the afternoon and have them serve punch and hors d'ouevres from the glass cases. She'd give a dress to the oldest grandmother; to the youngest grandmother, a war bond. Her father would present the bonds.

For her parents 53rd wedding anniversary, she paid tribute to them by unveiling their two portraits in the store. The portrait of Mr. Will is painted in such a way that his eyes follow you wherever you are in the store, acting as both an inspiration and a deterrent.

Today Ouida still does advertising for the store with her house turned into a one-woman ad agency.

Ouida says, "I have the best neighbors in the world. They never bother me." Her house borders the cemetery where, her mother, whom she nursed till her death, her father who died in 1954, and her youngest brother Lester rest. Pine trees shade their graves.

The retail lumber supply stores in Atlanta, Mt. Pleasant, Hughes Springs, and Dangerfield, and department store in Atlanta are still family run. The saw mill houses have been moved from the mill site to the town of Atlanta where they fit in well with the other houses. People have worked them over, building brick foundations and additions, and lives continue in them.

And though the last whistle may have blown closing the Grogan mills, ending the long dawn to dusk days, the name of Grogan survives in East Texas. It was more than just a payday—Grogan mills. It was a community of people, a way of life.

The Vision

by Jamie Frucht

Early on, Leo Richardson knew what he wanted to do with his life. "It never entered my mind to be anything but a sheepman." That decision was easy. Everything else that followed was hard, but possible, because of Leo's enduring determination.

Leo was born near Junction on August 13, 1895. His family history doesn't figure into his life's decision. Leo had to come up the hard way as a cowboy-rancher. Nobody was going to leave him a ranch. He inherited nothing from his family but the premise that you have to work to get by.

At the age of 17 he left home to start cowboying, working on various ranches for the Shreiner family between Junction and Rocksprings and in Kerr County. Though the wages weren't much, (just $30 per month for a cowboy, $35 for a sheep rustler), after three years he had enough put aside to buy a small herd of Angora goats. "I had to start somewhere." After an unseasonably cold rain, he lost all his shorn goats, even as they huddled under a shed for warmth.

This loss of three years work might have sent an ordinary man packing. But Leo's response was to get out and work, rebuilding what he had lost. Once more he lived to the rhythm of working and saving. In Sonora he found a job on the Hudspeth ranch. Hudspeth had a policy of letting his men keep any of the varmints they trapped. Leo accumulated additional savings from selling pelts.

After three years time, he had enough saved to invest in a small flock of sheep. He'd trade mutton lambs for ewe lambs and keep the increase, all the while building his stock. This was the beginning of a process that is still going on. He condenses some sixty-odd years into a single sentence. "You just build them up and build them up a little at a time, until finally you got it built up before you know it." It's much easier to summarize Leo's uphill battle than to have done it. Leo says simply, "I just got in the sheep business and hung on."

He didn't do it all alone. In 1920 he met Helen, a school teacher. When they married, she exchanged the hard work of teaching for the harder work of ranching. They became a team, Helen and Leo, managing the flocks themselves, only hiring extra hands around the marking and shearing times. The Richardsons had two sons. Their son Leonard died tragically in his early twenties. The other son Rod is in the sheep business with his father and has taken over the managing now. In October 1972, the Richardsons celebrated their 50th wedding anniversary. Two hundred and forty couples shared the day with them. "And we called every couple by name, except one." Fifty years of marriage haven't camouflaged his feelings any. "They say a wife is half of it, but she's more than half."

In the beginning, with their small flock, Helen and Leo went to Ozona where he worked on ranches for wages and made arrangements to keep his sheep in a horse trap or spare pasture. He never stopped trapping either. It was getting into the years of drought and Depression. With the Depression on, Leo recalls "I saw oats sell for 10 cents a bushel and cotton seed cake sell at $16 per ton, if anybody could get that $16." The dry land couldn't support extra herds, even his small bunch. There was no spare change or spare pastures. Men could force you off the land.

That's what happened to the Richardsons. They no longer could use the pastures of men he was working for. In the inauspicious year of 1931, when most things were closing down on account of drought, Leo and Helen pulled out on their own. They'd heard that part of the Yates' ranch in Iraan was up for lease. "So we went after it."

They had 1300 sheep when they leased 13 sections of Ira Yates' ranch, south of Iraan. The Richardsons lived in the headquarters house where they had to fight the termites for possession. By 1944 they had saved enough to buy some land, though they continued to lease land as well.

The country was, and is, not without problems. Iraan holds on at the foothills to the Rockies. Cross winds echo through the hills. The dry hot winds are hard on the south side of hills which are barely vegetated. The Pecos River wanders through the land. Seemingly dusty draws have the potential to flood up. This happened in 1974 when 25 inches of rain fell in one season. Usually the land averages only 13 inches of rain per year. In a drought year, such as this, grass fires are a weekly event. Black brush, salt cedar, wild willow and black walnuts dot the landscape, holding on to the hills. Arizona cypress really goes to town in this country. Around Sheffield, Italian cypress signals an old cemetery. Weathered grave stones graze like petrified sheep in the cemetery grass.

Iraan's location and lack of population cut it off from many things. The labor force was scarce. Sheep ranchers had to quit herding and were forced instead to fence the country with net wire. Leo and Rod have 500 miles of fence. They don't work with dogs. "When we work, it takes about 15 days, carrying about 12,000 sheep. The country's too rough on dogs. They give out after about three days."

This is not easy country. Leo says of it, "If we didn't work our country, it would just become useless. The brush would get it." But the country has been worked and grass has taken hold. Leo looks at a hill where tufts of dry grass move with the wind. There's no historical marker on that hill, and yet a struggle took place there. "We were ten years getting some grass on that hill. It finally took."

The Yates oil field came in in 1926. By now, pipelines are part of the landscape. At first Leo and Helen thought it would be hard living with oilfields. "We didn't realize that we would get used to it and that the sheep would get used to it, but they did and we did." Harder to adjust to might be the fact that none of that oil is theirs.

The Richardsons have worked for everything they have. Perhaps the Maker doesn't want to spoil them at this point. Oil and gas are being discovered all the time, not however, on any of the 100-plus sections of land that the Richardsons own. Last year 200 wells were drilled all around them on land they lease. "But it doesn't make much difference whether you make it or don't make it; you just need enough to live on and after that it doesn't make any difference."

In the sixty-odd years Leo has been in the business, some ranching methods have improved for the better. When Leo started out, he was a rustler, overseeing three herds of Mexican sheepherders. He had to count a flock a day and if a sheep were missing he had to find it. The counting was done by moving the flocks out to an open area and setting up two sticks about eight to ten feet apart. Then the sheep, cooperating out of habit, moved through the sticks, and not around them. There is a joke circulating that most ranchers running a count, count the legs and divide by four, but Leo counts six legs at a time; that's a sheep and a half. Occasionally he comes out with an extra half. Today they count sheep in gates.

Problems can vary in a matter of miles. Leo says of another sheepman thirty miles away, "His problems are not my problems and my problems are not his." Bitterweed, for example, is kept down in Iraan. Varmints, especially bobcats, were Leo's chief problem. "The country has a world of varmints. We don't let them bother us." Leo has had to use steel traps. In a sense, he still traps for a living since he and his sheep wouldn't survive if he didn't. "We have lots of problems, but you know a person who can't overcome his problems doesn't stay in the business. He goes under pretty quick."

It was in Iraan that Leo made the transition from ordinary grade sheep to registered Rambouillet sheep. As a breeder, he knows how he got his animals and can build right up all the way with the same flock of sheep. Livestock traders, on the other hand, may keep animals a year or two, buying and selling, dealing in numbers rather than breeding up a herd of their own. It's two kinds of speculation—the livestock trader's day to day numbers game, and the breeder's lifetime pursuit after a certain animal. All he sees is that animal. "I started out with Rambouillet and I've been with them ever since."

Rambouillet is a breed of sheep, a desert animal. It's also a dream. It takes a certain kind of man to sustain a dream of a perfect sheep over so many years. As his wife says, "You could never paint that animal or ever draw it, but in your own mind you have a vision of what that ideal sheep would look like." With the dream, Leo started in breeding for that imagined animal that had never been. One day perhaps he sees a ewe that has got everything except she's too short-legged. She can't travel well. He looks around for a ram with longer legs. The slow process of improving the sheep through selection goes on. He never gets it, his perfect sheep, but he tries; he's still trying.

Just how close Leo has come to attaining the perfect animal has been chronicled by a world of logs and records going back to 1948, which Leo and Rod have assiduously kept themselves. Leo and other breeders were instrumental in devising a new testing system for rams with the help of Texas A&M's Agricultural Experiment station. Leo was dissatisfied with the show ring and blue ribbons even though he had collected about 1200 ribbons. "A blue ribbon is just somebody's guessing."

Twenty-eight years ago at the Sonora Research Station, the ram performance test was instituted. The animals live at the station. They are sheared at the beginning and end of the test and tested for a growth period of 140 days. The Wool Research Laboratory at A&M provides scoring results. Some of the values tested are daily gain in pounds, grease wool pounds, clean wool pounds, staple length, face cover score, skin fold counts. By this test, Leo gets his answer in pounds as to just how good his sheep are. Since the progeny test began, the Richardsons have put over 300 rams through it. The test has elevated the standards of the breed of Rambouillet throughout the country and has produced bigger smoother animals with more open faces.

Leo and his son Rod have three ranches around Sheffield and Bakersfield, plus their leased ranches. Last year they sent many sheep into Mexico. They have one of the largest registered ewe flocks as well as a large commercial ewe flock.

Leo's contribution to improving the breed is well known and documented. Elmer Kelton, editor of **West Texas Livestock Weekly** refers to Leo as "one of the tallest figures in the Texas sheep industry. His work in the development of the fine wool Rambouillet breed is evident from one end of the Texas sheep country to the other, on thousands of individual ranches."

Looking at a picture of a handsome but deceased sheep, Leo says, "I bred him one year and got 20 rams out of him so I didn't lose him altogether."

Leo has set high standards for the sheep and for himself. But the life of a sheep is not so bad. Occasionally it's hard to walk around with all that wool on. Leo and Rod have supplied lots of watering places on their land so the sheep don't have to walk too far for a drink. Despite their discomfort from being too woolly, the sheep are not happy about being shorn either and have to be pulled by the legs to their shearing appointment.

Years of chewing the tough but palatable West Texas grasses, which are nourishing to the belly but punishing to the teeth, have taken their toll. In sheep, teeth are the first things to go. Leo lets some of the finer animals live their whole lives. When the sheep are six or eight years old, he retires them to the "corn belt" or sends them to the green farms of Kentucky, as a reward. There the grass is tender and easy.

The Richardsons abstain from putting any coloration whatever on their animals' wool, not wanting to interfere with the quality of the coat. Instead, they attach markers to the animals' ears, giving them a number for life. If Leo tried to name his sheep (some 12,000 sheep), it would take a year and he wouldn't get to call them for 6 months while they grazed the pastures. Occasionally a sheep will be especially personable. He had one pet lamb that drank milk straight from a bowl. Sheep have a love of tobacco once they get the taste of it. And this particular sheep would go around searching all the boys' coats hanging on the fence, and eat the cigarettes he found, filters and all.

Leo has probably been harder on himself than on his sheep. There is no date, no time, when things got easier for the Richardsons. "It never did get easier. We just kept building. We wouldn't give up. We had struggled so hard and so long that there just wasn't any quitting place."

(photo by Jamie Frucht)

Leo excuses how he and his sheep look on a particular day: the sheep had been shorn recently and he didn't think he looked too good either.

(photo courtesy Leo Richardson)

Leo has suffered two strokes since 1968. One afflicted his left side, crippling him, making it difficult to walk and giving him the perfect alibi to let up. But it didn't keep him down. By using the leg, he has made it stronger and gets around with determination for muscle. November 15, 1975, a second stroke hit him in the throat. That took his voice. The date is significant because it severely changed his life for a time. "I trapped right up until this last stroke got me and I didn't think anything about it. That was just part of it." Though lesser men might fuss over their predicaments, Leo, with the patience of Job, goes on. He does not grieve. And his voice is slowly coming back.

Breeding 85 pastures worth of a woolly vision—that keeps a man busy. With all Leo's struggling and troubles, you'd think there'd be nothing left over inside him. It's just the opposite. Acceptance of struggle as a way of life has made Leo a strong man, not a hard one. He is a sure and open person. His body, which doesn't sit still well and rises early, is still tall. His eyes are a lasting blue, not faded by age. Leo has a gentle sense of humor. He excuses how he and his sheep look on a particular day: the sheep had been shorn recently and he didn't think he looked too good either.

The vitality that drove him as a young man is still part of him, though paced in an older body. He and his dream are both active. After more than half a century, he's still going after his vision. He can't quit it even now. Leo is a driven man—driven like a philospher, not after money, but after an ideal—a sheepman searching for his platonic sheep, looking constantly for perfection behind the fleeting appearances of his flocks.

Sadly, Leo's vision is not communicable or transferable. He says, "This business, it's something you can't turn over to someone else. They can't visualize what you're visualizing. They haven't got the dream." His son who has quite a determination will have to pursue his own ideas and vision, building what he wants to see. It's all left to him now to do it.

Helen says of her husband, "I don't have the **vision** that he has of Rambouillet sheep, but I do know what his **problem** is." Leo Richardson's **problem**, the vision of the perfect sheep and his work to attain it, have given his life a heroic dimension and a wholeness.

Our Daily Bread (from: A Sprig of Grass)

by Raymond Elliott

Papa was an early riser, his built-in alarm being humiliating to the roosters. This seemed completely unnecessary during the winter months when the family could have slept longer. But only lazy people lay in bed! Thus, Papa would get up before daybreak and build a fire in the fireplace and in the cookstove. Meanwhile, Mama would dress before the open fire and drowsily move to the kitchen to start breakfast. We had biscuits for breakfast every day, for commercially baked bread was neither available nor desired. And there were biscuits and/or cornbread for the noon and evening meals. Soon after the morning biscuits were placed in the oven, Papa called. He called once and you moved. Our bare feet immediately hit the cold floor, jumping like jack rabbits to the fireplace where our clothes had been left the night before. At breakfast we bowed our heads in gratitude for the day and for the meal. After eating we'd probably retreat to the fireplace and blink at the blaze until it was light enough to do the chores. The cows—the cows were always waiting to be milked, the horses wanted their feed, and the hogs were squealing for attention. We were servant to all these that they might be servant to us.

In my youth, children were expected to work. John Smith's directive that "Those who do not work, shall not eat" was still a practical philosophy. All members of the family worked in return for their keep. Work was an expression of gratitude for having been brought into the world. When parents were old, the children were expected to care for them. These concepts have all changed during my lifetime.

As children, our first jobs were feeding the chickens, gathering the eggs, cleaning the lamp chimneys, and helping Mama in the garden. As we grew older, we were gradually initiated into the more strenuous chores, such as slopping and feeding the hogs, feeding the horses, milking the cows, and finally working in the field. In the latter, we hoed and plowed cotton and corn and eventually operated all farm machinery, none of which was motorized.

Harvesting the grain was probably the major farm operation. The binder had to be put in working condition, the canvas and sickle repaired. At least five horses or mules were required to pull the heavy McCormick binder, three as a wheel team and two as the lead team. My job was to ride one of the three and drive the lead team, the other boys taking their turn when older. Papa sat on the high seat of the binder, like an overlord directing the operation. He operated the levers which controlled the height of the cut and of the reel, observed whether the knotter was tying properly, and released the bundle carrier at regular intervals, placing the bundles in rows. The other boys followed the binder, shocking the grain. The latter work was always behind except when the binder gave trouble as it usually did, especially the bullwheel and the canvas.

Thrashing followed cutting by about a month. This was an exciting time. The neighbor women united in feeding the thrasher crew, and what a table they set for hungry men—biscuits, cornbread, potato salad, pinto beans, green beans, fried chicken, ham, milk, pie and/or cake. The men traded work with each other so there would be a minimum of cash outlay. Seeing the Will Riza steam engine pull the grain separator up "Rocky Hill" was an annual treat for men and boys alike. Sometimes the front wheels would temporarily leave the ground, but calm Mr. Riza always managed without incident. Arriving in a field, the engine would be set in line and at the proper distance from the separator and the big belt from engine to separator adjusted. A "pitcher" in the field would fork the bundles to the bundle wagon where they were stacked in a manner to prevent them from sliding off on the way to the separator. Two wagons unloaded at once, one on either side of the separator. The thrashed grain came out of the chute on the side of the separator, and the straw was blown into a sack. During my adolescent years, I did most of the jobs associated with thrashing.

Hog killing was another neighborhood activity. The hogs were kept in the feeding pens for several weeks before, the weather determining their day of doom. A still, cold, frosty night was ideal for cooling the meat. On the appointed day, each neighbor shot his own hogs and immediately cut the animals' throats for proper bleeding. The hogs were then loaded and taken to a previously selected place where pots of boiling water were waiting.

Dousing a hog in a tilted barrel of hot water softened the hair as in shaving. The hair was then removed by scraping the animal with butcher knives after which the carcass was hung by its heels, head down, thoroughly rinsed, gutted, and carved. Certain cuts were set aside for immediate use with many trimmings going into sausage. The womenfolk ground, seasoned, and sacked the sausage meat. The men removed the joint bones from hams and shoulders and placed these along with sides on the barn roof for cooling overnight. These were removed the following morning and salted down in the meat box. The fat trimmings were rendered into lard which was stored in gallon buckets for use in cooking throughout the year. Like packing plants, we used practically all of the hog except the hair and the contents of the entrails and stomach.

Making cane syrup was also a communal effort. Each family would hand cut and strip its cane and bring it to the syrup mill. A mule hooked to a beam extending from the rollers moved in a circle. This turned the rollers through which the cane stalks were fed, squeezing the juice into containers. The juice was then cooked for several hours during which the hot liquid was skimmed to remove undesirable matter. When the juice had been properly cooked, the resulting syrup was stored in jugs or buckets for winter use.

Papa's blacksmith shop was a fascinating place for a boy. There were all kinds of tools including saws, drawing knives, planes, rasps, a drill press, and thread dies. Papa taught us to use each tool, but woe to the boy who did not return it to its proper place. One of my first jobs was running the forge. Later, I liked to help Papa when he was welding. As I operated the forge, Papa would work boric acid around the metal pieces, now white with heat. When they were ready, I'd take one of the pieces in the tongs and place it on the anvil. Papa would take the other piece, place it over mine and fuse the two with the hammer. It was amazing how he could shape the iron to his will.

When we were young, Papa milked one or two cows—enough to meet the table demand. As we grew older and could help with the milking, the herd was increased proportionately. During my upper teens we were milking eighteen to twenty cows. This was by hand, of course, and had to be done twice daily. That's a potential of forty muddy tails per day to unintentionally swat you on the head, eighty hind legs to kick and get in the milk bucket, and one hundred and sixty tits to get sore by chapping or other means. I've often wondered whether the Lord ever considered putting old Job through such a test. On the other hand, there's something very cozy about milking a cow on a cold day in a warm stall as you rest your head in her flank and she contentedly chews her cud, realizing you're on the receiving end of one of the most miraculous manufacturing plants in the world.

There's fun, too; that is, a peculiar brand of boyhood fun. Hitting your brother between the eyes with a stream of warm milk when he's already out of patience with a pesky calf, is fun beyond words. He can't say a word, for Papa who is relieving a cow nearby would find out. It's that surprise on his face—that disgusted you-go-to-the-devil look in his eyes that's so wonderfully rewarding. And you have twelve hours to enjoy it after which you will be paid in kind for your sin.

Churning was the most disliked of our household duties. The churn was a three-gallon crock with a beveled opening. The original top had been broken and Papa had replaced it with one he had made from wood but had not got the bevel just right. As a result, it would not remain in place under the strokes of the dash from the careless hands of a boy. To keep the top in place, we'd place our heels on a rung of a high-chair we used when churning and hook our big toes over the sides of the top. Pity us when Mama caught us doing this; she did on several occasions.

Mama had a full-time job processing the milk from twenty cows twice a day. It had to be strained, cooled, and prepared for churning, and all buckets and crocks thoroughly washed. After churning, she molded the butter, wrapping each pound in wax paper. The butter also had to be kept cool until taken to market. I'm not sure how long Mama endured this ordeal, but it was much, much too long. Mama sold the butter and eggs where she purchased the groceries.

Eventually Mama insisted on a cream separator, but Papa would have no part of it. Just another new-fangled idea! Papa was like that. Finally Mama and I went to Sam White, borrowed $80.00, drove to Montgomery Ward in Fort Worth and purchased a separator. Following the instruction pamphlet, I put the thing together piece by piece. Papa just pouted. Only when I had trouble leveling the contraption did he volunteer his service. "That floor's crooked as a dog's hind leg," he said, lending me a hand. After milking, we filled the milk chamber, and I started turning the crank. Immediately, a good stream of milk came through the one outlet, but no cream at all from the other. "Just like I told you—no! You wouldn't listen to me," Papa stormed out of the room. Papa was like that, too. I rechecked the pamphlet and confirmed I had correctly assembled the mechanism. After some anxious moments, I discovered I had neglected to adjust a certain little screw controlling the cream flow. With this correction, we had both cream and "blue-john." A test at the creamery the next day showed a perfect milk-fat content. Several years later I overheard Papa tell a neighbor that he didn't see how we had got along without a cream separator. Yes, Papa was also like that.

When I was about twelve, Papa told me to saddle a certain mare and take her to Nort Jones for breeding to a fine stud. My instructions were to cross the George McClung Ranch, turn on the Cleburne-Glen Rose road, enter a gate on the left, ride in a southern direction to another gate where the fence cornered, continue over the ridge to the south when I could see boulders in the distance, pass by these, cross the Meridian road, turn south, and follow the lane to the Jones place. The round trip took most of the day. I was later to go on many such missions.

With this sort of background, we needed no instruction concerning the birds and the bees. We lived with them. When necessary we helped or watched Papa act as midwife to many a mother animal. Each member of the family loved the baby things—colts, calves, pigs, chicks, puppies, and kittens, and we were never allowed to mistreat any animal at whatever age. One of my fondest memories of Papa was his care of the young. As the time of delivery drew near, a cow would withdraw to a secret and secluded spot where she could have her baby unmolested. After birth, she'd clean her offspring, feed it, bed it down, and guard it with her life. Being concerned because of wolves in the area and knowing the cow had to have water, Papa would watch the watering places. Once the cow was spotted, he'd tail her like a detective, convince her of his harmless intent, and carry the calf home with mama cow hard on his heels, bawling every step of the way. Mother and calf would get special attention for the next few days. We liked to watch the cow every morning as she gave her calf a spit bath, forming hundreds of curly ringlets or cowlicks, a cow style wave set. Just like a mother!

As stated earlier, we learned to operate all farm machinery. When my legs were long enough, Papa bought a wiggle-tail cultivator. This new device could be partly guided by maneuvering the seat from right to left. It was much easier for a boy to operate than the old type. Other such cultivators were acquired as the younger boys grew. At the height of our farm operation, we were running three cultivators. Papa spent most of his time in the shop, sharpening sweeps. With this new equipment, we needed more land, so we rented acreage from Pink Hudgins on the mountain beyond Grandpa Myres' place.

When I was about fifteen, Papa said, "You know that stumpy seven-acre piece beyond the Pink Hudgins field? Well, that also belongs to Pink, and I was wondering if you boys would like to rent it for a crop of your own." Of course, the idea appealed to me for we got no allowance (what's that?) and no pay for our labors. I told Papa we'd rent the land, expecting him to make the necessary arrangements. (I now feel certain he had already talked with Mr. Hudgins.) "No," Papa said, "you'll have to make your own deal." So it was that the three of us boys went to see the owner, who agreed to rent the land. And we had to make our own arrangements for hoeing and picking the cotton. I even had to haul some of the cotton to the gin and take care of the business affairs. We made a bumper crop that year, our net profit being $211.00 apiece. Papa introduced us at the bank and we made our first deposit. It was our money and we could spend it, but Papa's and Mama's experience in buying would be valuable to us—or so we were told. Renting the land and taking care of the business affairs connected with it was valuable training from a wise father.

Mule Man

by Donna Bearden

Oren Reeves is a large man, a gentle man—friendly, quiet, loving. His smile lines run deep, but on his cheek there seems to be a drop of wetness, perhaps well-earned sweat from hard physical labor, but more like a gentle tear. For Oren is a man of feeling. His strong hands are firm as he harnesses up his six matched, red sorrell mules, the only hitch like it in all of Texas. Oren loves mules, he always has, perhaps even more now than back when they were the work animals of America.

At one time there were 10 million mules in the United States. George Washington is credited with bringing mule-power to the developing nation. In 1785, "Royal Gift," a prize jackass was sent to Washington by King Charles III of Spain. Washington had heard of the fine qualities that blended in the offspring of Spanish jacks and horse mares. Soon other jacks and jennies were imported and the mule population grew rapidly.

The mules tilled the soil of the East. They pulled Conestoga wagons for the pioneers pushing westward. They dug canals and then pulled the barges along the canals. Deep in the mines, mules pulled loads of coal to the mine shafts. In the forests they were used for lumbering and logging. Mule-drawn stage coaches delivered the mail. And the mule was a trusted and indispensable help-mate to the early prospector.

This hard-working animal, with crude tools and a lot of endurance, helped build the railroads and highways.

Reeves recalls mules being used for delivery wagons also.

"The ice wagon had two big mules that were so well-trained they would walk on to the next house and stop while the ice-man made a delivery.

(photo courtesy State Dept. of Highways and Public Transportation)

"About ten or twelve years ago I was ashamed for anyone to know that I would drive 400 miles to look at a mule."
(photo by Donna Bearden)

"And you'd see two mules hitched to a wagon running, just a-flying to deliver groceries."

Oren Reeves' father, an East Texas farmer, owned six or eight mules that helped him plow, plant and harvest. By the time he was eight years old, Oren could harness one gentle old mule and plow the fields. He had to climb up on a box to get the harness on, but the mule was patient. In the evening, Oren would climb up on his broad back and ride proudly home like a king on a beautiful steed.

Sometimes when the weather was bad, Mr. Reeves would hitch up a mule to the buggy and the children could ride to school. As the children recited their lessons in the one-room school, the mule would stand patiently in the schoolyard waiting to carry his passengers home in mid-afternoon.

If the roads were too muddy, the ruts got deeper. At least once, the gentle old mule fell, depositing himself and his young passengers in the wet mud.

As Oren grew older, he found a new use for his father's mules and a way to earn some money on his own.

About the Fourth of July, the farmers in Camp County "laid by" their crops and there wouldn't be much to do with the mules until it was time to pick cotton or harvest corn. Oren bought a fresno, a dirt scraper, and hired out to help build roads. The Highway Department awarded road building contracts to big earthmoving companies. The companies would, in turn, subcontract with small mule outfits of six to a dozen or more teams. At first Oren had one spread of three mules pulling a fresno. He worked during the slack period in late summer and also on the weekends during the winter months.

Reeves was never really a "gyppo," living in tents and following from job to job. Through the years he kept with his farming and, at one time, leased as many as 30 mules out for roadbuilding. But, like the gyppos, he knew his mules by name, knew their temperaments, their strengths and their weaknesses. It ran deeper than fondness and appreciation—it still does.

And it still pains Oren to talk about what progress and automation did to the mule population, the powerful builders of America.

"Mules were used for everything, the lighter ones did all the farming, pulled supply wagons, and took folks to church on Sunday. The average farm mule weighed between 1000-1200 pounds.

"The larger the mule, the more he could pull and the longer he could stand it. Most road mules weighed between 14-1600 pounds.

"Mules then were the only source of power we had, built roads, hauled logs, until they invented the steam engine, the tractor. . ." (His voice cracks and that perpetual tear appears on his cheek. . .) "By 1941 or 2 everybody sold their mules to a dealer and they were shipped to a soap factory. At one time there were over 10 million mules in the country and now I doubt if there are one million."

But mule lovers are still around—mule men who get together at the big mule sales in Waverly, Iowa; Topeka, Kansas; and Lebanon, Tennessee. People come from all over the world to swap tales and mules.

Oren got into show mules about a dozen years ago.

"About ten or twelve years ago I was ashamed for anyone to know that I would drive 400 miles to look at a mule."

So he would make up excuses like vacations in the vicinity of good mule traders.

Then he bought a jack and four Belgian mares from a dealer in Lamar, Missouri, and raised colts for two or three years. But it was a slow process since he was aiming for matched pairs. So he bought two pairs from the man and got a four-mule hitch.

He continued buying two-year-old colts, training them for about two years, and selling them at a profit. (But it was actually more hobby than profit.)

From a four-mule hitch, he went to six and today Reeves is the only man in Texas to own and drive a hitch of six matched, red sorrell mules.

He thrills many an audience of old-timers and youngsters alike, especially as he races around the arena at the State Fair in Dallas. One of his mules, Kit, was named "Model Mule" at the Texas State Fair. He also won first place at the Fair for the best hitch.

He makes a lot of the small parades and rodeos in East Texas and has even taken his team to Houston, Fort Worth and Dallas.

Bedding down six mules is no easy task and it's expensive. So Reeves carries his own pens to Dallas. The State Fair is two weeks long and he rides in the torchlight parade every night.

Sometimes he's sponsored by a company, business or club and, in return for decking out his wagon with advertising, he gets his expenses paid. But paid or not, Reeves will continue to make as many parades and shows as he can. He's proud of his mules and it's just his way of sharing their heritage.

On the Firing Line for Human Rights

by Jackie Swindle and Donna Bearden

"As a small child I can remember my father, Handy Daniels, being interested in politics, although Negroes could not vote. My father had a hauling business, and he came in contact with men discussing politics. Every night at supper we would sit around the table and listen to my father discuss the events of the day. I didn't know that the events he discussed were called politics and I really wasn't interested. However, my mother made us sit at the table and listen. As I grew older and studied more, I began to realize the value of knowing about politics. Later, politics became a part of my life just automatically."

Handy Daniels and "Old Grant" as they earned the daily bread.
(photo courtesy Christia Adair)

Christia V. Adair was born on October 22, 1893 in Victoria, Texas. She spent her early childhood in Edna, Texas and attended elementary school there.

When she was about in the sixth grade she was sent to Austin, to attend Sam Huston College, which today is Huston-Tillotson College.

When she finished Sam Huston, she entered Prairie View State Normal and Industrial College. She finished in 1915 and went back to her hometown, Edna. She was given a job teaching at the school where she had gone to elementary school. She received about $35.00 a month.

"The building which I taught in was very inadequate, and I had to buy teaching aids out of my own little salary. I taught the fourth and the fifth grade. The father of Texas Congresswoman Barbara Jordan was one of my little boys in the fourth grade."

She met Elbert H. Adair in Vanderbilt, Texas. They were married in 1918 and moved to Kingsville. As her husband didn't want her to teach school, she began to participate in community activities.

"It became known in our community that the owner of a gambling house was using teenage boys at the place. The Negro women decided to put a stop to it. We were not strong enough to do it alone and we didn't have enough influence with the law enforcement officers. So we asked the white mothers club to join with us in this effort. The white mothers club and the Negro women united. Working with the law enforcement officers and the District Attorney, we were able to close the gambling houses in Kingsville.''

Also, about this time, she became involved in women's suffrage. ''Back in 1918, Negroes could not vote and women could not vote either. The white women were trying to help get a bill passed in the legislature where women could vote. I said to the Negro women, 'I don't know if we can use it now or not, but if there's a chance, I want to say we helped make it.' So the Negro women joined with the white women and campaigned. When the women won the right to vote, we (Negroes) won it too.

''We went to the polls at the white primary but could not vote. Negroes could vote in federal elections but were denied entry into the local white primary. We kept after them until they finally said we couldn't vote because we were Negroes. That's just what I wanted them to say. I had an instinct that we could use this.

''Up until around 1900, all Negroes were Republicans because Abraham Lincoln was a Republican. Around 1920, I personally made a change from the Republican Party to the Democratic Party when Warren G. Harding was running for President. My husband was a brakeman on the Missouri Pacific Railroad. Being a senior brakeman, he would always bring special trains to our section. One day he called me long distance and told me that all along the road, the school children were meeting the campaign train of Harding and shaking hands with him. He said the train would stop in Kingsville.

''I went over to the school and told the teachers about the campaign train. They didn't appear very interested. So I asked to take ten or twelve children with parents' consent to see the candidate. Since I was always meeting the train to pick up my husband, I knew exactly where the train would stop. I selected the spot and placed my children. When my husband opened the observation gate, my children were standing in front of it where Harding had to step out. When he stepped out, he reached over my children and shook the white children's hands. I became upset and decided at that moment that I would become a Democrat.''

In 1925, the Adairs moved to Houston. It was in the 1920's that the first Houston chapter of the NAACP was organized. Christia became the first recording secretary. In 1949, she became executive secretary of the Houston chapter of the NAACP. This chapter fought a lot of battles in the 1950's for the rights of the Negro, and Christia played a leading role in helping to fight these battles.

''One battle which I fought personally was getting permission for Negro women to use fitting rooms in stores. I bought a $27.00 girdle which I didn't need and insisted that I try it on in a fitting room. I won the battle of the fitting rooms.''

If a Negro woman wanted to buy a hat, the sales clerk would try it on for her. It just wasn't quite the same thing.

And at the Houston International Airport, "a Negro couldn't sit in the waiting room. They had to go to the door of the kitchen to eat. The only restroom was a block away and it was for men and women both."

When the new airport was completed, newly-elected Mayor Roy Hofheinz had the "White Only" signs taken down. He also opened the city libraries and blacks could check out books. Mrs. Adair and NAACP had worked for both of these rights.

"White only" facilities included the city hall and county courthouse cafeterias. No Negro could get a county or city job.

The NAACP also fought for school integration and against police brutality.

Mrs. Adair went to the police station time and time again with charges to be investigated, pictures and sworn statements.

"We had police and sheriff brutality 'way down in the '50's," Mrs. Adair said, a condition she does not believe prevails today.

"We cut out all those out-of-boundary whipping posts," she said, mentioning the "Barn" and the "Windmill" on the edge of the county, where lawmen allegedly took Negro prisoners for private questioning and beatings.

Later, the young people decided to open public eating and amusement places with sit-ins. Mrs. Adair said, "They protested, and we would get them out of jail."

In 1952, Mrs. Adair helped found the Harris County Democrats, a group breaking away from the regular "Dixiecrat Democrats" who had fought for segregated primaries.

"I think the Harris County Democrats have done more for race relations in Harris County than anyone," she says, "including the NAACP."

About the same time, the Harris County Council of Organizations, a coalition of Negro organizations, was formed to bring a halt to the practice of buying Negro votes.

The two groups working together called a public meeting.

"It was the first integrated political meeting that had been held in Houston and it was a full house, a League of Nations," she said.

The coalition worked well, but then came the McCarthy era. Racial tensions accelerated at a time when the NAACP was filing suit after suit about college education for Negroes.

In 1956, the State of Texas charged the NAACP with barratry, based on the common law premise that lawyers should not solicit cases. Investigators, accompanied by armed Texas Rangers and Highway Patrolmen, were sent out to confiscate NAACP records.

"When they came I didn't have the membership rolls or the receipt books on who had contributed, which included some prominent white people," she said. The lawmen were after names. "They knew if a Negro was identified with the NAACP, he'd lose his job," she said.

The state subpoenaed Mrs. Adair and kept her on the stand for five hours in cross-examination during the three-week trial in Tyler.

Somehow the national membership records for Texas were unaccountably lost.

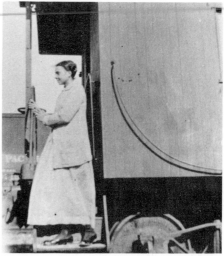

(photo courtesy Christia Adair)

Mrs. Adair called the trial a "soap box opera."

Thurgood Marshall, NAACP head attorney and later U.S. Supreme Court Justice, finally won the case two years later on appeal to the Supreme Court.

"But it created a tenseness, a mistrust and bigotry in our town. Negroes who were afraid of white people got more frightened. Nobody stood up for the NAACP," she said. "That would have been the kiss of death.

"The whites kept quiet because I wanted them to. I wanted to protect them. They never turned their backs on the organization."

In 1959, Mrs. Adair retired as NAACP executive director, emotionally, physically and financially exhausted, but kept on as judge of Precinct 25.

For 20 years she served as a precinct judge. She was one of the first Negro precinct judges. "There were always harrassments during the elections, but I always tried to conduct myself as a lady."

After she became a Democrat around 1920, she began campaigning for Democratic Presidents, beginning with Franklin D. Roosevelt to Lyndon B. Johnson.

"I worked very hard in those campaigns since I didn't have the money to contribute like a lot of people. I always gave service, which was helpful in getting the voters out. I have always thought that no matter how much money a candidate has, if he doesn't get enough votes, he will not get elected. As a precinct judge **I worked very hard** to get votes for the precinct."

She has a favorite story about the late President Kennedy. "On November 20, 1963, when President Kennedy was on that fateful trip to Dallas, his plane stopped at Hobby Airport in Houston. There were many people lined up to see him. When he got off the plane, he didn't look for any particular group but shook hands with all within his reach. There were many prominent Houstonians standing by and also various children's organizations. I began to push the children closer to see the President. There was a little black boy standing in front and a prominent citizen standing nearby with his hand extended. The little black boy was looking up with so much anxiety that his cap fell off. The President picked up the little black boy's cap and patted him on the head saying, 'You lost your cap, didn't you sonny?' He then

1916 Commencement week announcement postcard.

Christia Adair and friends at Samuel Huston College.   *(photo courtesy Christia Adair)*

(photo courtesy Christia Adair)

passed on to the others. I thought that gesture was very outstanding for a President."

In 1966, Mrs. Adair and Judson Robinson Jr. were elected as the first State Democratic committeemen of their race.

But the regular Democrats refused to seat the Harris County delegation. Then came word that two delegates were acceptable to the conservatives, Mrs. Adair and Robinson.

"I said, 'I don't want to go in if they won't let the others in.' And we refused. I never have been a 'good nigger' and I saw no reason to start then. They offered all kinds of fringe inducements. I don't know how anybody could live in Harris County and think I could be bribed. Judson held his own, too."

In 1970, when she retired as precinct judge, the Harris County Democrats honored her at a reception as the "Most Distinguished Colleague" of the Harris County Democrats, and she was given a life membership in the organization. She has been given several certificates and plaques for services rendered. Among these were a Women's Suffrage certificate, Woman of the Year plaque, and a meritorious award from the Texas Association of Women's Clubs, Inc.

It has been said that "Christia V. Adair fought for women's suffrage when it was a song on everybody's lips that women ought to have the right to vote."

She shrugged off threats, bad telephone calls, curses that ignorant people sought to inflict on her. She paid no attention when a lot of people would have panicked.

Mrs. Adair remembers: "Some of the Negro men tried to get me out of the precinct job. But I was always more afraid for the Negro men. I could get away with more. Many nights I didn't sleep. Living alone, wondering what they might do to me. I never had a gun in this house, but they thought I did. I did a lot of big talking."

In addition to working as a politician and civil rights leader, she has always worked in her church. Also, for many years she has been a member and worked hard with the Texas Federation of Colored Women's Clubs, which is affiliated with the National Association of Women's and Girl's Clubs. This organization was founded in the eighteenth century. Some of its earliest members were Mesdames St. Pierre Ruffin, Phillis Wheatley, Mary Church Terrell, Booker T. Washington, Harriett Tubman, and Mary McLeod Bethune.

In a **Houston Post** article, in 1972, Rev. C.N. Bonner described Mrs. Adair: "There were some tough years. And they left some scars on her. But you would never know they were there. I think it's because of her capacity for love."

"God has been good to let me be 82 years old and look back on so many of the things that have scarred my heart and brain," she said. "And I see so many things that are the result of suffering.

"As long as there is something to be done, I don't feel like I'm too old to do it."

"I don't want to please you; I want to tell you the truth."   *(photo by Mary Sherwood)*

The Doctor is a Fighter

by Helen Fischer and Jamie Frucht
from taped interviews by Hubert J. Miller

Dr. Octavio Garcia is a short man with delicate features and the long, steady fingers of a surgeon. He is a small, determined David who, at 77, takes on all Goliaths as he has all his life. In his battles against racism, stupidity and narrow-mindedness, among other evils, his character and powerful temperment have become all the stronger through the overcoming of obstacles. If he had not been a fighter, he could never have survived as a doctor—not in the Rio Grande Valley.

In the Valley, especially at the time of his arrival in the 1930's, an Anglo-Saxon name was more important to professional acceptance than ability and excellent credentials. But Garcia refused to be defeated by prejudice, refused to be forced out of his profession and out of town, refused to be controlled by others he considered less competent than himself, refused to accept the way Mexicans in the Valley were given second-rate medical care—or worse.

"I was wise enough to fight discrimination." How? "By knowing more than they did. I knew my rights. I knew my abilities. I refused to be cowed."

Though Garcia did not learn English until he was 17, he now speaks it with the swiftness and efficiency of a prizefighter's punches, as well as with the precision of a surgeon. His speech mirrors his temperament. The doctor is a fighter.

Octavio Garcia was born in Mexico in 1899. At the age of 10, after he had completed six grades in public school, he was sent by his family to live with an aunt in Saltillo, where he attended the **Ateneo,** a private school for boys.

The intellectual life of the school was quite vigorous. Sports, which are so typical a diversion for children of this age today, were little in evidence. The boys were instructed in mathematics, grammar, and history, with the addition of some art and natural sciences. In their free time, they gathered in the library, in the courtyard under a tree, or in the homes of their instructors for long and lively discussions of current events and classroom topics.

In the evenings they frequently played chess or attended the theater to hear the **zarzuelas** (operettas) and sneak flirtatious glances at the well-chaperoned daughters of the town's families, for dating was unknown, and boys and girls did not attend school together. Sometimes they rented bicycles and went on Saturday outings to nearby **ranchos** and **haciendas** belonging to the parents of boys at the school.

Though Octavio was still too young to have a very extensive understanding of the Mexican revolution, the political upheavals of that period had a profound impact on the subsequent course of his life, for they were responsible for his father's decision to take his family to the United States.

The elder Garcia, a **ranchero,** owned several large tracts of land on which he raised cattle. As the redistribution of land was one of the major issues of the revolutionaries, a great deal of hatred was directed toward the large landowners. In addition, the elder Garcia was suspected of opposition to President Carranza, because he had operated a stagecoach line which carried mail from Matamoros to Monterrey under the previous regime.

Garcia decided to take his wife, daughter and two sons across the border to the greater safety of the U.S. As soon as he and his brother had set up ranches on a 12,000-acre tract near Falfurrias, he sent a letter instructing Octavio, the youngest child, to come and join them there.

Time went by and no definite arrangements were made. The aunt wrote Octavio's parents not to worry because the political situation in Saltillo was still under control. They waited too long. The revolutionaries blew up the railroad bridge across the culverts and arroyas between Monterrey and Saltillo, and young Octavio was still in Saltillo.

"My father never intended to make Texas his home," Garcia said. "He did have interests there, because he owned land there. But he had no other thought but to go back to Mexico as soon as the fighting was over."

In 1914 it finally became possible for 15-year-old Octavio to rejoin his family. He went to live with them in a strange land with strange customs, where he did not understand the language.

"By the time I reached the ranch," he recalled, "my father had built a wooden house two stories high with a porch around it, as was the custom in those days. Around the house there was a fence to keep the animals out of the vegetable garden.

"After I had rested a while at the ranch, my father set me to work just like anybody else. He put me under the direction of the boss of the cowboys, who showed no favoritism to the owner's son. I worked just as hard as anybody else. There were some things I was not assigned to do because I was too inexperienced or not strong enough, but otherwise I took part in every activity connected with the care of cattle. My father wanted his sons to learn ranching from the inside.

"This particular spread was concerned with the buying, selling and shipping of cattle; they were not fattened there. When we received an order, we drove the cattle to the railroad terminal at Falfurrias, which was as far south as the railroad went at that time. It was 32 miles from our house and traveling there was always difficult. There was no road. The land we had to cross was all deep sand and it was difficult to drive a buggy or wagon; they had to have wide tires on the wheels to keep from sinking in the sand.

"We had to cross the Lasater ranch, the King ranch, and the Jones ranch, and of course all the ranches were kept fenced. There were gates at certain places and we had the key, or knew where the key was hidden, to each of the ranches near ours. Those familes, in turn, knew where our keys were. We were all very strict in the matter of the keys. We felt absolute freedom to go through nearby ranchers' land and of course everybody knew you and you knew them. But if anybody unfamiliar was seen trying to get through one of those gates, he was promptly asked his business. If it wasn't satisfactory he was just as promptly told to get out."

The cowboy's life was strenuous, and he had to be accustomed to hardships. Much of the work to be done on the open range consisted of riding fences to make repairs and tracking down strayed cattle.

"We had to organize that work very carefully. Nowadays, with good roads and pickup trucks, a cowboy's life is much easier. He can go many miles away, do his work, and come back to the house for lunch. We had to take equipment and supplies for days at a time. We might leave on Monday morning and not come back to the house until the work was completed, and it might take all week. We had to take along a cook and food, as well as materials for repairing fences. We slept out in the open with nothing much but a saddleblanket and a slicker."

Besides mending fences, the cowboys changed the cattle from one pasture to another, branded them, treated them when they were sick, and tracked them down when they strayed. They had to become expert in reading cattle tracks and trails. Sometimes cattle would stray from one ranch to another, making it necessary to notify the owner to come and get his cattle.

"There was no trouble over this because the cattle were branded and each cattleman's brand was registered with the county. Branding was an interesting time, although the work was very hard. The corrals we had then had no chutes like ranchers use now to control the animals better. A corral then was just a rectangular enclosure with a water trough, where the animals were confined before shipping or after purchase, or for other purposes like branding. We had to rope the animal, throw it and hold it down while the heated iron was applied to the left forequarter to make a spot where the hair would not grow. From then on the animal could be easily identified and so could the hide, so it was very difficult for someone to steal an animal and get away with it.''

The elder Garcia's workforce consisted of eight to ten cowboys and their **caporal,** or boss. Near his own house he built quarters for them—wooden houses for the married ones and their families, and a building to house the bachelors together.

About once a month, another task had to be taken care of and, though it involved a lot of work, it was regarded as something of a treat. Two of the cowboys would be sent to Falfurrias with wagons to fetch supplies. The ranch-dwellers were so isolated that this was a social occasion.

"Everything was carefully mapped out ahead of time, anticipating our needs for four to six weeks. My father used to send either my brother or me ahead of time on horseback to go to the bank, make a deposit or pick up money for wages and payment of the provisions, pick up the mail, and start placing our orders at the Falfurrias Mercantile Company. We had to buy staples like sugar, coffee, and lard, and also things like needles, thread, and sometimes clothing. The wagons would take two days getting there and another two days getting back, so it took nearly a whole week to bring provisions.''

On these trips the cowboys usually carried guns—not to protect their cargo against bandits, but to kill game.

"People tend to think of cowboys as wearing guns, but we went unarmed all the time. Nobody carried guns, except when they went hunting. And sometimes on the open range during the screwworm infestation, we would find an animal so badly infected that it was too late to treat it.

"We would have to shoot it and burn it so the carcass wouldn't be a place for more screwworm flies to breed. When we had free time, we would shoot at targets, competing in skill. But we didn't just carry guns around all the time.''

One of the major social occasions of the isolated ranches of south Texas was the arrival of the priest.

"We called them 'priests on horseback,' and they used to ride a circuit from La Lomita or Brownsville, going from ranch to ranch. Usually the priest had a helper with him and one or two mules to carry his equipment—the things he needed for Mass, and catechism books for the children, and any newspapers he could bring along for the ranch families. He was very welcome everywhere he went, even where people were not Catholics, because he was company and he brought news.

"People actually waited and looked forward to the time when the priest would come. Many celebrations took place then, particularly weddings and baptisms, and the rancher would invite all his friends to come from the other ranches. Usually a priest would stay not less than three days at a ranch, in order to carry out all these functions, and teach the children about religion, as well as say Mass. This was done in the house as we did not have a chapel on our ranch. In the evenings he would sit around and swap news with the other adults at the rancher's house.''

After Octavio had worked on the ranch about two years, his father decided it was time for him to continue his education. He chose a Catholic boarding school in San Antonio for his son and briefed him on what to expect there and on the customs of the Anglo-American people. Until then, Octavio's only contact with Anglo-Americans had been his friendships with the families on nearby ranches where there had been no racial or cultural conflict at all and everybody spoke Spanish.

He was astonished at the practice of racial segregation and at the discrimination directed against Negroes and the poorer Mexicans. He also had considerable difficulty making himself understood, for it had never been necessary for him to learn much English.

His father accompanied him to San Antonio and introduced him to his friends there, many of whom were Anglos, and took him to St. Louis College which lay about two miles west of the last streetcar stop. Because of its location, the boys had no contact with the life of the town. Life there was so regimented that at first Octavio mistook the place for a military school. It was operated by the Marian Brothers and great stress was laid on religion.

''A bell rang and we got up; another bell rang and we went to Mass; another bell rang and we went to breakfast.

''I was not used to being driven by a bell. We had classes all day, and after class there was no library or other place where we could gather to exchange views, like at Satillo. The teachers were much more aloof from the students, and I got reprimanded for asking too many questions. I found it very strange.''

He was there from 1916 to 1918, when he went home to the ranch, diploma in hand, and discussed with his father what plans to make for his future.

The family still thought of their stay in the United States as temporary. The elder Garcia offered his youngest the possibility of staying there and working the ranch on his own after the rest of the family went back to Mexico, and reminded him that he had also once expressed an interest in studying agriculture. But Octavio had changed his mind. He had decided he would like to study for a profession— only he wasn't sure which one. On the advice of one of his uncles, who was a doctor, he decided to study medicine.

''The better schools were in the North and East. I had decided, on my uncle's advice, to go somewhere and study biology and chemistry and things like that, get a B.A., and then go on to specialize. I told my father this, he gave me some money, and I just took the train and started off north with no definite idea of where I was going!''

At St. Louis he got off the train and went to talk with a counselor at St. Louis University. There he arranged to take some special courses at a local high school and perfect his English for a year, after which he would be admitted to pre-medical training.

"I was in for many surprises about the life of an American student. In those days there were no such things as dormitories. You found yourself a boarding house. And I had a hard time at first trying to understand the American student's mind and what was expected of me socially.

"I had a hard time getting used to the idea of the date. In Mexico, a young man did not take a young woman out. He visited her at her parents' home, under the strictest chaperonage. I was completely lost asking a girl to go somewhere with me all by ourselves, to a movie or a dance or a walk in the park. At first I refused to date at all unless I was formally introduced to the family of the girl, as had been the custom at home. But eventually I got used to it.

"At this time, the 'Roaring Twenties' were just beginning and 'roadhouses' were prevalent, where people could go and dance. Prohibition was at its height, but medical students could easily procure prescriptions for whiskey 'for medicinal purposes' from their professors, so we were very welcome for that reason. I was amazed very often at my fellow-students, at the informality and the type of dances and the type of music, and at some of their carryings-on. The pranks they played on each other—and sometimes on me—seemed to me very immature. But I tried very hard to understand their customs."

The first two years of pre-medical school were devoted to the study of anatomy, chemistry and other basic sciences. In the junior year the students were occasionally taken to a local hospital in small groups for demonstrated lectures on pathology and other clinical sciences. In the senior year they were assigned to a particular instructor at a hospital, where they were introduced to the tasks of obtaining a medical history and doing physical examinations. The discipline was rigorous and the pace rapid, yet Garcia found time to do more than was necessary.

He took advantage of the option offered pre-med students to attend non-medical lectures at the university, such as sociology and philosophy. He attended lectures of more advanced medical classes and observed the proceedings in their laboratory sessions. This exceptional interest was noted and encouraged by one of the professors, Dr. Fleischer.

In 1921 the Garcia family suffered severe losses in the stock market, and Octavio received a letter from his father telling him that he would no longer be able to support him in his studies. In need of a job, Octavio asked Dr. Fleischer for a letter of recommendation that would help him obtain work. Dr. Fleischer's letter of introduction to the owner of a local pharmaceutical supply house secured him a job as clerk in the warehouse.

Among the company's customers were a number of Mexican and South American buyers and young Octavio was soon making himself useful as an interpreter. Soon thereafter, he was translating for several other medical wholesalers on a free-lance basis.

However, what he was able to earn was insufficient to continue his studies. He took his problem back to Professor Fleischer who managed to prevail upon the university administration to grant Garcia a fellowship consisting of a tuition waiver and a job in a university medical laboratory which would pay him $62.50 a month for the school year. With this assistance, he was able to finish his junior and senior years.

After graduation, Garcia was selected for a rotating internship at the Jewish Hospital in St. Louis. Under this program, the interns spent a couple of months in each of several specialty areas. For room, board and $10 a month, they worked seven days a week. "There were no fixed hours. We worked until all the work was done. Lab work started about 6 a.m. and lasted until visits to patients began, which was about 8 o'clock, but often stretched to 10 or 11 p.m. On Sundays, since I was a Catholic, I was allowed time off to go to Mass. The conditions were terrible, but I have to admit that the training was excellent. It exposed us early to the hard work that is the lot of every doctor, and the need for dedication necessary to become a successful physician. By a 'successful' physician, I mean one who loves his profession and is more interested in being of service than in getting rich."

Understandably, this schedule limited his dating. However, he met nurses and medical technicians at the hospital. One of the technicians had a familiar face; he had met her at the university medical lab while she was learning technical work.

Cecile was the daughter of a Russian Jewish immigrant who had opened a drugstore in St. Louis. An uncle of Cecile's, who was a doctor, had persuaded the authorities at St. Louis University to let her study medical technical work at the university's labs, although no females were permitted to enroll as students. She and Garcia had little contact at that time. When she finished her training, she went to work at the Jewish Hospital and met Garcia again when he became an intern there. They saw each other frequently at work and began to date. They continued their courtship after Garcia became senior intern at St. Mary's Infirmary and then chief resident at the University Hospital.

Their decision to marry met with opposition from all quarters. Her father objected that Garcia was not Jewish; his parents and the Church objected that Cecile was not Catholic. At length a young priest who was a friend of Garcia's managed to get them a dispensation from the bishop to marry, though they were forbidden to marry in the church building. "It made me quite resentful of my Church that she was not allowed any of the dignity and pomp of the church like other girls. I didn't see any reason for it, because our love was just as strong as theirs." They were married in the parsonage in September, 1928.

Garcia had planned to enter private practice in St. Louis at that time, but in October his mentor, Dr. Fleischer, became very ill and had to leave his teaching post at the University. Garcia was asked to take over his classes for a short time until someone could be found to take Fleischer's place. Expectations notwithstanding, Garcia remained on this job all year. He also worked at the University Hospital and sometimes assisted the older, more experienced physicians in surgery or took over their offices while they were on vacation. At the end of the year he opened a small office of his own.

In the spring of 1930, Garcia's father died. The family's once considerable financial resources, eroded by the Depression in the U.S. and expropriation of their landholdings in Mexico, were exhausted. Octavio would have to take care of his widowed mother.

Meanwhile, his own finances had taken such a tumble in the Depression that he was unable to pay the lease on his office, and Cecile had given birth to their first child. In this crisis, he decided to move back to his native Mexico and practice medicine in Monterrey. There, however, his application for a license to practice was refused because of the revolutionary government's grudge against members of the old landed class.

Leaving Cecile and the baby with a cousin of his in McAllen, Garcia borrowed a car and scoured the Rio Grande Valley looking for a good place to settle. He applied for and was readily granted a license to practice medicine in Texas. As surgery was his speciality, he decided that the new hospital recently built in McAllen made that city the best prospect.

With the help of a loan from his cousin, Garcia rented an office and hung out his shingle.

"I considered it the courteous thing to do to let the city fathers and the mayor of the town know that I was going to settle in that community, and also to let the other doctors know that I was setting up practice there. So I went to the mayor, who happened to be a doctor, and told him my intentions. He told me, 'No! We don't need you! You should go to Mexico and deliver those women's babies! You are a Mexican and that's where you belong!' I was quite astonished at this cold reception."

For the first time in his life, Garcia found himself the object of discrimination. At that time, there was a great deal of interracial misunderstanding in the Valley. The differences between the Mexicans and the Anglo-Americans tended to obscure their similarities.

The Indian-tinged Spanish culture of Mexico contrasted sharply with the essentially British culture of the Anglo-Americans. In addition, intense religious enmities magnified the cultural differences, for most of the Anglo-Americans were Protestants, whereas the Mexicans were virtually all Catholics, and religious feeling ran high on both sides.

Differences of social class further aggravated the tension. Only after 1900 had large-scale irrigation been introduced to turn the chaparral basin of the Rio Grande Valley into a vast garden. It had been introduced by Anglo-Americans backed by large amounts of capital, who had hired great numbers of low-paid laborers from the rather numerous but abjectly poor Mexican population already living there. Many Anglo-Americans came to view all Mexicans as deficient in ability, ambition and intelligence, and to look down on them as an inferior race. They felt they had a right to consider themselves superior and to keep their supposed inferiors "in their place."

Into this feudal situation walked Octavio Garcia, a professional who insisted that everyone regard him as a professional, not a peon. Well aware that his ability, his mind and his education were at least as good as that of anybody else in town, he refused to have anything to do with "his place."

The hospital was largely controlled by the mayor and two other doctors. After his interview with the mayor, Garcia was refused an appointment with one of the doctors. The other received him courteously and took him to visit the hospital. He began the tour on the top floor, where there were two well-equipped operating rooms. Then he viewed the nicely appointed private and semi-private rooms on the next two floors. Arriving in the basement, where some six or eight beds stood next to an x-ray machine, he was informed matter-of-factly, "And this is the Mexican ward."

Garcia promptly revisited the mayor's office and inquired pointedly whether this city/county hospital had been built with tax money, and whether the Mexican people of the community paid taxes on the same basis as others. "Sure," said the mayor, "but this is **our** hospital."

Shocked and furious, Garcia complained of the situation to City Commissioner Guerra, a member of a prominent local family of Mexican descent. "You just don't understand," Guerra told him. "That's the way things are run around here."

"Coming from a Mexican, such a comment hit me rather hard."

He soon encountered other shocks. One day he was visited by a committee representing the local doctors and city officials, whose spokesman told him, "We don't put up with Mexicans telling us what to do—we're not used to being treated like this!" "I'm not used to being treated like this either," snapped Dr. Garcia.

The situation was no better for his wife. Many of the townspeople objected to her because she was Jewish. On one occasion Garcia was approached by some women of the Catholic church where he attended Mass. "They said to me, 'Don't bring that Jewish woman into this church!' Because they were women and I was a gentleman, I didn't say what I felt. I only said, 'The Virgin Mary, the mother of Jesus Christ, was a Jew!' "

The Garcias braced themselves for a long bout with the townspeople for social acceptance. Garcia was still unable to foresee the professional implications of "the way things were run." These surfaced the first time one of Garcia's patients required surgery.

The first case Garcia had to send to the hospital was a cowboy who needed immediate surgery for a strangulated hernia. The hospital refused him admittance. Garcia called the mayor for an immediate appointment. The mayor refused to see him, but agreed to call the hospital superintendent and instruct her to admit the patient.

The other physicians in town refused to assist Garcia or administer anesthesia for him. Determined, Garcia gave the patient a local anesthetic and operated unassisted. The cowboy recovered, and the story soon spread that Garcia had saved his life, and under what conditions.

The refusal of cooperation by the city's other physicians remained among the worst of Garcia's problems in his practice. Of the six doctors in McAllen at that time, all general practitioners who performed some surgery when necessary, only two were willing to assist him. Dr. Wharton offered to administer anesthesia when needed, and Dr. Balli agreed to assist in surgery—if Garcia could get him into the hospital. Balli was of Mexican birth himself and had been barred from the hospital and refused professional cooperation like Garcia. When these two were unable to be present, Garcia had to call in a physician from another city.

On one occasion, a girl developed high fever and distension after an operation performed by another doctor. As the situation became desperate, it was suggested that Garcia, as the city's only specialist in surgery, be called into consultation.

The patient's father went to Garcia and requested assistance. Garcia explained that, though he would be glad to help, he could not simply walk in and examine another doctor's patient; he would have to have the permission and request of the attending physician. When the anxious father made this request of the doctor in charge of the case, the latter refused to see Garcia or allow him into the patient's room.

As the girl was extremely ill, her father asked Garcia what to do. Replying that this decision was entirely up to the father, Garcia nevertheless pointed out that if he was that dissatisfied with the service of the attending physician, he could settle his bill with him, dismiss him, and call in another doctor.

He did so and asked Garcia to take the case. When Garcia arrived at the hospital, however, the nurse superintendent refused to allow him to see the patient. Garcia called the mayor, who replied that the superintendent's orders had to be respected, but said that the father could take his daughter out of the hospital and have anyone he chose examine her at her home, then return her to the hospital.

This was done. When the girl was readmitted as Garcia's patient, he ordered preparation of an operating room for immediate surgery. He was permitted use of the facilities, but as neither Wharton nor Balli was available and the other doctors refused to help, he was obliged to call in doctors from two other cities to give anesthesia and assist him in surgery.

Although the patient was in extreme condition by the time Garcia operated, fortunately she recovered. Her parents wrote an open letter of thanks to Garcia which was printed in the local newspaper, and the case was soon known all over town. Gradually Garcia was gaining a reputation as a good surgeon, and to his pleasant surprise other doctors began to call him into consultation on difficult surgical cases.

After a year or two, a new mayor was elected. Already familiar with the situation, he assured Garcia unobstructed access to the hospital. This helped Garcia in his running battle with the hospital superintendent, but the lack of professional cooperation from other physicians remained. Even after Garcia had become known for his surgical skill, extreme cases of racial bitterness sometimes appeared among the patients and their families also.

On one occasion when another doctor had called Garcia into consultation, both diagnosed the patient's problem as an intestinal obstruction in need of immediate surgery. The patient's husband, however, refused to let Garcia operate, declaring that he 'wasn't going to let any damn Mexican open up his wife's belly.' As there was no one else in town able to perform the operation, the husband took his wife to San Antonio. By the time she arrived, it was too late for surgery to save her life.

Sometimes the anger shows through. "It is always the patient who loses. It is not right for racial bitterness to interfere with the care of the patient. It soon became evident to people that the patient came first with me, regardless of color or creed, and they respected me for it, both Mexicans and Anglo-Americans, because they knew I would do my best for the patient—any patient."

Unfortunately, the other doctors in town did not seem to share this view. When Cecile was expecting the couple's second child, Garcia decided to ask another physician to give her obstetrical care, as this was an area in which he did not feel sufficiently competent. As Wharton had retired and Balli was on an extended visit to Monterrey, Garcia was obliged to take his request to another doctor. The latter agreed to perform the delivery, but told Garcia he would not do prior examinations, as Garcia could do that himself. Unable to persuade the doctor otherwise, Garcia was obliged to accept this state of affairs.

When Cecile was admitted to the hospital in labor, the nurse called the doctor to come and perform the delivery. "Hell, no!" he replied. "That damn Mexican can deliver his own wife!"

In desperation Garcia contacted Balli, who had recently returned to McAllen, and he rushed to the hospital—where he was refused admittance. Only after making a considerable disturbance was he able to get in and deliver the child.

Garcia's wife was his equal in her spiritual stamina. "I owe a debt of gratitude to my wife. She was a great woman. She withstood all the insults people here flung at me and at her as well. I know it was a great shock to her, after growing up in New York City, to come to live in a little hole in the wall like this, where people hated her because she was a Jew and because she had married a Mexican. But she stuck by me.

"Once she said to me. 'Octavio, you are either a great man or a great fool, to keep trying so hard in a place where people treat you like they do here.' And I said, 'Will you stay here with me?' And she said, 'Yes.' You can see what a great woman she was."

Overcoming the barriers to social and professional acceptance was a long, slow process. Garcia attributes his success to two traits: "The first was firmness. I knew my ability, I knew the extent of my education, and I knew my rights and insisted that they be respected. The second was competence in my professional field. I became accepted because the community needed my competence in surgery." Even so, the improvement of his relations with the other doctors was possible only because he did not let himself become bitter. Though he could not forget their past insults, he did not dwell on them or become vindictive. He concentrated on providing the best possible care for his patients, constantly expanding his professional competence—and insisting on his rights.

Such firmness is too much to expect of children, however, and the

Garcias soon decided that they would have to get their children out of McAllen if they were to grow up unwarped by the social discrimination to which they were subjected there. Further, Garcia was firmly of the opinion that education was the solution to the problem of discrimination, and he did not think highly of the quality of education available in McAllen at the time.

After the second grade, the Garcias' son and daughter were sent to parochial school, where there was less discrimination against Mexican children. After the sixth grade they were sent to school in San Antonio.

"It was not very agreeable either for me or for my wife, sending the children away to boarding school so young, because we missed being with them, but we had no choice."

From the very beginning, Garcia had been dissatisfied with the level of efficiency at which the McAllen hospital operated. It had no laundry facilities and the bill from the commercial laundry to which the hospital linens were sent was inexcusably high. The kitchen was across the alley. The laboratory couldn't handle anything but urinalysis and white blood cell count. And the X-ray machine sat idle because nobody at the hospital knew how to run it. He complained to the mayor.

The mayor, irate, chewed him out for being an uppity Mexican and the biggest nuisance in town, and declared that since Garcia knew everything, he (the mayor) was going to appoint him to the hospital board.

Nothing could have been more to Garcia's liking, of course. As soon as he was on the board, changes began to be made. He insisted, for example, that the hospital begin keeping permanent records covering admittance, diagnosis, treatment and dismissal. Previously, the 'records' had shown only the patient's name. This new system met considerable resistance from some of the older doctors who regarded it as a bunch of useless paperwork and a waste of valuable time.

During the 1930's, Garcia said, the practice of surgery was "rather disorganized." The hospital did not make doctors present their credentials and some incompetent doctors were allowed to operate. On a number of occasions Garcia was called in to complete an operation another doctor had begun, once after a doctor who had arrived drunk had walked off and left the patient on the operating table in the middle of surgery.

This was not the only adverse condition under which Garcia operated.

"For surgical cases originating in the small towns where medical facilities were poor or non-existent, and where the patient could not be taken to a larger and better-equipped city, I had to travel with my team. From 1932 to 1938 I was more or less an itinerant surgeon. The local doctor would assist me, but I had to have two nurses, one in charge of the instruments and one to administer the ether. Many times I have operated on kitchen tables."

He also took advantage of every opportunity to expand his competence. "There were two specialists in San Antonio to whom I would sometimes refer complicated cases. Sometimes I would line up five or six patients for surgery and take them up on the train. I assisted these specialists in surgery so that I could watch and learn.'' In this way he became quite knowledgeable, especially in orthopedic surgery and urology.

Poverty was rampant in the Valley. In 1932, when the Depression hit hardest in that area, many people in need of medical assistance were unable to pay for it.

"I don't know of any doctor in McAllen who ever turned anybody away because of inability to pay. Between 1932 and 1938, I'm sure at least half our work went unpaid. I've given thousands of dollars of free service, and I haven't starved yet. But most people tried to give something by way of payment, even if it was live chickens and produce.''

Poverty was not the only condition endemic in the Valley. "There was a wealth of clinical material here, exotic diseases that most medical students only read about, never encounter—things like leprosy and madura foot, and occasional cases of smallpox and typhoid fever, as well as a lot of tuberculosis.''

About 1942, another innovation was introduced at McAllen's hospital. Some of the doctors prevailed upon the administration to begin acquiring surgical instruments. Until that time, each doctor had had to provide his own. Garcia had collected several sets, each set designed for a particular specialty area. The hospital's instrument collection was begun by donations from various doctors—the first set from Octavio Garcia.

The vigorous training that made Dr. Garcia into a good physician and surgeon, also made him into a fighter—made him tough enough to withstand the tremendous opposition that he has had to face in his life. His strength is the result of that training, those circumstances and his own powerful temperament.

After half a century in the medical profession, Dr. Garcia is still practicing and still fighting. He is an American and feels that he has a duty to cure the ills of his adopted country.

"I think this is a great country, but they have also made a great big mistake: They have tried to make a melting pot out of the U.S. This country did one of the worst things—they denied the native population, the Indians, their culture and their religion. The greatness of the country is due to the variety of ethnic groups. Each ethnic group learns from the others. The U.S. should take advantage of the diverse cultures, and not try to suppress them, if it ever dreams of reaching maturity.'' And as for cultural background, in his opinion, "you can't beat the Spanish, no matter how you cook it.''

Garcia also questions the adequacy and advisability of medical education as it is today. For one thing, he says, doctors specialize too narrowly. He objects to the concept of the doctor as a highly trained technician "who can only treat a right ear or a left nostril. The narrow path is a disastrous thing.'' He advocated broader training, including education in the humanities, which he believes would produce "more humane physicians.''

"The U.S. has made a mistake with medical education,'' he declares. "They never subsidized it. They subsidized rivers and harbors and airports and every damn thing, but not medical education. And when they did give money, they tied the researchers' hands with so many strings attached to the grants! It is like a man who gives a very large sum of money to a church and specifies, 'Don't buy food for the children, don't buy medicine for old people, just use it to buy cut flowers to decorate the church.' They only care if the researcher writes papers—they don't care whether there is anything significant in them. A bureaucrat in Washington doesn't know any more than a flea about running a medical school.

"And I regret that they did not encourage women to study medicine. I think that's one of the biggest mistakes the country has ever made. There's no reason a woman can't be a good doctor. I'm all for women. There should be fully 25 or even 50 percent women doctors in this country, instead of six percent."

Some of Dr. Garcia's battles are not that large in scope. He won his eighteen-year battle to get doctors on the hospital board. "I fought like hell. Why do they think a furniture man or someone who owns an orchard knows more about running a hospital than a doctor? They always say having a doctor on the board would be a conflict of interest. That's ridiculous. Who hasn't got a conflict of interest? The furniture man sells furniture to the hospital, the fruit man sells fruit to the hospital. What is needed is men of integrity. A man of integrity is not going to sell his soul."

Dr. Garcia is a strong man with strong convictions. He does not argue for the sake of argument, but to change the way things are done. He has no patience with stupidity, inefficiency, superficiality, injustice. But he is not a revolutionary, advocating overthrow. "I want a little evolution, not revolution," he declares.

However, the kind of evolution Dr. Garcia wants is not the million-year variety that gave giraffes long necks. Within his own life span he has witnessed some human evolution: people becoming more humane, rationality overcoming irrationality, racism and injustice withering away. Education, in his view, is the mechanism of change. An outspoken advocate of learning, he advises the young (and the not-so-young), "Educate yourself—and keep on educating yourself!"

The "humane doctor" has a thriving practice in McAllen. His fifty years in the medical profession have given him enormous breadth of experience. People now come from all over the Valley to be treated by Dr. Garcia.

He continues to battle all the ills he meets, not all of which are caused by germs and injuries. The fittest stay fit by taking on all comers. He does. "I don't want to please you; I want to tell you the truth," he declares. "Go on—fight me if you want—it's okay with me. I'm rough, am I not?"

Grown up Loving

by Donna Bearden

It is ironic that Mary Moody Northen who, as a child, was frail, timid and shy, should one day find herself at the head of a vast financial empire consisting of more than fifty corporations. In 1954, upon the death of her father, W. L. Moody, Jr., she became the head of the Moody Enterprises. Although she was "past retirement age" and had never spent a day in an office, she suddenly found herself thrust into a man's world of business. An unusual woman with a multitude of unique experiences in life, Mary Moody Northen was **not** ill prepared for the position which resulted in her becoming known as "the First Lady of Finance." Born in 1892, Mary Moody Northen was the first child of W. L. and Libbie Shearn Moody. Frail of health, she did not attend formal schools but was educated privately. Although this afforded her a thorough education, it also presented disadvantages. It limited her social contacts with other children her age thus contributing to her timidity and shyness.

She became an avid reader at a very early age. Nothing suited her more than sitting in the house devouring book after book. "If I read every day and every night, all day and all night, I still would not have been able to read all of the books I was interested in."

The family physician was concerned about her health and urged her parents to encourage her to participate more in outdoor activities. The doctor suggested getting her some chickens and a pony. The chickens became her first experience in business that led to a long and distinguished career in the financial world that is unparalled by any other American woman. The pony began a love affair with riding that led her to become one of Texas' most outstanding horsewomen.

Her grandfather gave her a subscription to a poultry magazine. Her father got her the chickens, and her mother made a contract with Mary to buy all of her eggs. Thus began her first business venture. About the same time, her father purchased a pony for her. She started riding on the beaches of Galveston and learning the rudiments and discipline of equestrianism. As her father acquired ranches in Texas, she quickly learned the skills of riding in the rough wild territory of Southwest Texas, and it was said that she rode like an Indian.

Each April and October she spent her time riding. She would ride every day in the early evening when the wildlife was out, and thus began another facet of her life which has paralleled that of her father's, her concern for conservation. W. L. Moody, Jr. never allowed the wanton hunting of wildlife on his property. Although he was a strong advocate of fishing and duck hunting, he was also known to take down fences to aid in the plight of other wild animals such as deer. Her love for animals followed that of her father's. Once when she was out at a ranch helping to drive up sheep, she noticed an old lame one lagging behind. Mary insisted that he be put in her saddle with her. She became the animal ambulance, with the old fellow riding across her

"I've just grown up loving."   *(photos courtesy Mary Moody Northen)*

horse in front of her as they headed back toward the ranch headquarters.

When Mary was growing up she was known as her father's daughter. He taught her about business, not so much in a teaching-learning sense but in sharing and talking about the activities of his day. Throughout her youth and adult life, her close relationship with her father exposed her to his business acumen and the activities of the business world. He would frequently give her problems to solve or assign her tasks that would prepare her for the future role she was to assume. She was carefully prepared for decision-making by being given difficult decisions to make.

For example, on one occasion he sent her to Virginia to locate a farm nearby one of his hotel properties, Mountain Lake. She knew little about such a task, but she studied all of the available opportunities and made her recommendations to her father in the form of a written report. He accepted her recommendation and purchased the farm. Over the years Mr. Moody gave Mary similar assignments time after time. Perhaps one of the keys to her successful career as a business woman was a loving father who gave her responsibility and trust. People who knew them both said they thought alike, acted alike, and even looked alike. They were as close as father and daughter could be.

Mary Moody Northen is from strong pioneering stock. In fact her story cannot be separated from history. William Lewis Moody, Sr. came from Virginia to Texas in 1852 through the Port of Galveston, purchased a horse and started up country. At Fairfield his horse died, and he remained there and opened up a law practice. During the Civil War he served valiantly in the Confederate Army and was severely wounded. For his acts of gallantry he was promoted to the rank of Colonel. Immediately after the close of the Civil War, he moved to Galveston where he established a cotton factorage business in the old Henley Building on Galveston's Historic Strand. Soon after he added banking. In 1883 Colonel Moody built the W. L. Moody & Company Building on the corner of 22nd and The Strand. He was joined in business in 1886 by his son, William Lewis Moody, Jr. With the subsequent additions of insurance, ranching, newspapers, hotels and other enterprises, The Moody Interests expanded into one of the largest financial empires in the United States.

Mary Moody Northen's mother was Libbie Rice Shearn, a descendent of the Shearns from Bath, England. Charles Shearn, his wife and two young children came to Texas before its independence was won. He was once taken prisoner by the Mexicans and tied back to back, to be shot with another Texan. His young son, John, who could speak a little Spanish, saved his life by telling the Mexicans that they were British subjects. The Mexicans, afraid of chancing trouble with England along with the growing rebellion in Texas, released the prisoner. Charles Shearn later was among those who signed the first Texas Declaration of Independence at the altar of a small Spanish Mission in Goliad. He was also the founder of Methodism in Houston. The First Methodist Church, formerly known as the Shearn Methodist Church, was organized by Charles Shearn. John Shearn, who was Mrs. Northen's grandfather, became involved in the navigation business, running ships up and down Buffalo Bayou from Houston to Galveston.

Galveston's history of this century has been lived first hand by Mrs. Northen. "I guess I'm the old woman of the Island," she laughs.

Mrs. Northen remembers vividly the devastating hurricane of 1900 though she was only eight years old at the time. The great Galveston storm was the worst natural disaster in United States history. Six to eight thousand persons lost their lives when the high storm tides covered the Island. Since there was no seawall for protection, not a single structure escaped damage.

Mrs. Northen recalls going to her grandfather's three-story brick home as the storm became more intense. They stayed downstairs until the water began coming up through the floors. With others who had come seeking shelter, they went upstairs and remained until the storm subsided.

Over the years Mrs. Northen has supported the promotion of history. She has long dreamed of presenting Galveston's colorful history in an outdoor epic drama. She feels that Galveston is the perfect setting for such a drama because of its rich colorful background. She recalls that Galveston as far back as 1528 was the location of a historical first event in the western hemisphere. The Spanish Conquistador Alvar Nuñez Cabeza de Vaca shipwrecked on Galveston in November of that year. He befriended the cannibalistic Karankawa Indians by removing an arrow from near the heart of a young Indian brave and the son of the chief, thus performing the first recorded surgical procedure in the Western Hemisphere.

The Frenchman, Jean Lafitte, known as the gentlemanly pirate of the Gulf, ran his pirating operations and slave market from Galveston Island in the early 1800's until he was driven off the Island by the U. S. Navy.

Galveston served as the headquarters for an interim government of the Republic of Texas for a short time in 1836. By 1860 Galveston was the most important shipping port on the Texas Gulf Coast. Much more advanced than its small neighboring town of Houston, it was the financial center of the Southwest. It is known for many other historical firsts in Texas. Galveston is recorded as having the first public school, the first library, the first national bank, newspaper, and many more.

In December of 1975, Mrs. Northen began to see the realization of her dream of an outdoor drama when she broke ground for an amphitheater to be constructed in the new Galveston Island State Park. It was the first time she had ever broken ground using a bulldozer. Much to the amazement of her many friends who came for the occasion, she pulled levers and dug up and dropped more than a ton of earth. Unfortunately, she could not add another shovel to her already large collection of ground-breakers.

Mrs. Northen is an advocate for historical preservation. She is Honorary Chairman of the Galveston Historical Foundation and has supported efforts to save Galveston's architectural treasures. Many of Galveston's fine old homes and commercial buildings that withstood the 1900 storm's fury are now being restored to their original grandeur. She has had a great deal to do with raising the consciousness of the community about the importance of historic preservation. The restoration of the old homes has great sentimentality for her because she knew the families who lived in the homes; she attended many cotillion balls and other social events in them.

Mrs. Northen has a great sentimentality for a number of things. The Texas Navy is one of them. She has researched its history and was responsible for placing a marker honoring the Navy at Galveston's Menard Park. She is an Admiral of the Navy and Honorary Chairman of its Board.

Another project dear to her heart is the restoration of Texas' first capital, Washington-on-the-Brazos. It was the recipient of one of her first personal efforts in philanthropy. She awarded a grant to do archeological research at the historical site. Now, at long last, rebuilding will soon begin, restoring the city as it was more than one-hundred years ago.

Mrs. Northen met her husband, Edwin Clyde Northen, on Friday, October 13, 1911. It turned out to be her lucky day. Mr. Northen had come to Galveston to study medicine at the University of Texas Medical Branch. However, soon thereafter he changed his mind and went into business, establishing the E. C. Northen Insurance Company. He married Mary Elizabeth Moody on December 1, 1915 in the ballroom of the Moody Home on Broadway. After she married, she

lived only a couple of blocks down the street from her father's home.
She was frequently at her parents' home for breakfast and drove with
her father to work, returning to her home after dropping him off.
They would spend their time talking business, with her father
answering her endless questions. After her mother's death, Mrs.
Northen and her husband had dinner with Mr. Moody every night,
during which they would discuss the events of the day and aspects of
the various businesses.

Today Mrs. Northen leads a more active life than most persons many
years younger than she. She is a member of four State boards and is
active in over twenty-five national and local historical and patriotic
organizations. She still maintains an active role in the business affairs
of the Moody enterprises. She is Senior Chairman of the Board of the
Moody National Bank of Galveston, a member of the Board of
Directors of American Financial Corporation and its subsidiary,
American National Insurance Company, a member of the Board of
Gal Tex Hotel Corporation and Silver Lake Ranches Co., Inc.

In addition, Mrs. Northen is Chairman of the Board of the Moody
Foundation, which has contributed in excess of seventy-five million
dollars to education and charitable causes throughout Texas. She is the
only original member of the Board of Trustees. During her tenure on
the Board, more than thirty-six million dollars has aided educational
institutions, thirteen million dollars has supported the expansion of
health care services, eleven million dollars has brought the arts and
humanities to people in small towns in rural areas. More than five
million dollars has supported new frontiers in the sciences bringing
benefits to the general public. Over ten million dollars has
helped the economically disadvantaged through new community and
social service programs.

Mrs. Northen has also contributed personally to many projects
throughout Texas and the nation. She has a keen interest in character-
building and youth organizations. Following the great interest of her
late husband, she has actively supported the Boy Scouts of America.
Among her many contributions, she has given the E. C. Northen Scout
Service Center to the Bay Area Council of the Boy Scouts of America
in memory of her husband.

Like her beloved Galveston Island, Mrs. Northen has also achieved a
number of notable firsts in her lifetime. She was the first woman in
America to receive the coveted Silver Fawn Award of the Boy Scouts
of America. She is an honorary member of a Boy Scout Troop and has
been named the troop's sweetheart. She is the first and only woman on
the Board of Virginia Military Institution Foundation and the only
Honorary Woman Alumnus of that all-male institution. She is also the
first and only woman on the Board of the Marine Military Academy at
Harlingen. Her latest distinguished "first" is the first woman to be
recognized for her contribution to business and finance by the
University of Texas Graduate School of Business Administration,
which has named the Graduate Student Learning Center in her honor.
Many other achievements, honors and notable affiliations are listed in
the Marquis "Who's Who in America."

Mrs. Northen maintains an active interest in a number of educational institutions. Two of her favorites are Hollins College near Roanoke, Virginia and Virginia Military Institute. She has given a building in memory of her father to V.M.I. and another building in memory of both of her parents to Hollins College.

The story behind the Moody family's interest in Hollins College, an all-girls' school, is quite unusual. Mrs. Northen's father, Mr. Moody, was a frail child in his youth. His parents felt that a colder, more vigorous climate might be more beneficial for his health. The President of Hollins College was a friend of Colonel Moody's and offered to take the young Moody as a member of his family. For several years, young W.L. Moody, Jr. lived at Hollins College and was privately tutored. In later years, Mr. Moody delighted in telling stories about when he was a student at Hollins College and roomed with Miss Martha Pleasants (a lady who was actually in her seventies and was responsible for looking after the lad). Later, Mr. Moody attended Virginia Military Institute. He remained devoted to both schools and visited them often, taking his daughter Mary with him.

There is another spot in Virginia dear to the Moodys. In fact, it almost became a second home. Mountain Lake is a beautiful quaint resort, highest natural lake in Virginia where the fishing is good and the air is cool and crisp in the summer. Each summer the family would spend a month at Mountain Lake. When Mrs. Northen was a child, the roads were unpaved and the resort was difficult to get to, but each summer, year after year, many of the same families returned and stayed for a long period of time. It was like a homecoming.

During Mr. Moody's youth while he stayed at Hollins College, he was taken by the president to Mountain Lake to go fishing and hiking. The original hotel was built of wood and put together with wooden pegs. No one knew for sure how old it was. Because of his fondness of the area, Mr. Moody acquired Mountain Lake. Years later, fearing a fire disaster, he had the wooden structure replaced with one made of stone. It nearly broke Mrs. Northen's heart, and she refused to go to Mountain Lake the following summer, but the stone structure was beautifully built, and she was finally reconciled to the handsome new structure. After the death of her father, when it appeared that the property would be disposed of, she purchased the resort because of her great fondness and wonderful memories of times past. Although she knew that it would not be a profitable investment, it was too dear to her heart to risk losing it. Mountain Lake is one of her favorite spots to visit.

During her younger years Mrs. Northen never traveled farther than Houston alone. However, after her husband's and father's deaths, she began a series of travels which eventually took her on a trip around the world. She prefers to travel alone. It gives her more flexibility, and she enjoys meeting new people. Mrs. Northen has never traveled by air. She prefers to travel by motor car, rail or by sea. However, on one occasion she took a ride in a hot air balloon.

Besides horseback riding, she has also ridden a giant turtle in Seychelles Islands and an elephant in India. During one trip she became somewhat indignant after mounting an ostrich and a camel in Africa when the tour people refused to let her ride because they feared it too dangerous. She did persuade them, however, to let her sit on the animals and have her picture taken.

Although Mrs. Northen has visited many strange and wonderful places around the world, the small towns of her native Texas remain close to her heart. As Chairman of The Moody Foundation, she liked to give especial attention to the small communities in Texas "because they have such small populations, few resources, and need help so badly." As a result of her conviction, The Moody Foundation has funded more libraries in small towns in Texas than any other foundation. Medical services are also a critical need in rural Texas, and The Foundation has built numerous clinics across the state. "I have never known people to be more appreciative than those from small towns," says Mrs. Northen, and it is obvious she enjoys making dreams come true for folks who would otherwise just have to do without.

What's really special about Mrs. Northen? She enjoys—she enjoys life, enjoys doing, enjoys making possible. She never had a child of her own and yet she has thousands—and she enjoys her sons at V.M.I., at the Marine Military Academy and in the Boy Scouts. She just enjoys, and she sums it up with, "I have just grown up loving."

Although she is one of the most distinguished living Texans, she is still a little shy and a little timid, which somehow just adds to her warmth and her charm.

Rough and Rougher

by Jamie Frucht

The years Walter Russell spent on his own have freed his mind, face and clothes from mannerisms. The rough experiences of his life are not hidden away behind a veneer of years. All the weather he passed through has gone into his face's coloring. The style of clothes that were comfortable fifty years ago, still look good on him, though he dresses up for occasions. The years have not diluted him. His chiseled face still confronts the out-of-doors on a daily basis. Walter Russell is in his element around horses, pasture, cowboy wilderness. But he's so nice, you're glad he came into civilization.

Russell and the Rio Grande have never been too far apart. An only child, he was born on August 22, 1903 up the river in camp about nine miles from Presidio, Texas. When only a month old, he made his first drive, his mother carrying him horseback as her people drove cattle northwest across the river and into Arizona where Russell was reared.

At the age of three, with both his parents dead, his aunt ("meanest woman ever pulled on a pair of prairie boots") sent him to a boarding convent in the desert below Tombstone. He ran away from that "outfit" when he was nine. In three or four other "little old schools in the west," he was either running off or being run off by the teachers. He lived up on the White River with the Apache Indians for about two years. Russell is a quarter Comanche himself—"You got to be something."

He now laments his lack of education. "I should have gone to school instead of continuing to work on ranches. When I was little, someone should have told me, but they didn't. Mr. Crocker, who had an interest in the Double Circle Ranch where I worked, asked me, 'What are you going to do when you grow up? If you're going to be a cowboy, you should stay on the ranch, but if you're not, if you want an education, now's the time. We'll send you to California.' "

It was a foregone conclusion. "Well, what boy wouldn't say that he wanted to stay with horses? Whoever heard of a boy wanting to go to school?" And so Russell went on to work for all the big cow outfits including the XIT, Matador, and Chiricahua Cattle Company.

Most kids grow up to mother's home cooking. In those cow camps, the men cooked. The conditions and men were not too sanitary, and the food—not too savory. But as Russell recalls, "your choice was either eat it or do without." As a result of that early "grub," Russell has a permanent distaste for men's cooking.

With cowboys taking the place of parental guidance, Russell was susceptible to "mischief." Just as Russell was about to get into trouble again, Governor Hunt of Arizona, who'd been raised by Russell's people, gave him a choice—either go to war or become a ranger. "I was 15, too young to go to war and that's why Governor Hunt hired me." Governor Hunt, originally from San Antonio was partial to Texans. In fact the only people who worked for him were from Texas.

The Ranger Service in Arizona was full of ex-Texas Rangers who'd gotten themselves fired. When Texas would elect a new governor, they'd come back to the State and re-enter the Ranger Service.

The transition from being a "sure enough" cowboy to a Ranger was a natural one for Russell. "If you're reared out in camp, you have to protect yourself, even though you're not an officer. And then you come up and you're an officer and you do it, just like you'd do something else. You just do your work."

In those early days in Arizona, the work was hard and unheroic. Russell at 15 served an apprenticeship for four years with a group of older rangers. "I was the only young kid in the bunch. The other men were 50 or better, up to 75 years old." The situation was kind of like Cinderella only a cowboy version in the mountains. He worked for these older men and his part of it was "washing their clothes, dragging wood, building fires, shoeing horses—old rough work. Any man, if he told me to do something, I had to. Before I was allowed to go out on my own and make arrests, I had to be qualified."

That outfit of five men didn't stay together all the time. Ranger-fashion, they split up, going out on their own. What was life like for these scouts? For hygiene, there was plenty of cold running water. "I stayed in mountains but the rivers are plentiful and you never go a day without pure snow water."

The Rangers fared better than cowboys in terms of provisions. "The ranchers paid for our chuck. We had beef and flour. If we were staying in a place for any length of time (two or three days) we'd cook beans. We didn't have any air-tight goods (as canned goods were called). We had no garden stuff. We had no milk. We had no cream for the coffee and no sugar."

The only sweetening they had was white Karo syrup which they packed on their mules. Russell has only bad memories of the stuff. Until he'd been to town he didn't know any better. In town a friend treated him to hot cakes with syrup—two new tastes. Once he'd experienced the real syrup, it was hard going back to camp and Karo. He asked the captain why the rangers couldn't have syrup like that.

"You know what the captain said? (He was an honest man too, but I think honest men kinda get over the hill a bit.) 'This Karo syrup is thick and packing it on the mules, it won't shake. Cane syrup and those other kinds of syrup shake and then explode. They don't pack.' Well, why they used Karo was cause it didn't cost anything. The other syrup was a little expensive. I found out later you could pack good syrup just as well as any other. Since then when I got to where I could afford it, well, I have no use for Karo."

Those early years were powerful preparation for Russell's later officer life. He had learned to respect his elders. The most powerful elder was Governor Hunt who took a personal interest in the boy, making sure he was reared right. Was the Governor like a father to him? "No," Russell answers without bitterness. "If I'd been like his son, he'd let me dance with the girls and have a little fun in my life and come to town Christmas. I never seen nothing like that."

Governor Hunt never allowed Russell to drink. The Governor was also particular as to how young Russell dressed, not allowing him to wear his father's gold and silver jewelry and pearl-handled pistol. "He wouldn't let you put handcuffs on anyone cause he said it didn't look good; it looked gaudy. On occasions when you arrested someone and took him in, you could use buckskin string to tie him with."

This plain dress code, imposed on Russell, did not go unnoticed. Once, when he and another man, also under Governor Hunt's jurisdiction, had to make a court appearance for some little infraction of the law, a witness described the men like so:

"I saw two men coming. One of them, the one that was in the lead, we thought he was Tom Mix. Well, he had all this pretty stuff—shiny sterling silver." When asked what the other one looked like (referring to Ranger Russell) the witness said, "He looked like an Indian. Black-headed and long-haired. He had on Levi clothes. We thought he was an Indian but he talked English." Russell says that man's description was accurate.

From the Governor and the Rangers, Russell learned a code for living that has stayed with him. He learned that you sure had to respect the women folks. "You go to harming a woman, that's bad. A lady is a lady as long as she's living." Even today Russell is wonderfully chivalrous—kind of like a knight in chaps. He could have easily fallen in with King Arthur and his gang without so much as missing a step. If he'd been around during King Henry VIII's time, the likes of King Henry would have been gunned down personally by Russell for his treatment of "the little ladies."

The Governor also taught him "The Golden Rule" adapting it to the tough circumstances of rangering. In the "do-to-other" phrase, "the others" were often outlaws and life-term convicts. Russell learned— "You treat 'em like people, like you like to be treated; but then, if they won't accept it, if they get rough, well, you treat 'em a little rougher."

As an Arizona Ranger, Russell performed a great variety of duties. He had a stint for a little while as a scout for Zane Grey on a reservation. Russell was young and had never heard of Zane Grey. He remembers him as a quiet man who'd sit in one place for hours at a time and never speak. Unfriendly-like. "Not a bloomin' thing was happening. It was too slow, nothin' exciting."

More exciting was going down into Grand Canyon and gathering up the outlaws who had congregated there from all parts of the country and world to prospect for gold. Arizona was plagued by desperadoes and also by posters, wanting them dead or alive.

A bizarre assignment in the Mid-1920's still gives Russell the shudders. A single lady from New York, 25, red-haired, beautiful (so he was told, having only seen the corpse) came to the Hopi Indian reservation to live with and write about the Indians. She didn't want any "gringo guards" to accompany her. In the mountains, 10,000 feet elevation, they killed her. The Agent at White River, with orders from the Governor, sent Russell up there to assist the government Indian trailer and trucker.

Russell remembers. "It was terrible business." They brought one Indian back alive and one didn't make it. "You hate things like that."

And it could have been avoided if the woman had understood the Indians better.

While a ranger in Arizona, he came to Texas every two or three years to buy quarter stud colts to improve the Spanish horses. The Texas horses were put in stock bins and shipped back to Arizona. "Those Spanish horses wasn't much."

When Governor Hunt lost his race for governor, he got Russell a job in Corpus Christi where he worked as an officer for the electric company. But he missed the freedom of ranger life. City life was alien to him, so after about five years he quit, returning to law work again.

In 1935 he rode the Rio Grande as a scout for the Livestock Sanitary Commission of Texas. "I was sent up the River to Big Bend. Wasn't anybody up there and I had to ride that river front and camp up there." He furnished his own horse and equipment. His whole outfit was a tepee, canteen, pack saddle, dish pan, chuck box, leather deals and rifles. That was no desk job. He'd be on patrol working out of a tepee, packing up and leaving camp, patrolling the river, constantly on the move, just like the river. Once a month he could go home to his wife and children by riding the train from Marathon to Del Rio.

The life may seem hard and lonely, but Russell's not complaining. It agreed with him. "I liked that job because I was by myself and I wasn't bothered. That's the way I believe in working. I understand that kind of business."

Pictures of the Big Bend, Salina Canyon, show a staggering landscape. That was Russell's "beat." How did he patrol it alone without being frightened? Russell is philosophical about it. "If you know how to bed down by yourself in a tepee, you can hear a man tiptoe outside; if you've got a good horse, he'll wake you up. You've got nothing to be afraid of."

Even though Russell was "awful careful constantly" there was one danger he was not ever ready for. Snakes. In Arizona, the men in his outfit had instructed him to carry a rope made out of mane and tail horsehair or a manila rope that hadn't been singed, to put around his bed at night and a snake wouldn't ever crawl over it.

"I carried that rope all the time and then I came to this bloomin' country and came down here on the river. Not only was there snakes on top of my bed at night, but I'd always been told rattlers won't get up in trees. Well, that's all wrong. Two rattlers were in one mesquite tree up in the limbs. I had to see it to believe it. I'd used these ropes all my life, and they was my protector. Well, they was no good in Texas. I been bit twice by rattlers. Like to died."

If you were a good lawman, another hazard of the trade was that you probably had made a world of enemies, and didn't have too many friends—maybe as many as you could count on one hand. Russell worked with river men, custom and border patrol, specializing in cow smuggling cases. On the river, along with the desperadoes, was an old breed of lawbreakers. Cow men had found a giant loophole—the border, across which to get duty free cattle. There were just as good hereford cattle in the open country in Mexico. Texans who owned an

"I liked the job because I was by myself and I wasn't bothered. That's the way I believe in working. I understand that kind of business."
(photo by Mary Sherwood)

interest in Mexican land would buy up the yearlings from Mexican ranches and put their Texas brands on them. Just before spring, about February or March, they'd round them up and bring several thousand head across the river, duty free. There was nobody there to stop them and make them pay. Besides, they owned most of the country along the river on both sides.

Well, Russell became the person there to stop them. By the time the cattle crossed the river, the brand had healed and haired over. "But they wasn't settled." And that's how Ranger Russell could spot them. "It would be like myself going to a big city. You could tell I wasn't from that part of the country." To scout across the Rio Grande, he had an outfit which he put on. Dressed as a Mexican, he could ride freely among the cattle, spotting the illegal ones. "And I stopped all that, and I lost a world of friends."

In addition to not having too many friends, (by now both Texans and Mexicans were mad at him), the pay wasn't too good either. To supplement his small salary, Russell broke horses and okayed loans on livestock and ranches for a bank. He also took advantage of his proximity to the college at Alpine. As was his habit, he tried to arrange for some education on the side. It wasn't the first time. While living in El Paso and San Marcos, he'd taken courses at night. "I needed a lot of things bad—I wanted to learn English and how to figure. . ." The opportunity to take non-credit courses was greatly appreciated. "I could go up there to Alpine to college for two or three hours and then come back to camp and do my work."

Even now, Russell is sensitive about his lack of schooling, having had little formal education til he was grown. He elevates education and perhaps underestimates his own brand of learning. There are Ph.D's who couldn't find their way out of a canyon even if the horse were pointing in the right direction. And many who would trade their punctuation and grammar rules for some of Ranger Russell's style and bravery.

As a Ranger, he sometimes had to resort to unorthodox practices. A ranger out there alone is in the business to win, to get his man. "If you didn't, he got you. You had maybe two or three seconds to assess your man." A ranger had to think on his feet, plan a strategy. He needed to know the peculiarities and manners of the criminal and the terrain. A combination of Sherlock Holmes (tracking with eyes) and Emily Post-of-the-Brush was needed.

If a ranger does good work, there's very little he can tell about. (Which explains why a ranger's best friend is his horse, not a tape recorder.) Ranger Russell sometimes had to improvise with the law to get his man. A desperado kills his wife, tries to romance another woman and finally flees across the border. The Ranger "persuades" the woman to write to the bandit, saying she's changed her mind and will meet him a few miles this side of the river. The bandit falls for the ruse and writes back. But it is the ranger who keeps the rendezvous with the killer. Ranger Russell gets his man and justice is served, though the letter of the law is a little crumpled. But then the lawyers and judges live in town where they can sit down to civilized tables and discuss the shadings of the law. It was the Ranger who was alone, tracking the criminal, one on one, and sometimes one against more.

Being a Ranger was a kind of calling, something you did because you believed in justice in the raw. Rewards and riches were not forthcoming. The strain between custom, natural laws and the legal system often got to Ranger Russell. For instance, in the early west it was custom that, when a father was killed, the older son revenged him. An older son did revenge his father. Ranger Russell had to capture the man who put up no resistance. "I sent a man to the penitentiary. He needed to go." But the man bore him no bitterness. Russell proudly shows a beautiful steer horn carved with his initials WAR (Walter Arthur Russell). The kid he'd sent up to the penitentiary had learned to carve while serving his sentence. "When he got out, I got him a job and a friend of mine gave him a place to stay."

In 1976 Ranger Russell retired from the Ranger service. It took Walter Russell 73 years to settle down. He's covered a lot of territory in those 73 years. Finally he's in his own pasture in Riviera, where he's got a small place bordering the King Ranch. The climate is friendlier than Big Bend's. Now Russell's got a solid, non-movable house, and a wife, who teaches history at Texas A&I University in Kingsville. "I was smart enough to marry a woman who could support me when I retired." No longer constantly on the move, he's got time for a big cat named Fluff. There's 20 pounds of Fluff. And of course he has his great love—horses.

He bought the Rocking R brand back from his uncle and today rides and raises gray quarter horses—"wide powerful little buggers." Retiring hasn't hobbled Russell any. Up until last fall when a horse threw him, he broke the horses himself. He still takes care of the Rocking R alone.

With a little more time to whittle away, Russell can indulge questions about his genealogy which is fascinating and far flung. His relatives however, except for his aunt, had nothing to do with bringing him up. On the other side of the Atlantic his people came from "that little ole island—England." They owned interest in the big English cow outfits in the U.S. Bertrand Russell is related and you can see the resemblance if you squint and imagine how Lord Russell might have turned out if he'd been reared on horses in Texas, instead of books in Cambridge.

On this side of the Atlantic, his mother's people were Slaughters. John Slaughter was his grandfather. Sen. Russell in Georgia was his father's first cousin. But the most colorful relative is "old man Charles." That would be Charles Russell, a contender for greatest cowboy artist and writer. For a long time, Walter Russell didn't want anyone to know that he was kin to Charles. Charles was half-Indian, lived in buckskin and moccasins, squatting down to eat. "He didn't care about anything but foolin' around, drinkin', paintin' and visitin'."

The English side of the family sent Charles Russell off to the Dakotas with 5000 head of steers. After not hearing from him in a long time, they were anxious as to the whereabouts and condition of their cattle. Charles sent a postcard picture he'd drawn of a lone steer

". . . on patrol, working out of a tepee, constantly on the move, just like the river."
(photo courtesy Walter Russell)

surrounded by lobo wolves. Under the picture Russell had written "The last of the 5000." And sure enough he'd sold half of their holdings. Charlie's aunt had to pay.

Walter Russell remembers visiting his uncle who had some peculiar habits like not taking a bath but twice a year—in the fall and then again in the spring. An English lady fell in love with Charles Russell, long distance, after looking at one of his pictures. She came to Great Falls, Montana, and married him. "He wasn't worth a dime when she married him, but she put him to work sketching and she wouldn't let him sit and talk to cowboys three or four days at a time and she cleaned him up."

Now Walter Russell doesn't mind confessing he's related to old man Charles. He inherited 12 original Russell paintings which he sold for a pittance compared to what they drew in the art world, but to Walter Russell, in hard times, the money was welcome.

Though retired, Russell can't leave law work alone. He thinks and theorizes about the turn of events. Russell is critical of the way the Ranger force has evolved—"too many chiefs and not enough Indians. What is needed now are about forty privates, two captains and one lawyer, all hand—not politically—picked men whom you could put on the square to discuss the truth." He would prefer a little of that old time pride when a man was on the job because he had convictions. "A ranger needs a loose rein. If he makes a mistake, correct him; if he makes another, fire him."

Walter Russell has not stopped being concerned about law and order. His solution to the border problem is simple and old fashioned. But it just might work.

"All you need is the horse and a handful of honest men. Good men who know how to track. They say now there are no more horseback outfits, but until they put up a fence and a passable road, the way I see it, they'll always be a place for horses on the river. Airplanes, helicopters, that's great business but you still got the ground to work on. If you don't go in there you can't see tracks. So many things come across that river besides dope. If you're down there along the river, just a riding along—it's a pleasure to ride a horse—you can pick up those tracks and figure out just about what you're going to run into."

Not too many men have been interested in taking those risks, in sticking around to figure out what exactly was coming across the river. As Russell says, "In this life, you either do or you don't." Walter Russell, retired Texas Ranger, did.

She Shoed the West

by Donna Bearden

In 1879 a young man arrived in Spanish Fort with 25 cents and some boot making tools. He worked hard in his shoe repair shop and, as soon as he had enough money, he bought leather to make a pair of boots. He sold those and bought more leather. And he was good—a perfectionist with every detail of his fine handcraft.

"Daddy Joe" started a fine tradition of bootmaking which has lasted almost a century.

In 1887 "Daddy Joe" moved his family and his boot plant to Nocona. The railroad had just come to Nocona and he would have better shipping facilities. By then he had built quite a reputation throughout North Texas and Oklahoma as an exceptionally good bootmaker.

So it was with H. J. "Daddy Joe" Justin. So it is today with his daughter Miss Enid, "the world's only **lady** boot manufacturer."

"Daddy Joe" had seven children and trained them all in bootmaking. Several followed in his footsteps.

Enid started working in her father's shop in 1906, when she was 12 years old. She dropped out of school in the eighth grade—her rebellion for being expelled for dancing at a party in her own home. She went to work full time and hasn't quit since. She designed her first pair of boots when she was 14. "I got the idea for the pattern from a velvet brocaded couch."

She worked close to her father for the next 12 years, learning the fine points of the trade, absorbing his knowledge and his love for beautiful, hand-crafted boots.

In 1918 "Daddy Joe" died. Several members of the family kept the boot company going until 1925 when Miss Enid's three brothers decided to move the H. J. Justin and Sons factory to Fort Worth.

Miss Enid felt so strongly that her father would not want the factory moved that she stayed in Nocona, determined to make a success out of the Nocona Boot Co. Her brothers warned her she would fail, but that word was just not a part of her vocabulary.

To say that she was and is a remarkable woman is not enough. She looked forward, believing in people, believing in herself. She worked hard—still works hard.

Through a banker friend of her late father, she borrowed $5000, enough to keep seven loyal employees and her 25 square-foot shop.

During those first lean years, Miss Enid became a "jack of all trades." Her home became a rooming house. At the shop she worked as shipping clerk, stenographer, credit manager and traveling salesman.

"I guess it was during those times that my attitude about life really inspired me to try harder. I have always looked for the silver lining in the clouds that have come my way."

Her first sales trip was to West Texas in 1926.

"The roads looked like cattle trails," she said. "And for good

1924 H.J. Justin Boot and Shoe Factory.

(photos courtesy Enid Justin)

It's a well rehearsed orchestra of movement and sound.
(photos by Donna Bearden)

reason—they **were** cattle trails. Our old Model T took a pretty good beating on that trip. In fact, we lost a back wheel once. It came loose and jumped over a fence.''

Despite the hazards of the road, the trip was successful and Miss Enid came back with a book full of orders.

Miss Enid does admit there was a hesitancy to buy boots from a woman. But that all soon changed.

The discovery of oil near Nocona meant oilfield workers needing good strong workboots—the kinds with 16-inch tops laced all the way up.

"And they didn't care if they were made by a man or a woman."

As usual, Miss Enid put out a quality product. As workers moved on to other fields, they wrote back to Nocona to order their boots. And there's no better advertising than word of mouth. The boot business boomed with the oil.

PONY EXPRESS RACE

March 1, 1939, more than 5000 persons lined the streets of Nocona to witness 17 cowboys and a cowgirl take off on horseback for California, in a Pony Express race sponsored by Miss Enid.

Fort Worth businessman Amon Carter fired an old style ivory-handled .45 caliber pistol to start the race.

Equipped with duplicates of the regulation Pony Express mail bags, riders picked up mail bearing the 50-cent Pony Express stamp and the three-cent Golden Gate stamp. The Pony Express stamp was cancelled "Nocona, Texas, 9 a.m., March 1, 1939." The Exposition stamp was cancelled at San Francisco on the day and hour the winner crossed the finish line. Then the mail was dispatched by regular mail to its destination.

Each rider was allowed only two ponies and there was a Pony Express Station each 25 miles to allow the riders to change horses. Each rider had a truck or trailer and his crew of helpers. The rider made as many exchange stations as his ponies could stand each day.

Shannon Davidson, a 22-year-old cowboy from Matador reached the finish line first at 2 p.m. March 24. Miss Enid presented him with 750 newly minted dollars.

PLANT EXPANSION

On July 29, 1947, Miss Enid and her employees climbed into the back of a truck and rode through downtown Nocona waving shovels. They were on their way to break ground on "Boot Hill" for a new plant. There was no room left to expand at the downtown location.

The new 33,000 square-foot building opened June 9, 1948. The *Nocona News* of June 4, 1948 described the new building, including its air conditioning system, intercommunication system, public address system over which football games could be broadcast ("Nearly all the factory employees are ardent football fans."), parking lot and landscaping.

"New equipment has been generously sprinkled throughout the

entire factory, with such machines as an automatic cut-out machine in the cutting department that automatically cuts out the intricate designs as used in fancy inlaid patterns. Another new machine for closing the boot top in the fitting department has been added, as well as the addition of new Singer sewing machines for stitching the tops in this same department, and several new machines in the lasting departments for shaping the insoles and giving them a uniform thickness. Also added are new trimming machines and finishing machines for the soling and finishing departments and new dust collectors for removing all dust particles from the machinery air and at the same time return to the factory proper this same clean air.''

The plant has been enlarged several times since 1948 and now covers 100,000 square feet. It includes a retail shop which attracts travelers from all over the world. At the entrance to the shop is Miss Enid's little museum, a collection of mementos, boot making implements used by her father, plaques and awards, and old boots of various sizes and shapes.

Boot history is naturally one of Miss Enid's favorite topics.

"Boots have been a part of nearly every culture. Although the western style boot is part of America's heritage, its predecessors go back over 4000 years. The cowboy boot of the mid 19th century, which was directly influenced by the Spanish, was much like that worn by the Asiatic plainsmen.

"The high-heel type boot has historically undergone style changes in every culture. The men who rode the range in the 1800's weren't concerned with how their boots looked but with how they lasted. Boots were designed in solid colors and for durability only.''

When her father was making boots, they were brown, black or tan. Today, they are all colors of the rainbow. And reading the materials is like calling role at an exotic zoo: anteater, lizard, ostrich, elephant ear, snake.

Boots have come a long way from the early civilizations where they were considered a status symbol to be worn only by kings and nobility. The cowboy no longer has an exclusive option on them. Today boots are worn by housewives, doctors, and truckers.

Miss Enid has seen many improvements in bootmaking in her lifetime.

"Daddy Joe" was responsible for one important innovation which is still in use today. A rancher friend in Montana wrote that his cowboys would be glad to buy boots from Mr. Justin, if they could be fitted. Montana was a long way from Nocona—too far to fit boots. To meet the situation, "Daddy Joe" originated the unique system by which the customer could do the measuring and do it accurately, so that perfect fits could be had. Mr. Justin was urged by his friends to have the system copyrighted.

But he declined, with the argument that his system would be a great thing for the bootmaking industry and that his system would be his contribution. It proved a boon to the industry, with every major bootmaker in the country using it today.

Miss Enid and the Nocona Boot Company have been responsible for other innovations. The Thin-Line Cushion Shank was introduced in 1960 and was patented. The Seamless Saddle-Side was developed in response to track exercise boys who spent long hours in the saddle. The boot has no seam on the saddle side and can stand up under heavy pressure and rubbing. The Flex-Line Sole was introduced in 1963.

In 1964, Nocona produced a "Needle Toe Cushion" to solve the break-through problem of narrow, sharp toes popular on cowboy boots.

Miss Enid looked to R. S. "Ruff" Lemon, her vice-president and general manager, for many of these advancements. He had worked for her for more than forty years until his death in 1971.

And many of her employees are that loyal, working thirty, forty years. She has no mandatory retirement clause—a person can work as long as he wishes. Some may opt to go half-time after they get older. But a tour through the plant shows as many older faces and hands as younger ones. And they're all busy, fingers flying as they cut, sew, turn, hammer, glue, dye, box and ship. It's a well-rehearsed orchestra of movement and sound.

More than two-hundred steps are involved in producing a boot and many are still done by hand. Miss Enid built the company on pride of craftsmanship and she continues to run it that way. She doesn't cut corners that would result in an inferior product.

Automation has helped speed up some areas of production. The British high speed stitching machines have been a big boon to more production. Automatic sole stitchers have also helped.

Perhaps the most fascinating pieces of equipment are the computer stitching machines added just recently. The machines can top-stitch complex designs in multi-color at the rate of about 30 pairs a day or the equivalent of five workers. But Miss Enid is quick to point out that machines do not replace people at Nocona. In fact she held out on buying the stitchers until she was sure that they would benefit production without putting anyone out of work.

And production is up to about 1250 pairs a day. Back in 1925, it took six or seven employees one whole day to produce one pair of boots. And it took all seven of them working to do it. By 1940 production had risen to about 80-100 pairs a day, primarily because automated machinery was available. Production dropped during the war when leather and thread were hard to get.

After the war, production zoomed up to 300-400 pairs per day. In the 1950's, a rapidly changing style revolution caused a drastic drop in the demand for cowboy boots. By 1960, production was just between 400-450 pairs per day; and by 1970, production was up to 500-600.

The 1970's saw a style shift toward western wear and, in five years, the production level doubled to its present 1250 pairs per day. Unlike production in 1925, when all seven employees worked to make one pair of boots a day, today each person has a specific task. Today it takes about six weeks for a pair of boots to go through the individual production steps starting with cutting the leather to boxing and shipping the finished product.

(photo by Donna Bearden)

Countless celebrities and dignitaries throughout the United States and the rest of the world have worn Nocona Boots, including King Gustav VI of Sweden; former U.S. Supreme Court Chief Justice Earl Warren; George Burns; Lawrence Welk; Henry Ford II; Carol Burnett; President Lyndon Johnson; John Connally; and country and western singer Glen Campbell, who is one of Miss Enid's favorites to make boots for.

There are currently 52 stock styles available and more than 200 pairs of special order boots being made on any given day. More than 100 styles are possible in made-to-order boots. (One musician had inlaid violins stitched on his boots.)

In addition to managing the company and promoting her product, Miss Enid is very much a part of her community. Every year she buys a new piece of playground equipment for the children of Nocona. She has recently provided a bandstand for the park for the enjoyment of all ages.

Miss Enid has received numerous awards and commendations and she treasures them all. She seems to collect awards just as she does little boots of all shapes and sizes from around the world. And she collects incidents which she jots down in a little black notebook. She pulls out the notebook from time to time and smiles as she reads her one or two liners which stir a whole flood of memories.

There was the time she heard a radio newscast about an amnesia victim, hospitalized in Olympia, Washington. The young man had no identification, but was wearing a pair of Nocona boots. Miss Enid wired the police department in Olympia asking for the serial number of the boots. By checking the company records, she found that the boots had been shipped to a store in Pomona, California and then transferred to a store in Twin Falls, Idaho. This information led to the boy's identification.

There are other stories, other incidents, other awards. But Miss Enid doesn't have much time to recall them. She enjoys them, but she's busy looking forward. Her Nocona Boot Company has just celebrated 50 successful years and she's started on another one. She lives today, enjoying her "family" of workers. The lady who cut her teeth on leather has one major focus, to build "the better boot."

(photo by Donna Bearden)

The Man Who Set Texas to Music

by Donna Bearden

David Guion had been called "the man who set Texas to music for all the world to hear." Everyone from school children to professional musicians sings, plays and enjoys his folk songs, cowboy ballads and spirituals, which number more than 250.

Guion, now 83 and living in Dallas, is still composing. His musical career started about 77 years ago when he was a five-year-old boy living in Ballinger, in West Texas.

The "Mollie Bailey Circus" came to town and all the children flocked to hear the old steam calliope, which played out of tune. Young Guion was fascinated, and when he returned home he climbed up on the counter stool (they didn't have piano benches in those days) and played perfectly the calliope melodies—out of tune, just as he had heard them.

This so excited his family that his mother, an accomplished musician with a beautiful soprano voice, began giving him piano lessons. Then he studied under Charles J. Finger in San Angelo. Every Saturday, he boarded the train in Ballinger with a big placard around his neck telling his name and address. Finger would meet him, give him a lesson, and put him back on the train. San Angelo is about 30 miles from Ballinger, but in those days the trip took almost two hours. Many years later, Guion arranged some sea chanteys and folk songs that Finger had collected in his travels.

At the age of 12, Guion played piano in an open-air motion picture theatre, earning six dollars a week. That same year he won a scholarship in piano at the Conservatory of Music at Jacksonville, Illinois. Then after studying at Polytechnic College in Fort Worth, he spent three years in Vienna, studying piano under Leopold Godowsky at the Royal Conservatory.

Guion's father, the Hon. John I. Guion, was an influential judge well known in Texas. He served several years as president of the board of regents of the Agricultural and Mechanical College of Texas, and one of the halls there was named for him. Guion's paternal grandfather and great-grandfather were governors of Mississippi. The Guions are also related to Benjamin Franklin and the Taft Family. On the maternal side, he is related to U.S. President James K. Polk and Oliver Wendell Holmes.

Had Guion not become interested in music, he might have followed his father's footsteps in law or ranching. In fact, his father once tried to send him away to a military academy. His trunk was packed and the ticket was bought. The day came and the boy was not to be found. He had saddled his pony and ridden off onto the range. And that was the last he heard on that subject.

(photo courtesy David Guion)

Guion's father finally resigned himself to the fact that his son was going to be a musician and told the boy, "If you want to be a musician and starve to death, why go ahead."

But Guion never starved. In fact, he had published a few things before his father died and the Judge began to think his son might even "make a go of it."

Looking back, Guion admits, "Even then, I didn't have any idea of making a livelihood out of it. I never did take it as a business. My music has always been an avocation to me, something that I enjoy."

From the time Guion began playing, he began improvising. He drew from "material right at his back door," namely cowboy ballads, old fiddle tunes, and Negro spirituals.

Guion "grew up in the saddle and can sit with as much ease there as he can at the piano," Finger, his early music teacher, once said. He is "the only American composer who can boast of breaking his own horses, riding in rodeos and carrying off first prizes. He knows the cowboy at work as well as at play . . ." Finger went on to say that "Guion's cowboy songs ('Bold Vaquero,' 'Home on the Range,' 'McCaffie's Confession,' 'Range of the Buffalo,' 'All Day on the Prairie,' 'Cowboy's Meditation,' 'O Bury Me Not On the Lone Prairie,' 'Ol,' Paint,' 'Roy Bean,' etc.) are of the greatest importance to American folksong literature."

Of all the beautiful things Guion has arranged, everyone wants to know about "Home on the Range." It was written in manuscript form when he was about 15 years old, although he had actually been singing it since he was about eight. There were several different versions of it as a cowboy song, claimed to have been written in Kansas, Colorado, Wyoming, Arizona, New Mexico, etc. Each version had different words, a different title and a different tune. Guion heard the words from two or three of them, rewrote them, adding more verses, and composed the melody that became so popular. It was first performed at the Roxy Theater in New York City, then on nationwide radio.

When President Roosevelt heard it, he announced that it was his favorite song and called Guion to tell him so. Roosevelt continued to be a Guion fan and at various times sent Guion wires and letters and an autographed steel engraving of himself. (The photograph is one of Guion's prized possessions and still sits on the composer's grand piano.)

Guion once sent Roosevelt a wire asking if he could dedicate his "Yellow Rose of Texas" to him. Next day he got a phone call from the White House. F.D.R. greeted him with "Hello, Mr. Home on the Range." He said officially he couldn't accept the dedication, but unofficially he was delighted.

Another popular composition is "Turkey in the Straw," written in 1919. He had heard the old fiddlers play it and cowboys whistle it "before he could talk." It was the first old fiddle tune ever arranged for the piano by a composer.

"As to my arrangement, it was just in my soul and had to come out. Part of it was gotten by hard 'diggin' while at the piano. A certain little part popped into my head one morning between 2 and 3 o'clock. I arose and ran downstairs to my piano to write it down before I forgot

(photo courtesy David Guion)

it. Then our neighbors knew I was crazy. I managed to get back in bed without being murdered and, by the end of the day, my 'Turkey in the Straw' was finished and I was almost as glad as the neighbors.'' (Dallas News, Oct. 14, 1923)

Another old fiddle tune Guion arranged for piano was "Sheep and Goat." On the jacket of the piece of music published by G. Schirmer, Inc, in 1922, the composer notes, " 'Sheep and Goat', like 'Turkey in the Straw,' was written, whistled, sung, or played, once upon a time, by someone, somewhere in America . . . . I have used, aside from the original old melody of 'Sheep and Goat,' a little snatch, here and there, of other old familiar cowboy breakdowns, and a few 'side-kicks' of my own."

Guion's parents were both raised on old-time Southern plantations and learned many of the old Negro spirituals from their "black mammies." Mammy Nepie was slave in his father's family and didn't want to leave the Guion family. She came to Texas with Guion's father and grandmother. She cared for Guion when he was small, sang the old songs to him and even took him to church with her where he listened to the Negro songs, and clapped his hands and swayed to the music.

In this way, the old tunes became part of him and he couldn't help but write them down, he said. "Many of them are very plaintive and have a haunting strain of minor key running through them. This is true of the folk music of races that have suffered. It is noticeably true of Russian folk music," Guion said.

"Shout Yo' Glory" is one of the oldest negro tunes in existence. Guion learned it from his mother, who learned it from her mammy. "De Ol' Ark's a-Moverin' " was the first of his spirituals to make a real hit in New York.

His spiritual arrangements include: "Run, Mary, Run;" "Swing Low Sweet Chariot;" "Little David;" "Nobody Knows De Trouble I See;" "John de Baptist;" "I See Lawd Jesus a-Comin';" "You Jest As Well Get Ready;" "I feel Lak a Motherless Chile;" and "Praise God I'm Satisfied;" to name just a few.

Guion's first published song was "Old Maid Blues," which he wrote for Nora Bayes in 1917, and which she performed in the Ziegfeld Follies in 1918.

In 1924, Guion, who had moved to New York by then, tucked some manuscripts under his arm and went to the Roxy Theater with an idea for a cowboy production. Two weeks later he was rehearsing the show. With Guion at the piano accompanied by the orchestra, western music was heard for the first time in New York City. On the stage was a typical western setting with cowboys and cowgirls singing around a campfire. Square dancers, a rope dancer, singers and orchestra put on a rousing performance. It proved so popular it was held over for a second week. The show opened with "Turkey in the Straw" which was soon to become very popular.

While he was on stage, he received a call from the General Electric Radio Program wanting him to give an all-Guion program on a coast-to-coast hook-up. With only 15 minutes to get from the Roxy to the radio station, Guion, still dressed in cowboy regalia, got into Mr. Roxy's chauffeur-driven Cadillac convertible. With a police escort and sirens blowing, they raced to the radio station where a special elevator was waiting. The audience was arranged and the orchestra was ready. And Guion's first show stretched into 32 weeks of hour-long shows on NBC, followed by 32 weeks on WOR.

And then there was Carnegie Hall, musicals at the Baltimore Hotel, "Night of Stars" at Madison Square Garden, and the NBC Artists Bureau.

"They were all singing my songs, from the Metropolitan Opera Company to Bing Crosby. I even heard Caruso sing 'Home on the Range.' " After several years of New York City night life, Guion left his Greenwich Village apartment for a homestead in the Pocono Mountains in Pennsylvania. He remodeled an old home, furnished it with beautiful antiques, and named it "Home on the Range." The doorbell even chimed the first few bars of the famous song.

Situated on a trout fishing stream, it was quiet and peaceful and allowed Guion to devote full time to composing. It was also a gathering place for artistic people and he often had a houseful of friends. He lived there until 1970, when he moved back to Dallas.

In 1952, Guion was commissioned by the Houston Symphony to produce a major work. Texas Suite premiered on February 5, 1952. The 14 sections include "Prairie Dusk" ("A Concerto for Crickets"), "Camp Meetin' Along the Brazos," and "High Steppin' Lula Belle May Ida Brown of Lyons Avenue Steps Out."

Critic Hubert Roussel of *The Houston Post* wrote, "It was one of the gala evenings of the orchestra's season, very narrowly closing the gap between the high ridin' of high music and the rodeo a few blocks to the east. One heard in the hall that Trigger himself had been invited, but that was probably rumor. Everybody else was there. The auditorium was filled with more than 3000 good, colorful Texans . . ."

Guion also wrote the scores for two ballets. "Western Ballet" was performed for four successive seasons in Europe and America by Catherine Littlefield and the Philadelphia Ballet. "Shingandi—A Primitive African Ballet" was composed for Theodore Kosloff and his ballet company and was produced in the Hollywood Bowl and Dallas Bowl.

In 1958 the National Federation of Music Clubs declared Guion second only to Stephen Foster as America's most significant composer of music in the folk vein. The Texas Federation of Music Clubs had previously honored him (1950) with both a David Guion Week and a David Guion Month. At the same time, Howard-Payne College in Brownwood awarded him an honorary degree of Doctor of Music.

Guion has presented over a hundred of his original manuscripts, including "Home on the Range," to the College of Fine Arts at the University of Texas at Austin. History can be a tune, as well as dates and places. Guion set history to music so that even after the buffalo have stopped roaming, we can hum along to our own history.

Listenin' In

by Paul Cravens

As a country boy living in the small Texas town of Anna in Collin County, I experienced a happening barely understandable and almost unbelievable. I arose two hours before sunup and had been tinkering with a device I had put together the day before, in the fall of 1926. Clamped over my head, a pair of headphones fitted against my ears. Distinctly I could hear the jangling of a cow bell followed by a man's voice. He said, "I am janitor for the Fort Worth wireless broadcasting station WBAP. As I finished cleaning the building, I noticed that the transmitter seemed to be fired up, ready for operation. Laying my broom down, I stepped to the microphone and pressed the talk button. The ready light came on so I decided to talk a little, sing a little, and try out my new French harp. Now, here goes!"

At that second I bumped the table and the sound died. By adjusting the "catwhisker" on the small chip of lead ore called a galena crystal, I soon found a sensitive spot and the harmonica came to life, sweet and sharp.

Daddy, who had come into the room and started a fire in the black cast iron stove, walked over to see what had waked me so early. I slipped one earphone off the headband and handed it to him. He put it to his ear. His expression of surprise and disbelief, in a few seconds, became a grin as he started tapping his foot on the wooden floor.

The talkative janitor continued his monologue with the request that anyone who had heard his doings send him a card or letter, addressing it to Janitor, WBAP, Fort Worth, Texas.

This near miracle began when a classmate described in detail to me a wireless receiver he had seen in operation. He said that it was called a crystal set and with it one could hear all the way to Dallas and Fort Worth. When I asked my physics teacher for a piece of galena he found a small gray rock about as large as the end of a small thumb. He told me that it was lead ore and if he remembered his Latin correctly it was labelled as galena.

Using a dry wooden plank about four by six inches for a base, I mounted the galena crystal with glue and fastened one end of a copper wire around it. A second wire, mounted near the crystal, had a straight pin soldered to its loose end with the pinpoint resting on the galena which had been split to expose a fresh surface which was bright and shiny.

For a tuning coil I wound number 22 enamelled magnet wire tightly around a Quaker Oats oatmeal box 125 times and fastened the wire ends through holes punched in each end of the box. This coil was mounted near the back edge of the base and the crystal detector had been mounted near the front. Near the coil, a stiff copper wire with an eye formed in one end was anchored loosely with a screw so that the free end could be bent to slide along a path that had been scraped bare on the wire.

Paul Cravens listenin' in.   *(photo by George Sappenfield)*

The 75 foot metal clothes line mounted in the yard on six-foot posts was isolated from the ground by having inserted in each end the neck from a broken glass bottle. A lead-in wire attached to the end of this improvised antenna was brought through the window and soldered to the slider on the coil. By moving this slider, the number of turns connected to the antenna could be varied from one to one hundred and twenty-five. With the left end of the coil connected to a ground wire fastened to a metal rod driven into the earth, a tunable circiut was completed which could be adjusted to resonate with the frequency of the broadcasting station.

By adding a parallel circuit consisting of a magnetic earphone and the crystal detector, for changing the radio frequency waves into audible frequency waves, a working receiver was completed. This was done by wiring one side of the detector to one side of the ear phone, and by connecting the second side of the detector to the junction of the coil and the antenna, while the second side of the earphone went to the junction of the coil and ground wire.

Having assembled and connected the parts, I put the headphone on my ears and listened—to nothing! I wiggled the catwhisker around on the crystal until I found a faint noise. By moving the slider slowly from one end to the other of the tuning coil, I found a man talking. I let out a yell and ran to find someone. I had built a receiver and it was working.

After a few of the early morning sessions which I shared with other members of the family who were willing to rise at four a.m., I looked for results during the daytime. I discovered the world series of baseball in progress. Finding a scratch tablet, I ruled off some lines and kept official score for each of the series games. In the evening, after a day of labor in the field, my daddy, who loved baseball, would sit before the fire and study the score sheets. After listening to the newscast on the little radio for a few minutes, he would doze off to sleep in his chair.

My first set was built for a cost of 75 cents for three coils of door-bell wire and a lot of cut-and-try persistance. The first earphone was the earpiece from our crank up telephone. Because it was needed for its original purpose, I ordered by mail a pair of radio headphones plus a hundred foot copper antenna wire and a pair of factory made porcelain insulators. Installing this new antenna about thirty feet high atop the house to the barn, resulted in louder reception.

The quality of the sound received was such that in the succeeding forty-nine years I have never heard any sound reception or reproduction so clean and clear. I have heard louder sound but never truer sound. No electricity was used with this receiver and since motor cars were few and far between, spark plug static was absent. There was no getting away from the static of lightning, but we were afraid to use the set during stormy weather so we disconnected the antenna and tied it to the ground wire.

In May of 1927, about four or five o'clock in the afternoon, I heard through my earphones a live broadcast from an airfield near Paris, France. This was a first for me. It was the arrival and landing of Charles Lindberg after his thirty-four hour flight across the Atlantic Ocean in his single engine airplane, Spirit of St. Louis. I could hear the wildly cheering crowd of more than a hundred thousand persons who greeted Lindy at the airfield. A news commentator gave details of the landing and of the take-off from New York. By contrast the take-off had received scant mention in the United States.

Of the largest and more versatile receivers I have owned and operated since 1926, not one has generated the absolute amazement and excitement produced by the home-made crystal set.

El Aeronauta

by Jamie Frucht

A farmer who's grown old has at least the outline of his fields, a peeling barn and his faded overalls, certain indelible early rising habits, plus the whole complexion of his face to prove it. A few roosters might still echo the past. But what about an aviator? No remnants of wooden planes in the garage. The acreage he plied was the sky.

Fidel Vela's lasting sense of humor is the compass that has allowed him to keep his direction. His face has a serious aspect when it seems to express all his conscience and convictions. Then he will toss that smooth, serious face into its opposite extreme, a face that rocks with laughter. Obviously, Mr. Vela needed both extremes to get so high in the air against a gravity of difficult conditions and doubters. After all, what was a Mexican kid from South Texas doing with the likes of the early aviators—Billy Parker, Doolittle, Goebel, Lindbergh? Not just watching. This kid from "Mustang Prairie" said, "I didn't want to go out there and dig potatoes. I wanted to fly."

Fidel Vela was a foreigner from Mexico, even though, from the age of four, he had been on American soil. When his people came here in 1900, there were no restrictions. One could go over the border any time. "My ancestors had a place close to Hebbronville by the name of La Florida. It was a Spanish grant. To make the story short, these people from the north, what you call the 'carpetbaggers,' started buying up land for taxes. So eventually my people didn't have any land. All they had was 200 acres of homestead, and it was just sand. You could raise nothing on that land. And finally we had nothing."

As difficult as things were for the Velas in the United States, the situation was even worse on the other side of the border where Villa's insurrections were erupting. The family stayed in Texas, living first at Hebbronville. From 1903 to 1911 Fidel attended school in San Diego. The family settled in Falfurrias in 1911, and Fidel continued his education there until 1914.

Even as a young boy Fidel was fascinated with engines. His memories of early friends in Falfurrias include recollections of their Model T's, Mitchells, Overlands, Jacksons, Essex and other cars that have disappeared as totally as dinosaurs.

It was his interest in cars that took him to Detroit, Michigan in 1916. There he went to auto school. He remembers visiting the Model T factory and seeing the cars come out on the assembly line, their engines running, their radiators steaming.

"When I was up in Detroit, I was just a kid from South Texas. I didn't know much. (I don't know much now.)" He supported himself by odd jobs, such as working for American Express for 25 cents an hour. But since he knew about engines and knew how to drive, he was hired by the U.S. Government as a civilian truck driver. The Motor Truck Co. 42 Storage Detachment of the Quartermaster Corps used the

"It's unbelievable, you know, what people will go through when they have some kind of an ambition. I wanted to learn to fly and I learned."
                                                                    (photo by Mary Sherwood)

first mechanized trucks in the Army. Fidel was under contract, working for the Army but not actually in the Army (more like a scout from the Old West). The Corps was supposed to help in General Pershing's chase of Pancho Villa. "And I gather the Army didn't know that I was a Mexican citizen." Things could have gotten pretty sticky if they'd found out. But they were short of drivers, and very few people could drive trucks. Fidel Vela did all the work that was required of him—hauling ammunition and troops, whatever. Before the trucks could make contact with Pershing, however, World War I had broken out and the Army had bigger problems than Pancho Villa.

It was during his stint as a truck driver with the Army that Fidel Vela first set eyes upon his true love.

"One time I went with a load of equipment to Remount 1 Cavalry Training Field. At that time the U.S. Army had a cavalry; we didn't have any motorized equipment. And we were transporting some big boxes, long boxes. I remember loading these boxes and found out it was an airplane. This was when the U.S. started flying. And I'd never seen an airplane before. They had one sample in one of the hangars, and I looked it over and looked it over and I was in love with this thing, you know. And I saw them flying around and I said, 'I'm going to learn to fly someday!' "

As with a true love, one's family may not be as taken as you are.

His family didn't think much of his ambition to fly. Unfortunately, neither did his country. When the U.S. entered the First World War, that should have been a perfect opportunity for a would-be aviator like Fidel to get his wings. But instead, because of his Mexican citizenship, his pinions were tied. "I couldn't join the Army. And I tried the Navy and it was the same thing, you know, I just couldn't get in. And finally, another friend of mine from Falfurrias, we both tried to get into the Navy. Well, it was the same old story. He could join because he was a citizen of the U.S. but I couldn't."

A man who saw how much he wanted to join, said to him, "Well, you can talk pretty good English. You can say you was born on this side." So Fidel tried to join the Navy, "Some way or another, I approached these officers. They started asking me a lot of questions, you know, about this and that, and well, I just couldn't lie. I told them that I was born in Mexico."

Fidel's honesty kept him out of the Navy. He still had the problem of how he was going to fly. It was neither the right time nor the right place to learn flying. All the airfields were closed for security reasons. Then one day Fidel saw an ad in a Sunday magazine section for a flying school in Dewey, Oklahoma that was accredited by the U.S. Government.

This field was out in the middle of nowhere, where the politicians probably felt no one could do any harm, or even get to the edge of the county. "We had a lot of rejects there. There were Chinamen and people from the U.S. Army that couldn't learn how to fly for some reason or another, and we had a lady from Seattle, Washington." This strange assortment of people shared one strong ambition: to fly.

It was at that school in 1918 that Fidel's friendship with Will D. Parker began. He was a pioneer aviator and an instructor who had been trained with the British Royal Flying Corps. Parker was working on the government's experiments with reversible propellers. He promised to take "Pancho," as he called Fidel, under his wing and teach him to fly, if "Pancho" would assist him in the experiments. "Pancho" grabbed at the opportunity.

Fidel had to pay dearly for his ambition. He had to scrape up about $1000 for tuition to be trained for his international license. In 1918, no particular government regulated the licensing. It was a global license issued by all governments of the world.

Fidel had taken a gamble that he would be reimbursed by whatever government (French, Canadian or British) hired him to fly, for the school had worked out an arrangement for rebates. "I done it on my own. The Government wasn't backing me. I was spending money of my own. So it's a foolish thing to do, but you know young people, they do that."

On August 20, 1919, at the age of 23, "Pancho" received his international license from the Aerial Club of America. It read, "Fidel Vela has fulfilled all the conditions required by the Federation Aeronautique International for an aviation pilot and is bevetted as such." It meant that "Pancho" had his papers to fly anywhere in the world.

And then, just as he was about to enter the war, "the war expired, ended. And there I was with my license, but I didn't know what to do with my license." His disappointment was tempered by the knowledge that the worst of wars was over.

For a short time he toyed with the idea of joining the Mexican army as a flyer. Fidel had a relative who was a colonel. "I had an appointment to meet this man in Victoria in the state of Tamaulipas, Mexico, just across the river. Anyway, I didn't see him because something happened. (Good thing I didn't, because I'd have been dead by this time.)"

In Mexico, there was a revolution with a rebel army conspiring against the government. A train full of rebels was coming from Tampico to Monterrey, Mexico. "My uncle, Col. Jose Mario Ramirez, had orders to dynamite the train, but he let them go by because he had so many friends on that train. That didn't help him any, and they arrested him and took him to Mexico City to be executed. But his army record was so good that they pardoned him. And this was the man I was supposed to present myself to. Maybe I would have been arrested with him. When that happened, well, I said, 'Why not leave good enough alone. I'm not going to Mexico.' "

That still left Fidel with the problem of how to get his flying career off the ground. He did what all the other daring young men with flying licenses did—started barnstorming. The airplanes they flew were the surplus biplanes, "Flying Jennies," left over from the war, which were being sold at airfields like Love Field in Dallas. Barnstormers made their money by charging passengers $5 a ride. Airplanes were such rarities in those days that people would flock from miles around to see one, and the most daring would pay to ride.

"The people I worked for—they was people that wanted to invest a little money on some adventure and they'd buy an airplane to make money with." They got their adventure. "It was an open cockpit. It was tandem, the pilot would sit in back and the passenger in front. and so we'd go to different little towns and fly around and take pasengers for hire. We'd just take off with this airplane and we didn't know where we was going. When we'd see a little town and a good field where we could land, we'd land on it."

The fields Fidel refers to are not airfields (there weren't any in the small towns) but cow pastures, cornfields and the like. Sometimes they landed in inappropriate fields. He remembers a farmer who was having a big auction in his field. When the crowd saw the plane land in the opposite field, everybody took off, leaving the farmer to talk to his cows. "That farmer really was mad that time."

The pilots usually tried to come to a compromise with the farmer whose field they'd appropriated, either by paying him outright or offering him a free ride. That didn't always work. Fidel recalls landing in a field in Shamrock, Oklahoma.

A man in overalls came to him and said, kind of mad like, "Are you the people who own this plane?"

"Yes, sir. You want to take an airplane ride?"

"I'm not going to take any airplane ride."

"Well, I guess if I want to use your field I'm going to have to pay you whatever it is."

"Well, you can use the field. But you're not going to take **me** for no ride!"

So Fidel started taking passengers and this guy started getting more confident. Soon he called Fidel to one side and said, "Listen, I'm a man with a wife and family. I'd like to take a ride, but I want you to fly low."

It was more dangerous to fly low than high, but of course the farmer didn't know it. Fidel couldn't take him low. He took him aloft and gave him a good ride.

Fidel would make a living barnstorming until he'd wreck the plane, then he'd have to look for a new job. "We had mishaps and bad luck and all that. A couple of planes, we wrecked them and I'm lucky to be alive today, but at the same time, why, we had a lot of fun. We laughed a lot."

After much flight experience as a barnstormer, Fidel went to work as a pilot and mechanic for the Phillips Petroleum Company in Bartlesville, Oklahoma. He was in good company. He worked with some of the best early pilots—Clarence Clark, Billy Parker, Arthur Mills.

"We'd fly to Chicago to sell gasoline to the airlines, and then from Chicago on to Cheyenne, Wyoming; from Cheyenne to Salt Lake City. . . make the rounds you know, like a traveling salesman." On one of these trips he was teamed up with his friend Billy Parker. They flew to Bartlesville from Cheyenne, a distance of 600 miles, in 3 hours 40 minutes, at an average speed of 177 m.p.h. in a Travelaire Biplane with a 200 horsepower motor. It was a remarkable speed for the day. A strong tail wind helped them all the way.

While more respectable than barnstorming, working for Phillips Petroleum was almost as risky and no more lucrative. "I don't know if the company was making any money or not, but **we** weren't, anyway."

For $200 to $300 a month, they risked their lives flying in snow and ice over the mountains. Parachutes were more a psychological lift than a real safety device. "Chutes don't do you any good in the mountains, if you jump or fall—if you get lost in the snow you'd freeze to death. So I told Mr. Parker that it had to be a very hot fire for me to jump."

Although Fidel did not get to test his mettle against foreign enemies in his flying career, he has flown against many natural enemies, weather being the most formidable. Once he was co-pilot taking Frank Phillips, president of the company, and his secretary on a flight from Columbus, Ohio to St. Louis.

"It was wintertime and the ceiling was very low, and so we had to climb on top of the clouds. The only communication we had was a one-way communication of the weather report every hour. We got right on top of the clouds and couldn't see the ground. And so we tried to fly non-stop to St. Louis, over the clouds—if we had to, we could land at Terre Haute, Indiana, which was by the river.

"Mr. Phillips punched a button, a light went on in the cockpit, so I went down to see what he wanted. And he says, 'Where are we?' I couldn't see the ground, I couldn't tell him. 'Well, I don't know,' I started to say. Then I happened to look through a window of the plane and I saw a hole in the clouds. Now I recognize Terre Haute, you know, because I've been over it so many times and I know the river. And I said, 'We're over Terre Haute, Indiana,' and he said, 'Oh, okay.'

"I went back to the cockpit. We started getting reports from St. Louis. Well, I was scared, because it was raining and the ceiling was less than 500 feet. Supposing when we try to get through the clouds we get to a rainy spot and can't see the ground? We had to hear the beam—a long signal and a short one. If you get out of the beam you get a long one and then when you get to the other side, you get a short and a long. You're supposed to go right between them. Anyway we hear a buzz and we know we're in St. Louis. Clarence Clark who was first pilot said, 'Well we have to make it some way because we're practically out of gas. You get a hold of your control and I'll get a hold of mine and look ahead. We're going through the clouds.'

"We couldn't see the ground because it was raining and I knew we probably never would see it. But it happened that it was clear right on top of the river and we straightened out and landed in East St. Louis, in Curtis Field. We couldn't go on to Lambert Field because we were afraid we'd be out of gas. I'm telling you, I was shaking. And Phillips and his secretary didn't know a thing about it. And so they got out and went to eat something, and we started filling the plane with gas and just kept on pouring gas in it. It was practically out of gas. If we had tried for Lambert Airport, we would have cracked up, we would have crashed."

As part of his job with Phillips, Fidel went to air shows and national air races to boost the Phillips products. These races attracted an international crowd and cheers were in all languages. Fidel enjoyed these meets but he never had an ambition to be a big shot. "I always wanted to be a little guy flying airplanes." Nevertheless he got to meet many of aviation's greats.

Phillips also had a wilderness lodge. Fidel and Clarence Clark flew many celebrities there, including Will Rogers, in Ford Tri-motors owned by Phillips Petroleum Company.

In his flying career Fidel did many types of things, becoming acquainted with planes inside and out. He tested and worked on the Cavalier plane for the Star Aircraft Company of Bartlesville, Oklahoma. For a brief period of his life, being of Mexican descent worked for him. The Cessna Aircraft Company of Wichita, Kansas hired him as an interpreter for their business transactions in South America.

Fidel also went to Arcadia, Florida, to teach flying and work for the Army as a mechanic. He remembers the boys practicing night flying with no landing lights, only two navigation lights, one on each side of the wing.

"You know how they used to practice flying at night? We'd pour some gasoline on the field—the field was not a concrete field, it was just grass and sod. And then we would ignite the gasoline and this pilot would go around and land by the light of the fire. And no chute, no nothing. And a lot of them boys got killed, but that's the way it was, you know.''

Fidel himself had some close calls. In 1929 on a flight from Dallas to Austin the plane started vibrating. "And then I smelled something burning and then there was some smoke coming out of the floorboard and I said to the co-pilot, 'We're on fire.' We were not very high, I saw a cotton patch and the rows of the cotton patch were just that wide. And so I had to land with the rows of cotton because if you would land crossways, the plane would be liable to turn over. I was flying it and he was just sitting by me and I was—I didn't remember I was scared maybe he was, but I wasn't anyway—I was just thinking about landing.

"When we got it on the ground, what we wanted to do was just get out of the plane because we knew it was on fire. Well, the propeller was made of wood in them days. And it came loose in the hub, and the friction caused the fire. Anyway we landed, and we were lucky that the plane wasn't upside down like I thought it would be. And the hot coals from this propeller got on the grass and the grass caught fire, so we had to run with the plane—good thing it was a light plane—we had to run away from the fire to save the plane. And in the meantime, the owner of the cottonfield came down and with some gunny sacks, we put the fire out.''

Fidel credits God with helping him out of some tight places. Years ago they had "pusher" planes, the kind the Wright Brothers invented with the engine in the back. Those planes were before his time, but in 1921, he did get to fly a pusher's plane.

It was around 1922 and Mr. Beech (of Beechcraft) was showing him a new plane—the Laird Swallow. He took Fidel for a test ride. Shortly after they landed, Fidel took off again, piloting a plane for a man "who had some business in El Paso." The motor was turning over fine but the plane wouldn't get off the ground.

Fidel recalls it was one of those long August days when hot air currents run up and down the afternoon. "So I start pulling the stick, and pulling the stick, and pulling the stick, and the plane is still on the ground, it just barely misses a fence. And then I can see where I'm going to hit a house, a farmhouse. On the other side of the house is a chicken coop. I decide to hit the coop and the chickens. So I got the wing down and it hits one of the coops. All I can hear is bang, bang, bang, and that's it.

"We didn't turn over. We didn't catch fire. And Mr. Beech when he saw this plane fall, he started rushing over the field in his Cadillac. When he saw me with blood on my face, he thought I was badly hurt. We went to a doctor's office and I waited and waited and waited and nobody came so I said, 'I'm all right. My head isn't broken.' And I went home. Later I found out that the man I was flying for was hauling heroin, but I didn't know anything about it. Good thing I wrecked.''

Eventually Fidel's own mother warmed up to the idea of her son being a pilot. He never could take his mother up in a plane, though; but then, she wouldn't even get in a car. Fidel's homecomings were celebrated. Of course he would come home in a plane, a little craft. There were so few planes in those days flying over Falfurrias that every time his excited mother heard one, she'd cry, "Here he comes, here he comes!" She had a girl named Ninfa helping her around the house. And when she heard the plane, she'd cry, "Ninfa, Ninfa, go catch a chicken."

"And Ninfa goes and catches a chicken and wrings its neck. Many times it wasn't me, the airplane would just go by, you see, but the chicken was dead anyway. So I don't know how many chickens I killed."

When Fidel flew in from Oklahoma to Falfurrias he hadn't been home in such a long time that he didn't know where the airport was. He didn't even know if the town had one or not. "I was flying and I saw some big pastures out there by Burdette's so I landed. And Mr. Burdette drove me to town to my mother's. Garland Lasater, owner of the Dairy and Falfurrias Butter, let me use his hangar and gave me gasoline for the return flight."

There was a time when Fidel decided to stop flying. It didn't last too long. He threw his decision to the wind, and once more became an aviator. However, when he resumed flying, he had to contend with the U.S.Government. His international license was no longer valid as the Department of Commerce now issued all licenses.

"It was terrible the way the new license was acquired. We had to do all kinds of stunts, spins and loops." It was when he was spiralling around in tighter and tighter spirals to satisfy a capricious government inspector that Fidel realized he was spinning too close to the ground. "I knew that I was going to crash. It just went through my head that way." The plane disappeared between some hills. Fidel pulled the plane up from some corn stalks. Everyone was running from the hangars expecting to see a broken plane and pilot. But instead Fidel emerged from between the hills and landed. The inspector flunked him for his fancy handling, but later he passed.

Number 14599 is not just another number. It is the transport license issued to Fidel Vela on January 15, 1936 by the Department of Commerce. It was an all inclusive license, the highest a pilot could get, qualifying him to carry passengers and to give flight instruction. It represented ambition that wouldn't quit.

With the license, Fidel could instruct Navy pilots during the Second World War. But he himself could not get a commission; though, for the second time in as many wars, he volunteered. The law was such that a person had to have been a citizen for 10 years to qualify. (Fidel, by now, had his citizenship papers, but not his 10 years.) Later this law was revoked as unconstitutional, but not in time for Fidel to see "action" or to serve his adopted country. Once again Fidel experienced deep disappointment. His patriotism was unwanted.

Fidel retired in 1959 after 25 years in the civil service of the Army and Navy. He has kept up with developments in the aviation industry through reading and through discussions with his youngest son, who is a technician for Eastern Airlines in Houston. Fidel may have started in planes with a top speed of only 75 M.P.H., but he can tell you all about the Concorde's 1500 M.P.H., 35,000 foot-high flights.

"I didn't want to go out there and dig pototoes. I wanted to fly."
(photo courtesy Fidel Vela)

It is astonishing and gratifying to Fidel to see how far planes have come. He became a flyer because he felt compelled by his youthful infatuation with planes. But in time his love matured and was found worthy. "You know, I never thought that this thing (flying) was going to get where it is today. I thought it was just something like a passing fad."

Planes still give him a bad time occasionally, as when he went by Boeing 747 to Seattle to visit his daughter.

"I went to the door of the plane and the stewardess didn't ask me for my ticket. She let me on. So I sat down. Finally we took off, And we kept on going and going and didn't go no place. I was thinking that we were going to Tulsa, then from Tulsa we'd fly on to Washington. When I was airborne about an hour and a half, I called the stewardess and said, 'When are we going to get to Tulsa?' She said, 'Tulsa? We're halfway to Los Angeles.'

"Can you believe that? I was just by myself, and I said, 'I'm not going to Los Angeles. I'm going to Washington, **State of Washington.**' And then she got all excited and she went to the head man in the cockpit. He came to talk to me. 'We're going to Los Angeles, but don't worry. We'll transport you back to Houston as soon as we get to Los Angeles.'

"Well, I didn't care about the plane ride. But some of those people must have thought I was kind of an old, crazy man. A young kid says to his mother, 'He's kind of nutty. He's likely to jump off of the plane or something.'

"There comes a good-looking stewardess who sat down by me and started conversing with me and trying to, I guess, forget that I was on the wrong plane. She thought something was wrong with me I suppose. When we got to Los Angeles, I called my daughter in Washington. 'What are you doing in Los Angeles?' she wanted to know. 'Somebody made a mistake so I'm going back to Houston.'

"Soon I was on the plane, but it was the time of the Hemisfair and a lot of people from Los Angeles were going to San Antonio. And a lot of drinking was going on, and champagne and all that. I didn't want to sit down in the first class place because it was usually all rich people drinking. There was an old man there who was really pretty tight. And finally I got to Houston and I think that morning I got away to Washington. By four o'clock the day after I started I was there." He could have made better time in one of his two seaters.

Fidel is proud of his three children. Like some of his remarkable flights, he seems to give credit to forces outside himself—tail winds, good engines, God.

"I don't try to get credit for any of these kids." Paul, the oldest, is a professor at Goddard College in Vermont. He's been to Russia, Italy and France, and Fidel is proud that he's "not stuck up. He lives simple, he dresses humble, and he loves Mexican food more than anything." Paul was very ambitious when he was a kid and he "wanted to learn."

His daughter Irene, living in the suburbs of Seattle, is a teacher of Spanish, having gone back to complete her college degree after her own children were grown. John is a technician with Eastern Airlines in Houston.

Fidel Vela is a good man who has followed his own dreams and voices. In spite of some close calls, there's no nervousness anywhere in his face. He is totally at ease. He's capable of long, serious explanations but always there's a parenthetical laugh. His face is at the command of that laugh, which just takes over. The dome of his head is smooth as a stone in the sun—the kind of stone people keep and rub for good luck. He wears a golf cap, and has always favored caps of one kind or another.

As a young man, Fidel was handsome in an easy way. Once at an international balloon race, Fidel, on account of his smooth face and get up, was mistaken for an aristocratic balloon racer.

"I was walking by the hangar. I was young and maybe I have presentable clothing, gloves and so on. This fellow motions at me, 'Hello, Count,' he said to me. I said I thought he was mistaking me for some other person. You know, Italians are funny people. They embrace you and they kiss you. And he embraced me and kissed me and said, 'Hello, Count so-and-so.' And I thought, 'Well, what's the matter with this guy?' 'Count, when are you going to go up?' he asked.

" 'I think you're mistaking me for somebody else. I'm no Count. I'm no Count. You've mistaken me. I work for Phillips Petroleum Company.' And that was that."

Fidel is tolerant of jokes. He likes to talk to friends and to tinker with motors, anything that runs. Falfurrias is a good place to be at ease and tinker. It was also a good place for a young man to leave to become a flyer.

Falfurrias is mostly sky. It is a town of wide boulevards in search of crowds. There's much land and not much town. There are wooden houses with well tended yards. Most people simply pass through it on their way to the Valley. It's been called "The Gateway to the Valley." Fidel lived for a time in Corpus Christi when he worked for the Navy, but after Hurricane Carla, he decided to come inland, back to Falfurrias.

The sky that has surrounded him so often in his life, baffled him, and kept him aloft, now, like a hangar, arches over him. His long-run luck has been good. He's still alive today, having logged over 2000 flying hours at a time when every flight was a life or death affair. He has no regrets.

It is remarkable that Fidel Vela could persevere against the red tape, the elements and a world of extenuating circumstances that plotted against his flying career.

"I do not consider myself a hero. God had ended W. W. I in 1918 and I had to follow a way to make a living at that time." Fidel Vela put himself through his own maneuvers. "It's unbelievable, you know, what people will go through when they have some kind of an ambition. I wanted to learn to fly and I learned."

There are other heroes besides war heroes. And Fidel Vela is one.

Wild Things in Caddo Lake

by Wyatt Moore as told to Donna Bearden

I was born in nineteen-and-the-year-one—you can't get much older than that, you know. In two, three, four years, I thought I was big enough to go to the river. In commercial fishing, I started when I was about two years, I thought. I used to go to the lake with my grandpa and he called it his lake. Told us it belonged to him and I believed him cause I always believed Grandpa. It was only a couple of miles and my grandpa would bring us. This river here has little inlets where we'd land the boats, wasn't any outboard motors or any of the things that we have now. When I was 12 to 15, I was fishing commercially. I haven't fished in the lake much the last 20-25 years, but I did fish in it for 20 or 25 years before that.

People couldn't even imagine today the pollution that went on in Caddo Lake and the lake survived it.

The oil field pollution occurred from 1910 to 1920, for ten years or so there, and we caught thousands of pounds of fish those days.

I had some pictures of wells blowing clear over the top of the derrick, a six-inch stream of pure oil. Gulf Oil drilled over 500 wells in the lower part of the lake. Once there was a well that blew out so much oil on the water that the boats' propellers would spin and run fast. If they would have had a fire, they'd have burned up the country. There was oil a foot deep for a mile or two from the well to the bank, killed trees, supposed to killed all fish. And we would catch fish when that drilling was going on and the wells blowing out. We would catch buffaloes with their fins eat off where they couldn't hardly swim, but they'd be in good shape and fat.

When the war plant was established at Karnak immediately after Pearl Harbor, the wash water from making TNT and other chemicals was dumped into a creek which ran into a section of Caddo Lake. It ran into an arm of the Lake, about 100 acres, and every bit of fish, frog, any kind of wildlife whatever just disappeared. There was a third or a fourth of Caddo Lake completely killed of any fish. But it came back and got over it.

Mr. T.J. Taylor here in Karnak, Lady Bird Johnson's father, was a shipper of fish. There was four passenger trains a day here then, two in the day and two in the night. About two days a week, Tuesdays and Fridays was fish delivering days, and the trains would sometimes be an hour and a half loading fish on the express cars. There would be eight or ten of those express fish wagons loaded with barrels of fish packed in ice to ship to Dallas, Greenville on up north of here, maybe some into Oklahoma and Shreveport. That Lake would furnish enormous amounts of fish.

One day Mr. Taylor shipped 5200 pounds of white perch or carp. That would go on about seven or eight months of the year, mostly through the winter and spring, and next year you could put your nets back in there and catch by the boatloads again. Once an uncle of mine

Wyatt Moore: boat builder, fisherman, moonshiner . . .   *(photo courtesy Wyatt Moore)*

that I was fishin' kinda on shares with and I had 1800 pounds of white perch, more white perch than people get to see these days in a lifetime. Things do change around, I don't think the lake produces that way anymore.

There was quite an industry in spoonbill catfish, that's a shovel-bill cat that seems to be almost extinct here now. They would catch them mostly for their eggs. They would have 30 or 40 pounds of eggs in them at a certain time of the year. Later the fish meat itself got to be valuable along in the late Twenties.

Up till 1910, there wasn't a dam and the Red River was dammed up by logs and jams. When overflows came, it would pool back up in here and enormous amounts of buffalo and catfish apparently drifted here from Red River or Mississippi or anywhere in the whole United States. They would come here and there was tons of those caught. Now with the dam in the lake and its being a landlocked lake, it doesn't produce the catfish, buffalo or carp that it used to.

The water was controlled by the rise and fall of Red River; and in the summertime, the river and this lake would go about four feet lower than this, which meant you could walk way out there on a sandbar ledge. Caddo Lake is a very shallow lake and probably over half the lake would go completely dry and grass would grow up out on the dry sandbars and islands. Cattle would graze out there and people would cut hay there. Then when Red River was cleaned of the log jams, which caused the water to back up to Jefferson, the steamboats could come here. So there was a dam built about 10 miles from Red River over in Louisiana, and it lasted about 60 years. I lived long enough to see a concrete dam wear completely out. Now they got a new one over there, about three or four years old, and it maintains this level here.

Around '21 or '22 people in this area got the recipe for making alcoholic beverages. I was 20 years old and a lot of us turned toward that as a sideline, and sometimes it was a complete line. The method of operation here was usually kinda small outfits, comparatively small. Over in Mississippi, they would dig a hole in the side of a hill and put a still there that would hold several thousand gallons, and make it in a big way and haul it off with trucks. But here, our method was mostly to put a platform out over the water in Caddo Lake, in thickets where only a small canoe-like boat could go into it, and would carry five or six barrels of mash.

You put water and hops and yeast cake together and then you cook it in a container, preferably a copper still. But most everybody used oil drums—cleaned 'em out good. There was 110 gallon drum could be had from an oil company in Shreveport. I had several of them and some of them rusted out during the eight or ten or fifteen years of operation. I maintained an outfit on a platform that I could set up on some sort of carpenter type workhorses and then lay the decking down and wouldn't make any noise establishing a location like hammering and building a platform.

We usually used wood to burn and put this drum into a brick furnace and fixed it up with this old chimney mud that you can get around here. There is a white looking post oak clay—they mix grass with it and build mud chimneys. Anyway we brick it up, make a furnace, put a smoke stack around the end of the drum and it was a pretty efficient burner. Usually the best whiskey to be made is to boil it once and run your fluid out through a copper tubing in the lake (let the lake cool it) and back on the platform and run up a bunch of it. Then you put all that you've got back in your drum and run it again to get it real strong. You could get up to 170-80 proof, almost pure alcohol. Then you cut it down with, preferably, rainwater to where it's about 100 proof.

Then you could buy a proof gauge, a little hydrometer type thing, and put it in charred oak kegs that you could buy anywhere and age it awhile and it was pretty good material. In fact, I expect it was as safe to drink as any they've got now.

Then it got to be that the price of the product was so low that we got to making it with a thumper. A thumper is a smaller tank that sits between your copper boiler and the coil that goes in the lake to cool it that acts as sort of a settling bulb. That way, at one run, you can make pretty strong liquor. It's not as good as the complete double run, but it is pretty fair if you'll fire it slow.

Alcohol leaves fluid at 180 degrees. You seen the old-time car gauge where the heat indicator was painted red at 180 degrees. Well, at 180 degrees, the old time alcohol antifreeze would boil out of your radiator. Well, water don't make steam till it reaches 212 degrees; therefore, the secret of making good liquor was to keep your temperature between 180 and 212. Then only the alcohol would come out and you wouldn't get boil over of mash or non-alcohol. Some of them didn't know that, but I had a doctor friend and he liked the material we was making and he showed me how to put a temperature gauge on it to hold it in the proper perspective, or what they call now the proper quality control. Lot of people have told me that my product was as good or better than most.

I never was arrested. I was nipped at a few times. I always managed to dodge them. It was just pure luck. If you operated truthfully, they got what they called for and sampled it. I gave them a swig out of mine. I never did sell around the house or have any drunks around. In fact, we lived on the lake and operated a fish camp and built boats. I used this operation as a sideline, but at times it was just about the mainstay.

Once it brought eight dollars a gallon. Finally people got to selling it for as low as two dollars a gallon, but I never did sell it for less than three. I figured it cost me a dollar a gallon to make it and if I sold it for three, and sold half as much as those who sold it for two, I'd still make just as much clear money and do just half as much work.

At one time I had a still so close to the house that I could see the smoke from the house and the thumper would make a bump, bump, bump noise when you fired it up on a cold morning. I had an irrigation pump on the bank of the lake and I irrigated a little truck farm. When I had people around the house, I'd fire up the little water pump to drown out the noise of the thumper down there. And anyway, I never did have any trouble.

The smell never did go anywhere other than right close by. I could

Wyatt Moore still knits his own fish nets.   *(photo courtesy Wyatt Moore)*

smell pretty good cause I never did smoke—haven't yet—and I never did notice a smell to amount to anything. Sometimes I guess I smelled like whiskey and duck and money and fish all at the same time.

If you operated right, you could sell it to doctors, lawyers, bankers and people who really didn't want other people to know they were getting it. You could make a kinda pest out of yourself by not using it carefully and making poor stuff and getting in the wrong kind of company with it. But the sheriff liked good whiskey, you know. However, I don't know anybody in this county who actually had a deal with any of the law enforcement officers, whatever, in order to get by. It might have been that they was nice to them or took them a mess of fish or something, but as far as any actual payoff, I don't believe there ever was. The Federal revenuers was the only ones the people in this area was ever afraid of. But this is a large area of Caddo Lake with lots of swamps, shallow water and big trees where you could go back and build you a platform whereby an airplane couldn't even see it down in the thick cypress trees.

I went down to Huntsville once and tried to spring my uncle who had moved to town and went to selling in town and they got him. If he'd stayed on the lake where things was wild like he was, he would never have got caught. I didn't spring him, but he got out later. A lot of my neighbors went to the Federal Correctional Institute of Texarkana and Tyler, but somehow I managed to squirm by, myself. I guess you might say I'm really the only uncaught one in the area. I don't attribute it to anything uncanny except that maybe they didn't as many people know about me as I thought knew. And people wanted to know, wasn't I scared? And I told them, "Yessir, I'm scared, I stay scared." Maybe that's the reason I didn't have any trouble. I never did have a trial, I had a grand jury vote to bill me once and I got kinda underground wind of it and I pulled a few strings that night and the next day they voted that maybe they didn't have enough evidence for conviction and believed they'd throw it out.

I had a winter-time spot and a summer-time spot. I'd move in a little paddle boat at night and haul a little at a time. I'd move as I was making a run and as the barrel would get empty, I would put it over into my little paddle boat and move the whole outfit over a half mile or so to another platform and set it up on the platform and then when I drained the cooker I'd drain some of that hot fluid out in the boat and just use it for a tanker, and paddle over to this other place and pour it in. So when the next run come off, I was moved. I moved sorta while under operation.

People would get their stills tore up—I never had one tore up. People would get brazen and put it out in an open spot and let it get found and, of course they had to tear them up. They didn't refuse to tear them up. To satisfy the Christian Temperance Union and the bootleggers, too—they had to have both sides make a showing. It still goes on that way everywhere now—you scratch my back and I'll scratch yours, though I never did scratch many backs. I figured if it got to where I had to obligate myself, I'd just do something else, but there wasn't anything much else to do then.

Toggling, Railroading and Fourteen Other Occupations

by George McCants

In 1895 my oldest brother and I bought a nice farm about three miles north of Chatfield. Most of the family had already married or gone out to make a fortune on their own. There were only my mother, brother Walter, sister Fannie Lee, twin sisters Nellie and Winifred, and I left at home.

In the winter of 1896, after we had gathered our crop, we had an opportunity to trade our farm for a hotel in Rice, a town about six miles from Chatfield. We moved to Rice and took charge of the hotel. As I didn't have anything to do, I went with a friend who said there was lots of cotton to pick in Dallas County—we took the train to Wilmer, a small town near Dallas. Sure enough there was lots of cotton there and we had no trouble getting a place to room and board, and pay of 40 cents per hundred pounds. We stayed until all the cotton was picked and, as it was nearly Christmas, we went back to Rice on the train.

After this, another man and I contracted to load cotton from the wharf onto flat cars and into box cars at the price of 15 cents per bale, also to load cottonseed into box cars from the warehouse for 15 cents per ton. This was very poor pay for so much heavy, hard work but wages were very low then.

My next work was building bridges and grading roads for Navarro County for about two years. This also was very hard work and required camping in tents near streams such as creeks and rivers, with exposure to all kinds of weather. Once we were camped near a creek across which we were building a bridge and it rained for three days and nights causing the creek to overflow the channel and run through our tents. So we took our tents down and loaded everything onto wagons, but our bedding and all got wet before we could get the "tarps" on.

We had a crew of seven men and we had to load two road-grading machines, large plows and other equipment into two wagons. By the time we were ready to go, the water was running over the tops of our rubber boots. We had four mules to each wagon and four to the grading machine. We had four small mules and we put them in front so if the water got too deep they could swim if they had to. We had to cross a slough before we could get out of the low land and, sure enough, the mules had to swim! We spent the night in a small country school house, built a fire in the stove to dry our clothing and had only crackers for supper.

We were building a suspension bridge across the Trinity River at a point known as Porter's Bluff. A ferry boat had operated at this place for a long time as this had been a Stage Coach route. When the bridge was completed the ferry would be out of business.

The ferry boat had to make long trips from shore to shore (a distance of about a mile and a half) and the man in charge gave me a job helping him run the boat, which was very nice for me. During stagecoach days there had been a town on the high side of the river but it was completely destroyed by a flood in 1867 and was never rebuilt.

Then I worked for a season at the largest cotton gin in the world which was in Corsicana and was owned by a man named Scales. It consisted of one engine large enough to pull twenty-five saw gin stands, four double box square presses, and two round bale presses. It required two men at each press, and I worked at one of the round bale presses. Five bales of cotton were ginned every thirteen minutes and the entire machinery was pulled by one belt from the engine.

From the job, I went to work for an oil well drilling company owned by two men named Lowery and Winn who were drilling wells in the Corsicana oil field. The first well was discovered accidentally when the city was drilling an artesian water well and struck oil—that was the first oil well in Texas!

We had a tent camp in the oil field and there were seven in our crew. We agreed that one of us should stay in camp each weekend to take care of things. It happened that the weekend that I was to take care of the camp, the worst storm ever to strike Galveston occurred—this was on October 8, 1900. However, when the rest of the crew left to go into Corsicana for the weekend, we knew nothing about the storm.

About eight o'clock that night, the storm struck the camp and it is useless to try to describe what a time I had trying to keep the three tents from blowing down! Finally two tents blew away, but I managed to keep one staked down and it withstood the fury of the awful blasts of rain driven by the wind, lightening and thunder. Oil well derricks were being blown down all around me—seventeen were blown down—in fact the only one that stood was the one we were drilling and the reason it didn't go was that the driller had left the string of the casing and drilling bit all suspended to the toggle block on the top of the derrick.

I stayed with the camp all of Saturday and up until about 2 p.m. Sunday, not having slept any all night or all day. There was a little country school house about a half mile away and, as the tent was flapping and popping in the wind and rain, I decided to go to the school house for the rest of the day. By night the storm was about over so I returned to camp and slept, as I was completely exhausted—worn to a frazzle—just pooped!

The company decided to move their machinery to Spindletop, which was about nine miles south of Beaumont but I didn't stay there very long as I thought it too dangerous because the wells were too close together.

Some of the companies would build as many as twelve derricks in a row and after the first one was built they would start another so close to it they would let one set of the foundation rest on the ground and the other rest on the first derrick about twenty feet high. I saw one row of twelve derricks all drilling at once and they had twelve boilers lined up close by—one for each well being drilled. There were many companies drilling and each was trying to get as much oil and gas as they could while the getting was good!

Ever so often a well would be blown up—when they struck an extra pocket of gas, it would blow the casing out through the top of the derrick and the casing would break into pieces in the air and fall, some landing end-wise and some falling flat.

I was working as a derrick man and my place was seventy feet high in the derrick—I was known as the toggle man. So altogether, I decided the danger was too great for me, so I went to the foreman and resigned after explaining to him my reasons for doing so.

Some months later, I went to the Indian Territory seeking a job with McCabe & Stein, Contractors, who had their main office in St. Louis, Mo. They were advertising for men to work on the construction of a railroad to be built from Ashdown, Arkansas to Ardmore, Indian Territory. Since I was experienced, I secured a job with a pile driving crew which was camped on the Washita River.

That was the year of 1901 and my pay was $2.75 per day—I had one of the best paying jobs in the crew. I also received my board and the meals were well balanced and very good—we had a good cook. The working hours were from 7 a.m. until 5 p.m. I worked with this crew of twelve men for about a year, and while I was there, not one of the men was sick or injured!

The Railroad Company that was having the road built had a man who boarded with us and who recorded the penetration measurement of each piling driven. The company paid so much per foot or fraction thereof. The Indian Territory was controlled by the Federal Government and whiskey was prohibited. Therefore the field was good for bootleggers and moonshiners.

There were places all along the roads where anyone could get moonshine whiskey—such places as a hollow stump or a hollow tree where you could go and put your money for a quart or more. Then you could come back in about a half hour and your whiskey would be there!

There was also a bootlegger that came to our camp regularly at 9 o'clock on certain nights each week selling Old Crow liquor for $2.00 per quart. This same liquor could be bought in Texas at such towns as Texarkana, Paris, Denison and Wichita Falls for $1.00 per quart!

This bootlegger always rode a large black horse with leather saddlebags in which he could carry about sixty quarts. His signal to let the men know he was coming was to fire three shots from his 45 Colt pistol so they could have their money ready. He had a Colt 45 in a scabbard and a 30-30 rifle across the saddle between himself and the saddle horn. He wore a black scarf over his nose and mouth and he would ride up and stop under a large tree. Each one who wanted whiskey would tell him how many quarts and hand him the money—he would examine it to see if it was genuine and the right amount before he would hand over the whiskey.

Well, the recorder in our camp was his best customer—he always tried to buy enough each time to last until the bootleggers came again. He stayed drunk almost all of the time and the foreman of our crew would record for him. So whenever we would get a pile driven down to where it didn't go much when the 4000 pound hammer would drop 48 feet, the foreman would cut the pile off, roll the piece into the river, and record it as that many more feet than was actually driven! That was where one rascal took advantage of the other and made an easy profit for his contracting company.

We were paid twice a month—on the first and the fifteenth—and about two days after payday the recorder would be flat broke as they would all shoot craps each night in our bedroom tent until the foreman and his assistant would have all of the money from all who joined in the dice game. Each Saturday night the foreman and his assistant would go to the closest point in Texas where whiskey could be bought and return Sunday night "broke." I was the only one in camp who had any money and I had to stake them each time the bootlegger came until next payday.

After the men had lost all their money, they would use tobacco as stakes in the dice game—Bull Durham, Duke's Mixture, plug tobacco, and Old Virginia Twist—which they could buy from the Commissary on credit. I have seen the winner of the crap game have a large tub full of tobacco which he would put in the Commissary for safe keeping. The next night he would get his tub and stake all who wanted to get in the crap game and they would give him I.O.U.'s which would be paid by the company at the next payday.

There were contractor camps every five miles the full distance of the railroad camp being built. Each contractor had a camp for his laborers—men and women—and each camp had a table about 50 or 60 feet long and four or five feet wide, with a 1x6 board up on each side to keep the dice from falling off. Above the table was a string of electric light bulbs running the full length of the table.

There was always a game with men and women standing on both sides of the table shooting dice and, now and then, there would be a fight. Sometimes one would catch another cheating in the game and other times one man would get mad at another for trying to take his woman away from him.

Just take into consideration all the camps and the number of people being paid twice a month, and the moonshiners and the bootleggers cashing in on them! It was really a wild life in wild territory.

Once we were camped in a small town by the name of Madill— we were on the railroad right-of-way near the depot which had been built before the railroad was completed. The first night it began to rain so we all retired about 9 o'clock. About 2 o'clock I woke up and heard water running under my bed—so I got up to see what was wrong and stepped into water about knee deep!

The water was very swift so I sounded an alarm. You can imagine eight men in two tents without lights trying to get enough clothes to put on so we could get outside. The foreman said we had better go to the hotel for the rest of the night so we all took our Gladstones, valises and grips and started. We waded in water up to our shoulders with our grips on our heads—don't you wonder what the night clerk thought when we walked in? He must have thought he was having a nightmare or something worse! We lost a lot of our clothes and all of the groceries, but our tents were not washed away.

The next contract was in Texas for the Texas and New Orleans Railroad in January, 1903. When the work was completed, I heard that the Pacific Express Company was looking for a man.

I had no trouble securing the job which was meeting all trains, delivering express from the city office to the trains and picking up incoming express and delivering it to the office. I also delivered express to various places in the city and picked up all outgoing express and delivered it to the office.

I was courting my sweetheart of sweet sixteen, Sadie Hodge, who lived at Chatfield, and I had a special black horse and buggy at the livery stable engaged for the fourth Sunday of each month. I would go to Chatfield, spend the day with my mother and family, and take Sadie out for a drive.

There was always lots to do with all the friends and acquaintances— never a dull moment! Usually I spent the entire afternoon and evening with Sadie—until midnight. Then I would go back to see my mother and visit with her until 2 a.m. Then I would get in the buggy, buckle the lines together and put them around my neck, hook one arm around the rod at the side of the seat and that little horse would go like a blue streak to Corsicana. There they would wake me up at the livery stable about 3:30 a.m. and I would take the express horse and truck and take off to meet the 4 o'clock train, get the express and take it to the office. Then I would go to the boarding house for breakfast and then I was ready for the day's work!

This went on for about eighteen months and then I was promoted to Express and Baggage Master from Corsicana to Hillsboro, which is a branch road of the Cotton Belt Railroad (which ran from Waco to Texarkana and on north to Memphis and Cairo.)

Leaving Corsicana at six p.m. I would arrive at Hillsboro at eight, spend the night, leave there at 7 a.m. and get back to Corsicana at 9 a.m. Then I had the rest of the day with nothing to do, so I would visit various stores and banks, or stand around on the street corners and visit with friends. Having worked for four years building roads and bridges all over the county, I knew a great many influential people, and of course they all came to Corsicana sooner or later, so I was never bored. Then too, Sadie would come to town to visit an aunt and since I didn't want her to be lonesome, I would naturally visit there also!

Soon after I started on this railroad job, I met some young people in Hillsboro. Pretty soon they would all meet the train and escort me to the express office and, after I had checked my run of business in to the agent, we would have an evening of fun.

Well I soon learned that with every night at Hillsboro and every day in Corsicana, I was burning the candle at both ends so I had to put out some of the fire! I asked the company to give me a run on the main line from Waco to Texarkana and they did just that and I left without letting anyone know what had happened or where I had gone.

As Baggage and Express Messenger of the run to Texarkana, I handled all the baggage of the passengers and all the collections of money for tickets and prepaid express by each agent from Waco to Texarkana. Consequently I always had a lot of cash by the time I reached Texarkana, but, fortunately, I was never robbed.

One of our men was robbed and almost lost his life. The last station before Texarkana was Redwater, about twelve miles distance, and each agent had to close his day's business and be ready to check off his entire collections of baggage and express to another agent at Texarkana. As he began to get ready to check everything over at Redwater, he opened the stationery safe to transfer the money into his portable safe and he was hit on the back of the head by a man who had gotten into the car with a key. They fought from one end of the car to the other—there was blood in the safe, on the floor and the walls—and finally the robber opened a side door and threw the express man out.

When the train rolled into the station at Texarkana and no one came to open the baggage car, the porter unlocked the back door and discovered what had happened. So the train crew took an engine and one car and went back to look for the express man. However, some men who worked on a section of the railroad about three miles from Redwater were on a handcar going into town for supplies and saw the injured man. They picked him up and took him into Redwater. Pretty soon the crew arrived and took him to the railroad hospital in Texarkana where he was taken care of and was able to go back on his run in about a month.

The conductor of the train thought the robber was a porter who had worked for the railroad but was no longer with the company. A man who was a passenger in the first coach told of seeing a man come through the car with a valise and said he lay down on the floor between the coach and the baggage car so he could see underneath the door. In this way, he could watch the express man as he took the money out of the safe. He had a key so he opened the door and went into the baggage car. The man later identified the robber after he was caught by two detectives who trailed him for two weeks. They caught him spending some of the stolen money at Laredo, Texas, as he was getting ready to go into Mexico. He was convicted and sent to prison for 99 years.

After the robbery, the company sent a cab for me and I had to take the express man's place on the run back to Waco—not a very pleasant trip in a blood splattered car! I spent the night in Waco and on the trip back to Texarkana I was carrying $350 cash in my pocketbook, $150 of which I had collected for a fellow worker. As I was winding up my day's work near Redwater I turned a trunk on end to put my keys, pocket knife, change and purse on while I changed clothes. As I was in a hurry, I didn't notice that my purse must have shaken off the trunk; anyway, I checked my run over to the other expressman and got off the train. I didn't miss the purse until the man for whom I had collected the $150 came in from his run and I said "I'm sure glad to see you so I can pay you and get that much out of my pocket."

So I went to the station agent and wired the man that I had checked over to and asked him to look on the floor and get my purse. He wrote from St. Louis saying that he had looked the entire car over after it was unloaded but could not find my purse. I believe to this day that he got the money because he had just told me a few days before that he had been sick and had some bills past due. I saw him six weeks later and finally cornered him—he said he was sorry for my loss and that he had done his best to find my purse and I am sure he did!

This happened about a month before I was to be married and I almost had to marry on a credit plan. But I never asked my Sadie to wait and we married on the date appointed—I just had to dig deeper into my savings to pay the man the $150. If I had it all to do over again I would still marry my Sadie!

On June 6, 1906, Sadie and I were married. We made our first home in Texarkana which was my headquarters. At that time I was depot Express Agent with sixty-five express messengers under my supervision. My work was to see that each train leaving Texarkana had an express messenger on it. Each train had a regular messenger but if one had to be replaced because of sickness, etc., I had to get a man to take his place and that was what was termed "doubling back" as the substitute would be leaving 12 hours before his regular run.

Also I had to see that each messenger checked all the express that was to be loaded into his car before it left, plus check each train that came into Texarkana which did not terminate there. I also had the combinations of all of the stationary safes in the express cars and had to open each one so the money packages could be checked from the incoming messenger to the outgoing one. All of this had to be done on schedule as the trains only had thirty minutes in Texarkana. It really kept me rushing around to see that all was done and ready when the conductor said "all aboard!"

This was not my job permanently and, when the time came to accept or reject it as a permanent job, I went back to my regular one as a messenger on the road. The trains were hardly ever on time as the road-bed would get soft when it rained because there was no ballast beneath the cross ties which held up the rails and the engineer would have to run the train slow to keep from wrecking it.

One time after I was married I remember that I left home at 6 o'clock one morning to go to Fort Worth—this was in the month of May, 1908—and it was raining and had been for several days. All rivers were overflowing and when we had gone about 70 miles to the town of Jefferson we had to stop as a bridge had been washed out between there and the next town, Marshall. There were three trains loaded with people stranded in Jefferson and we couldn't telegraph or telephone anywhere, as all lines were down on both sides of town. Twice a day all the people had to go about a mile from the depot to get something to eat. A few of us had all we could do to take care of everything.

After that I took a vacation for two weeks and Sadie and I went back to Chatfield to visit our families. While we were there, Sadie's father who had a blacksmith and wood shop made me an offer to go to work in his shop, learn the trade, then he would sell the shop to me and he would move to Rice and run a shop there.

So I wrote the Agent at Texarkana and asked for a leave of absence. They held my job for me for four months before I decided to buy the shop. I received a nice letter from the headquarters of the Express Company at St. Louis, Missouri, stating that they were sorry to lose me, but wishing me well in my new business.

"Eye as a camera, ear as a trumpet, brain as a warehouse. Sit straight. Grow like the pine tree grows." (photo by Mary Sherwood)

Tonk-Wonda
(Sioux: one who tells history, storyteller)

by Jamie Frucht

Chief William Red Fox is 105 years old. So much age might act like a gauze screen, isolating, softening the Chief's existence. But Chief Red Rox is not remote. He is as pungent as his cigar, and his voice is a traveling theater of infinite memories.

His age is not visible. His face wouldn't remind you of 105, nor his mind. Only his jaw, lacking any teeth, gives a clue of his age, and it's a false clue. It was not age, but a bronc in Buffalo Bill's circus, that took his teeth. "One day a bronc shook hands with me, smacked me in the jaw, and broke out almost all my lower teeth. I got false teeth, but I didn't have a good gum there to keep them in place, so they kept sort of sliding around in my mouth. So one day on a train to Kansas City, my teeth slipped around and pinched my jaw, and I took them out of my mouth and threw them out the train window."

That was in 1924, when Chief Red Fox was 54 years old.

It would be wrong to typecast the Chief as a very old Indian. He is above and beyond 105. In life, he's played so many roles—student, sailor, actor, teacher, writer. He is a traveler nonpareil who was "on the road" for 101 years, criss-crossing America and the world. He is a man who did not gather roots, and yet all of America was his home at one time or another. He knows the innkeepers of each city intimately, having stayed at the hotels off and on over many generations. His address book, indelibly committed to memory, has streets in all towns, friends in all places.

Where to dip into his worlds of experience?

An Oglala Sioux, he was born on a reservation on June 11, 1870, at Thunder Butte in the Dakota Territory. His mother was White Swan (New-Evaw). His grandfather was the original Crazy Horse, who was not a chief but a holy man of the Black Hills. After the grandfather's death, New-Evaw's brother, Little Curly took the name Crazy Horse and later became Chief and top warrior of the Battle of Little Big Horn.

Although there was no formal, enclosed school at the Pine Ridge Reservation, Indian families taught one another. Children learned from their grandparents about Indian customs and migrations. "We also learned how to care for those who cared for us when we were weak and they were strong."

Then too, history was not something remote in a textbook. The Indians were being engulfed and subdued by the history that the white race was writing. There was only a scattering of buffalo in the Black Hills but, unfortunately, there was a lot of gold in those hills. It was for the gold that the U.S. Government violated the treaty of 1868, which had upheld the Black Hills as the Holy Land of the Indians. The year of this Nation's centennial, 1876, was also the year of the great battle of the Little Big Horn Mountains, in which Custer was defeated. As a boy of six years and 14 days old, the Chief heard the guns of that battle. The tragedy of Wounded Knee had yet to be written.

At the age of seven, he was sent 200 miles away to a boarding school, the Fort Yates Indian school in the Standing Rock Reservation, returning only during the summers to the Indian's way of life. It was there that his Indian name To-Ka-Lu-Lu-Ta, meaning Red Fox, was exchanged for the name William.

After four years, when he was 11, he went to the first government Indian school at Carlisle, Pennsylvania. There were no appropriations for Indian education, but the Civil War Arsenal was converted into a school. (Afterwards, it reverted to its military origins and became a War College to train military police.) At Carlisle, they cut off Red Fox's long hair and outfitted him in white man's clothes and shoes that hurt his feet. Before, Red Fox had only known moccasins which cooperated with his feet. There, Indian children from all the tribes learned the ways and history of the white man. The Indians had their sign language, a superior **Esperanto**, and could communicate in spite of the diversity of languages. It was his experience at Carlisle that gave the Chief the "credentials," the familiarity with white man's ways, to go on and take an active role as liaison between Indians and the white race. (For example, when he was 21, he went to Washington for two years as an interpreter for the Bureau of Indian Affairs.)

During his years at Carlisle, he spent the summers as a hand on sailing ships, square-riggers. His was not a sit-still geography lesson. "I've been around the whole world—from the Seas of Gaspar to the China Seas. I've been five times around Cape Horn, coming, not going—going you have headwinds—you've got the tradewinds coming this way. We go by the Cape of Good Hope, we go to 44 degrees south of the equator, and we go up to 105 degrees longitude. And of course, south latitude, you go through the Straits between Java and Sumatra, to get into the China Seas."

The Chief credits his travels on the sea as his real education. "I got a better education going to sea than I did going to school."

At 14, he ran away from school to become a cabin-hand on a four-mast burkentine named Josephine. A seaman's life was not lucrative—he made $9 a month—and that salary got swallowed up by the supplies the sailors had to buy from the captain. The captain had quite a racket—two pair of socks for 10 cents; overalls 50 cents; plus oilskins and boots. Sailors would sign on for about 15 months of hard work and rough seas. Since there were no longshoremen's unions and no stevedores, the seamen had to unload all their own cargo.

The life of a seaman was just as dangerous on land as on sea. By the time the sailor got to port after a year, there was a good chance he'd blow his remaining salary in a bar. Some of those bars were built on piers that had trap doors. Unscrupulous people would roll the unsuspecting and drunk sailors. They would shanghai them in those bars above the piers by dropping them down the trap door and taking them out to a sailing ship that had such a tough name, no one with any common sense would go aboard, willingly or sober. Often the crew would be made up of farmers and bums off the street who'd wake up the next morning going down the Chesapeake Bay with a tug boat at heel.

Despite the risks, Chief Red Fox was enchanted by the sea. As a second mate on a packet steamer on a run between Alaska and Pacific coast ports, he struck up a conversation with a writer in a San Francisco bar. Over some beers, the man learned about the life of a seaman from one who knew. The writer's name was Jack London, and the Chief must have given him enough stories to fill a notebook or two. The two of them were kindred spirits, both accumulating the experiences of a life's worth of travel.

The Chief, like his Sioux tribe, is a supreme traveler. Hand-in-hand with his travels goes a superb memory—able to go long distances (back to the 1870's) or short distances, remembering everything. The expression "it slipped my mind" is alien to the Chief. He deserves a Nobel Prize for memory.

"God gave us (the Indians) that memory because, you see, we didn't have a pencil and paper, we didn't have any signs to put up—10 miles to here and 10 miles to there. We had to cross the plains, we had to remember this butte, this ravine, had to know directions by moon and stars. It's very artificial, what most people do today—use a pencil and paper. If they didn't, they wouldn't know what groceries to get."

Memory was a way to develop yourself, and the Chief stretched memory as far as it would go. His is a geographic memory that locates places exactly. And so, 96 years after he went to Carlisle, he still can pinpoint it as "about 25 miles from Harrisburg and about 35 miles from Hagerstown, Maryland." You don't need a dictionary to follow the Chief, you need an atlas.

The Chief's "I used to's" go a lot farther back than most people's. His 105 years give him a higher vantage point. He has seen the 'before and after' of great inventions—the first telephone, the first railroad. Also the 'before and after' of lives changing, cities growing, prices soaring. He is an everyman's archives, but unlike sealed, sleeping archives, his is a fluid, living presentation, available for the asking.

When Colonel William Frederick Cody (alias Buffalo Bill) came in 1893 to the Pine Ridge Reservation to recruit Indians for his Wild West Show, one hundred and twenty Sioux Indians from the Pine Ridge Reservation signed up. Thus Chief Red Fox embarked on one of his great adventures and opportunities. He traveled throughout the U.S. and Canada and visited Europe, acting as an interpreter and performer. Through the show, he met great men—McKinley, Edison, Bell. Teddy Roosevelt came backstage at Madison Square Garden and spoke to the Chief.

The Burlington Railroad took the show to the World's Fair in Chicago. The railroads, Burlington, B & O, Erie, became as familiar as horses, real companions. The Chief bedded down with them; they rocked him to sleep. He experienced early morning towns on them.

In those days, towns built to the railroads and railroads built to the towns. They courted each other like lovers.

The Chief can close his eyes and be lulled back to the memory of the train's rhythm. "Here I am in my roomette with my pajamas on and my slippers on and I'm going through town after town. I remember them, you know, going through—and how happy it was. Hearing the

wheels on that train—bu-bu-bu-bu-woo-woo-woo. Ding-ding-ding—
hearing those old bells ring at the crossings and people waving and we
with the circuses—in our rooms with curtains. And I think of those
things. . .The Arlington Car on the 101 Ranch had an old flat wheel
and until we could get that flat wheel fixed, I think about how many
a night it'd go kapop-kapop-kapop—kapop you to sleep, you know.
Yeah. Wake up in the morning and you were in another town. Those
beautiful, beautiful old days of traveling was fine."

Chief Red Fox also experienced the late night towns. He got to know
Baltimore when her boundary lines were Fulton, Broadway, and North
Avenue; before, like a matron, she began to spread—35 to 40 miles
into her county.

While the Wild West Show was in Baltimore, for a little extra money
on the side, the Chief broke horses for the streetcars of Baltimore.
"We'd get $5 apiece for riding those broncs and getting 'em calmed
down. Then, when they were broken, we'd hook 'em up with an old
horse to a street car and drive 'em through the town from midnight to
5 a.m."

None of the historians in 1894 were riding Baltimore's streetcars in
the early morning hours, but the Chief was, and remembers the quiet
of no-traffic streets, where occasionally you'd see a railroad man going
to work.

"Only thing you found in those streets about 4 o'clock were bakers
and milk wagons. In those days, individual farmers had customers for
their milk. The farmers had pint, quart and half-gallon measures
and had their milk kept up with ice, for there was no refrigeration, no
bottles or cartons. People put their pitchers out—little tin buckets."

The Chief remembers a dairy man, C. B. Wooden, telling him about
one of his drivers who tried to fool the customers after some cow had
kicked the bucket over. The driver didn't have quite enough milk to
serve his customers, so he laced the milk with some creek water. That
morning when a lady came out and opened the lid of her milk bucket—
splatter, splatter, splatter, she saw some minnows swimming around in
her milk." The Chief's not sure that story's true, but he enjoys the
possibility that it might be.

The Chief is a comparison shopper, comparing two centuries. (He
still shops today.) He reports that butter was better then, and you'd get
a good pound of steak for 15 cents. "I used to buy a whole hog for $5
fresh, 150 pounds worth. Now I pay $5 for two slices. Three fryers
went for $1. You got all the liver you wanted for your cats and dogs.
Good soup bones too, with lots of marrow. Gold Medal flour came in
barrels. Corn was 15 to 18 cents a bushel."

Hotels courted theatrical people in those days of vaudeville and
theater, giving performers special theatrical rates. "For two and a half
dollars a day we thought we lived in luxury." In 1924, when the Chief
was working in the Criterion in New York, he stayed at the Waldorf
Astoria for $5, including three meals a day. The Algonquin, especially,
had a lot of professional performers living there. The hotels are still
in the city, unchanged. But the prices of $5 and $2.50 are gone forever.

"Like I told the manager at the Algonquin, last time I stayed in

New York, 'Geez,' I said, 'I like to broke my neck this morning.' 'You did?' he says. 'You can look at the records from before you was ever here,' I said. 'I had that exact room, that hole was in that rug, but I didn't recognize it until I got out of the shower and my big toe got caught in it. And now you're charging me $18 a day for that lousy room that I used to get for $2.' ''

Another price increase that riles the Chief is doctors in general and opticians in particular. It was cheaper to see in the old days. The Chief says, "Biggest graft in the world is eye doctors. Men used to come to country towns. Farmers would have their eyes examined with a card, then go down to the 5-and-10 cent store and buy their glasses. Here I've got a pair of those glasses I bought for $1 and I can see everything in them, better than with my $40 pair."

Of all the famous people the Chief met, his favorite was Will Rogers, who was with the circus for a brief spell before the Ziegfeld Follies grabbed him and his lariat and lingo act. Will Rogers, who was part Cherokee, made it more acceptable to claim Indian blood. The Chief recalls asking him once how big a part of him was Indian. Will Rogers replied, "An eighth or thereabouts, but one drop would set me to braggin'!"

The Chief hoboed with the "Cherokee Kid" on the way to a rodeo in Johnson City near Binghamton, New York. "There were crooked judges. He and I were the tops in those days with the lariat and horse catching. Lots of Mexicans were good, too, but they never got on the circuit like we did. I remember we only had $35 when we got into town. We paid $15 apiece to enter the rodeo. That left $5 between us. A room was a dollar and a half. And in those days you could get a good breakfast, two buns and a cup of coffee, for a nickel.

"At the rodeo I caught four horses and did the Texas cartwheel and Will was even better, but the judges robbed us. Gave the prizes to their native sons. Will says, 'We're in an awful fix.' We put our ropes and stuff in brown sacks and piled on the freight train. We called it the 'side-door pullman.' Well, at Elmira, the brakeman who knew us said, 'We'll be here an hour, fellows.'

"Geez, we were both hungry, so we went up and knocked on a lady's door. Will did the talking: 'Good morning, Madam. Would you give an Indian and a cowboy something to eat? We're not hobos, we've been at the rodeo up here and we didn't get any money.'

"The woman said, 'I wouldn't give it to you for your sake, or for my sake, but I'll give you something to eat for the Lord's sake.'

"She went in the house and came out with a big newspaper, all doubled up. And you know, Will always wore his hat on the side and he looked sideways as he opened the newspaper and said, 'Mum'—he didn't say M'am, he talked as Oklahoma boys do—'yes, mum'— 'Mum, **whose** sake did you give us this for?'

"And the lady said, 'Not for your sake, not for my sake, but for the Lord's sake.'

"So Will said, 'Then, mum, for God's sake, put something between the bread.' ''

In 1898 during the Spanish-American War, the Chief left the circus to join the U.S. Navy. With the Pacific Fleet, he went to China, Japan and the Philippines. He was discharged from the Navy in 1902 and came back to the show in 1903. In 1904, Buffalo Bill took his show to Europe for four years. The show played in all the large cities in Europe, and in England, Scotland, Ireland and Wales. As a finale for the opening night of the London Show, there was a mock stage holdup with Chief Red Fox tomahawking the King of England, Edward the Seventh.

Although this was just "show business" there was some justice to an Indian scalping an Englishman with a tomahawk, since both the name tomahawk and the practice of scalping were of English origin. According to the Chief, during the French and Indian Wars, One-Patch Hamilton had told Red Jacket and Corn Planter to organize the Mohawk and Iroquois Indians for the British side. For every lock of a Frenchman's hair and button off a Frenchman's coat, the English would give the Indians a sovereign (coin). The French turned around and enlisted the aid of the Mohegans and Hurons. And now Chief Red Fox got to "scalp" a real Sovereign.

While in England, the Chief visited the grave of Pocahontas, the first American to become an English lady—Lady Rebecca. At her grave at Crews, the grey-haired custodian took his hat off to the Indian and said, "The only true Americans, all the rest of them are citizens."

When American history comes back at you from the Indian's perspective, it is different from the historical pablum force-fed to schoolchildren.

The Chief's version of the Pocahontas story goes like this: Pocahontas was the 32nd child of Powhatan who had befriended the English when they first came to Jamestown. She was 13 at the time the English came, and visited their boat where she met John Smith and fell in love. After a mutiny, John Smith was thrown off the boat and had to live in the wild with the help of the Indians. The good feelings between the Indians and English were vanishing as the Indians realized the extent of the Englishmen's selfishness and their intention of taking over the Indians' land.

The Chickahominy Indians captured Smith and were about to kill him. Pocahontas interceded with her father. However, Powhatan could not persuade the Chief of the Chickahominy Indians, and the ax was lifted above Smith's head. (This is when the American schoolchildren come in on the story.) Pocahontas flings her body across Smith's, thereby saving his life, and by this inspiring and historic act, restoring friendship to the two races. (That's where the American schoolchildren leave the story.)

Smith returns to England and hostilities begin again. The commander in charge of Jamestown decides the only solution is to kidnap Pocahontas, which he does, luring her onto a ship and keeping her there as a hostage for a year to bring the Indians to terms while peace negotiations proceed. While on board, John Rolfe falls in love with the Indian. She asks about John Smith, and Rolfe tells her Smith is dead. She then marries John Rolfe and converts to Christianity. She is christened Rebecca.

The next year Rolfe and Pocahontas sail for England where she is accepted at the court of King James and elevated to Lady Rebecca. While at the court, she comes face to face with John Smith, whom she never ceased to love. Her husband tells her he lied to her about Smith's death "because I loved you as you loved him."

Pocahontas, meanwhile, is with child and gives birth to a son. She wants to return to her people in Virginia and pleads with her husband. He says, "You can go back to your red savages, but you won't take my son." The Queen intercedes with King James, but Rolfe will not relent about their son. While at Gravesend, awaiting transportation home on a sailing ship, she dies of smallpox on March 21, 1617, and is buried in the Church of England at Crews, the spot the Indians of Buffalo Bill's Wild West Show visited to pay homage.

The Chief tells how, years later, he was in a hotel lobby in Virginia, getting ready to address a Boy Scout meeting. Two ladies told him that a fashionable woman in the lobby was "the first American to become a Lady of England." The Chief said, "You mean that's Pocahontas?" Taken aback, they said, "No, Lady Astor." The Chief informed them they were mistaken about their American history. Lady Astor overheard the conversation and backed up the Chief's story. "The Indian is right. Pocahontas was named Lady Rebecca of England."

Upon his return from Europe, the Chief joined up with the 101 Ranch Wild West Show. In 1909, he was gored by a bull and had to take some time off. "I didn't figure there'd be any vaudeville or show for that winter." In Tacoma, he met a captain who said, "Come on Chief, come on over and sign up with me. This is the last trip for me and the last trip for my ship." So on the 4th of January, 1910, Chief Red Fox sailed around Cape Horn for the last time. Just off the Jersey coast, a northeast wind came up and held them offshore from the 1st of March until the 17th, when a tugboat picked them up. On St. Patrick's Day, 1910, they landed. And on that same day, the Chief took a train to Oklahoma to rejoin the 101.

The 101 Ranch Wild West Show wintered at Venice, California. There the Chief was scouted by Thomas J. Ince, a moving picture director, who was rounding up Indians and Mexicans to play in westerns. In the late teens, the movie companies were migrating from Chicago, the capital of the moving picture industry, to the cheaper and uncluttered properties of Los Angeles and its environs. The transplant was successful.

"We leased all of the horses and wagons, got redwood slabs off of big trees to make a stockade." With Ince he made one-reelers which took only three days to film, if the weather held. **War on the Plains** was the first picture Red Fox was in. Then he went to Chicago with the Selig Studios and did nine pictures with Bronco Billy (Gilbert Anderson).

With Warner Brothers he made **Daughters of the Tribe, Toll of the Warpath, Red Fox and Wild Flower, Perils of the Plains**, and **Medicine Boy**. While not in a starring role, Red Fox was more than just a face in the crowd. Chief Red Fox never became a movie star. He did appear in **Desert Gold** with William Powell and **Wild Horse Massacre** with Jack Holt. In **The Round Up**, Red Fox's name finally made the billboard along with Slim Hoover's.

In the movies he worked with "The Bison 101," and with William S. Hart in the Triangle Film Company. He played with all the old-timers—William Duncan, William Stowe, Bronco Billy, Jack Hartsick. "We got paid $35 a week and were glad to get it."

Chief Red Fox recalls the craziness of the movies. In the "biograph house," Hollywood "christened" its would-be stars with new names. You went in a Smith and came out a Pickford, as in Mary.

In **Under the Black Flag** (1920), the Chief played with Jessie James' son, who was supposed to jump off a boat and be rescued by Indians. The actor couldn't swim a stroke, so the studio built a platform and put boots on their star so he could stand on the platform and look like he was walking out of the water. Unfortunately he walked off the platform and fell into the water. Then the Chief had to rescue him in earnest.

"I grabbed him see, and put a blanket on him and he said, 'Gee ain't this water wet!' He meant cold—it was November. Luckily, it was no talkie. Anyway, we had a few tepees, lousy looking things that weren't the original, and he sat down by the fire and sat right on a hot coal and burnt a hole in my Indian blanket. I saw it and said, 'You got the seat of your britches burnt. You better get up.' "

The Chief appeared in **The Covered Wagon**, which was his most adventurous movie and took five months to make. He's most proud of having been in **The Vanishing American**, made in 1926 with Richard Dix and Malcolm McGregor, for it portrays the Indians' sacrifice in the first World War. The irony of the Chief's movie career is that, for the most part, Hollywood gave him the stereotype of the savage to play. The Chief has plans to direct his own picture, **The Rainbow Warrior**, about his Uncle Crazy Horse who defeated Custer. He thinks it would be better if people knew about the Indians who actually lived in this country, not the ones who lived only in the westerns.

In all, the Chief made 107 movies from 1910 to 1932, but he doesn't go to see movies. "Did you ever see a shoemaker watch another shoemaker tack on a heel? Then why should I go look at the heels, 'cause I was a heel myself."

Warner Brothers sent Chief Red Fox out on the road to promote **The Vanishing American.** The Chief, standing on stage with a young buffalo bull and an eagle, the three of them living symbols of vanishing Americans, would deliver the prologue to the movies. He opened in 1926 at the Criterion and on the tour hit all the big theaters—Hippodrome, The Loews Theaters—touring theaters in Cleveland, Zanesville, Ohio, Charleston, Baton Rouge, Shreveport, Lake Charles, Beaumont and Houston.

Until Al Jolson sang "Mammy" in Warner Brothers' **The Jazz Singer**, the company was going broke. During the difficult time before Warner Brothers succeeded with synchronized speech, many actors were suing them. The Chief didn't sue for salary. They gave him **Daughters of the Tribe** and **Toll of the Warpath** to furnish to various theaters for 50 percent of the box office take.

"I'd sell the films to big city theaters—Cincinnati, Detroit, Omaha, Kansas City—and also to the "sticks," as we called the circuit of little towns. I used to go up in the mountain country—places like Big Stone Gap, Appalachia. They all had a little old picture show. Sometimes I'd be ashamed to take their money. The commissaries were owned by the mining companies. And a man would come in and he was tired. He didn't want to go to no picture show and the commissary man would pull out a row of tickets, snap it off and drop it in the miner's basket and charge him for it. People don't know how bad off the miners were. They couldn't pick up and move since they owed everything to the mining companies. Those men were treated like slaves."

During his movie career, the Chief was also in vaudeville, working the Pantages, the Keith Albee Circuit, and all the "coffee and doughnut circuits." He worked from 1910 clear up to 1927, as a rope slinger, spinning his rope and jumping through.

There was a feeling of cameraderie among the actors on the vaudeville circuit. He numbered Sophie Tucker, George Raft and Bob Hope as his friends. He can remember when old Sophie Tucker, one of his favorites, got up on the piano. "She was pretty well schloshed and sang **Memphis Blues**. The Chief doesn't think any of the kids who sing today can touch her. He knew John Barrymore when he wasn't making but $25 a week. Chorus girls made $15 to $18 per week and the piano player a dollar a night. The money wasn't much, but the friendships were. "If someone died, we'd take up a collection to bury them." They took care of each other, for better or worse.

The Chief also worked for Wilson Company and Rath Packing Company, as a goodwill ambassador, and it was his picture they used as their emblem. Once more the job involved meeting people and traveling, going from country stores to big supermarkets throughout the country.

The Chief was steeped in vaudeville and he still delivers lines with a vaudeville beat. He can make complaints entertaining. He recalls how he and his friends would treat a bad cup of coffee. "We'd put the cup and saucer down on the floor. 'What are you doing with my cup and saucer down on the floor?' the owner would ask. 'Well your coffee's so weak we were afraid it would fall off the counter.' "

The Chief has his own version of the weak coffee **shtik**. When he gets a weak cup of coffee, he takes his handkerchief out and dabs his eyes.

"What's the matter?"

"I'm homesick; I'm homesick."

"What makes you homesick?"

"Your coffee."

(Pleased) "Oh? Why does my coffee make you homesick?"

(Even more pleased) "I live by the Gulf of Mexico, and this is pretty close to water."

At the height of vaudeville there were theaters in all the cities, and trains to take the performers there. "Railroads would send a dray to the hotel and move all your sets and luggage. You got a baggage car with 25 tickets. All you would have to say is 'I had a good trip on such and such a railroad that brought me in here.' " The competition brought out the best in all the companies. They outdid each other, fighting for customers. The passenger was always the winner. The system was called Free Enterprise.

Vaudeville created a kind of stamina in its performers—a vaudeville banter and resilience. "See, I'm a performer. I'm from the old school, we had good talent and we never called ourselves stars because star spelled backwards is R A T S."

Vaudeville was a temporary antidote and living for an Indian who had watched the Indian ways become extinct. Algonquins, Iroquois, Cheyenne, Arapahoes, Winnebagos, Osages—these are the names of the great stocks of Indians, beaten like third rate teams. "Cherokees, Chickasaws, Choctaws, Creeks, Seminoles, Pawnees, Shawnees, everyone of them was planted between 1820 and 1840 out there in Oklahoma in Indian territory—taken away from the east, sort of like cattle." Migrations toward extinction, the Trail of Tears, Wounded Knee.

The Chief never forgets his Indian heritage. Recently he became involved in the Congressional hearings about whether or not families of the victims of Wounded Knee should be compensated for loss of lives and property.

As though to dispel the image of the savage and to preserve the great contributions the Indians have made to the nation, the Chief lectured on the "Lost Chautauqua" circuit between movies in 1929 and 1930. In this circuit, out of Bloomington, Illinois, popular lectures, with the purpose to educate and entertain audiences which had gathered expressly for enlightenment, were delivered in tent-shows. It had some elements of evangelism, mixed with high ideas and culture. Its intent was serious, for the Chautauqua lived on ideas. The "Lost Chautauqua" was organized by Billy Sunday, a preacher, and Ruth Bryan, daughter of William Jennings Bryan.

Vaudeville and the Chautauqua were totally different presentations and entertainments. And the Chief sometimes felt as if he weren't in the same league as the other educated speakers. He described it this way, "My tongue has never been clever in speech or subtle in repartee; nor was I endowed with the spiritualistic fervor that underlies evangelism." The Chief wore his Indian costume and that made up for any lack of eloquence. He tried to teach people about the Indians, for few knew as much as he did. The Indians had "published" on buckskin, using symbols. It was up to the Chief to edify and enlighten the people about the richness of Indian life. He was privy to Indian lore that couldn't be learned from books, and held his own, even with college-educated folks.

Billy Sunday, who was usually in a rush of salvation, "did stop long enough once to warn me about the weaknesses of all flesh, including mine, after he saw me smoking a cigar," recalls the Chief.

In his heyday, the Chief smoked 100 cigars a week. Cigars were the Chief's trademark; and he has claimed, with cigar in cheek, that they are his vitamin pills. He has always been on a kind of cigar crusade against those who would try to reform him, including his own doctor, who said, "Chief, you have so much nicotine in you, you won't wrinkle. They won't have to embalm you."

In Charlotte, North Carolina, the Chief was sitting with a judge in the lobby of a hotel, enjoying a fragrant cigar, when an indignant lady accosted him. She said, "I notice you've adopted a filthy, dirty, white man's habit."

The Chief said, "Beg your pardon, madam, what do you mean?"

"Smoking."

"You don't know your American history. The Indians taught the white man to smoke."

"Well," she said, "You'll burn in hell's fire, just like those ashes. Greatest sin on earth."

"There's a greater sin than that, madam."

She said, "What?"

The Chief said triumphantly, "Meddling in your neighbor's business!"

The Chief has never really stopped traveling on his own circuit. He's a one-man Chautauqua, talking to various groups, demonstrating Indian dances and ways on lectures throughout the U.S. On one of his speaking engagements, he was addressing two groups in a hall in Birmingham, Alabama—on one side the Rotary, on the other some real estate people.

The real estate people were feeling pretty good and began chanting, "Heap Big Chief, Scalp 'em, Scalp 'em." Composed, Chief Red Fox took the stage and said, "Thank you. Thank you, Gentlemen, for your greetings and hospitality. Now, Brothers, I want to ask you—who did the Indians scalp?"

The group answered, "Their enemies."

"Yes, sir," said the Chief, "We sure scalped our enemies. But by God, you real estate men skin your friends."

After that the "Big Chief" had no more humbug to contend with.

Although Chief Red Fox adapted completely to the white man's ways, he is not a camouflager. He proudly proclaims his Sioux heritage and being. On occasions when he lectures and dances he wears his eagle feathers, which have been in his headdress at least 50 years. "And I don't know how long the eagle had 'em before I got 'em."

As was the Indians' way, the eagle was trapped alive and released unharmed after a few of his feathers had been taken. The colors in the headdress are all symbolic. "The red is for blood; the white is snow; black means clouds; orange means sun; yellow is for the moon; green is the earth; light blue is the sky; dark blue stands for loyalty." America adopted the eagle as its symbol. The Indians relationship to the bird was even more personal.

In Missouri, on Route 70 near Columbia, Boonville and Rocheport, the Chief had an Indian trading post and owned part of the Peach Cafe. "I had a cabin. I built it out of logs. There weren't no cabins toward town when we built it. And I went to work just for pleasure, to entertain people—children—I didn't care about selling anything. But do you know, an eagle used to fly over my tepee every day, going to the Missouri River. I'd see him flying and I'd get out there and 'Hya-ho-ho-, Hya-ho-ho,' and you'd see him coming right to me. He'd fly about 100 feet from my tepee—a gold eagle.''

The Chief had pictures of himself on postcards, but didn't take any money for them, just asked people to drop contributions in a sealed box. "Give anything you want, but make it at least a dollar.'' After three years he gave the money in the box to the Cerebral Palsy Fund.

Lately he's taken his "Chautauqua" to the TV circuit, where on countless talk shows—Johnny Carson, Tom Snyder, Merv Griffin—he describes the Indians' life and his own. The transition from vaudeville to TV was easy. The Chief is a real trouper and knows how to perform. "When I was on TV, I never had to be reviewed. They knew anything that they snapped to me, I'd come right back.''

Writing was another outlet for expressing all he knew about the Indians. The Chief had years of preparation and many Big Chief notebooks of accumulated stories from the time he had traveled with the Wild West Show. Whenever the circus hit a town, he would take the opportunity, in between shows, to check with the library and old country stores to see if there were any Indians living in the area. If there were, he would go out to their farms and interview them. In this way, Chief Red Fox met many Indians, Geronimo among them, and learned about Indians' lives of all the tribes, not only the Sioux.

In **The Memoirs of Chief Red Fox**, 1971, McGraw-Hill Book Company, he's taken his "Chautauqua" into seven languages. The book details the Chief's life and the history and culture of the Indians. When he tried to go to London to promote his book, he found it was difficult for an Indian born in 1870 in Indian Territory to get a passport. The first time he'd gone abroad with the Wild West Show, there weren't any passport laws to fool with. The Chief explained his difficulty with the Feds at the Passport Office, using a little vaudevillian exaggeration.

"They wouldn't issue me any passport because I didn't have a birth certificate. Now remember, I was 19 years old when South Dakota became a state. They said, 'Don't you have your name in the Bible?' The Missionaries never gave us any Bible. They used to come down and sit around and eat the venison and quail and stuff like that what we had and they'd say, 'Hallelujah, glory be to God, thank you,' and away they would go. The hardest job they had to do was to keep away from the committee that was paying them a salary and sending them out there. My name in the Bible?—No.

"So they began to he-haw around, and I said, 'Give me that telephone, I paid for it.' So I called the Immigration Department, the head of it in Washington, his name was Johnson, and I said, 'Mr. Johnson, this is Chief William Red Fox. My ancestors was Immigration Officers before your ancestors came, but we let a lot of damned dumb ones in. Now send me my passport.' And I got it; but going down to the Immigration here—they he-hawed, he-hawed around like a bunch of children playing around, all passing the buck to one another.''

The Chief has always communicated with children, knowing that their ears are still young and hear few false echoes. In the last few years, the Chief has gone into Texas schools and spoken to the children. "Hello, boys and girls", he begins. "I'm going to tell you about the Indians. Now let us sit back in our seats. Right in this very city, but not this school building, when your mamas and papas and some of your teachers were little children just like you, I talked to them. And I remember them because, you know why? They kept their eyes open, their ears open, and their mouths closed. And I want to remember you as I do your parents."

He continues something like this: "Where you live today and play is where the Indians once lived and played. Many little girls and boys today love to play Indians and hear stories about the Indians, see them dance and sing. Some little girls and boys are afraid of Indians, but the Indians love little white children. The reason you are afraid is because you have heard some stories and have seen moving pictures that have made you afraid of them. The little Indian children were at one time afraid of the white men because they did not know them as you do not know the Indian. So let us be friends and learn to love each other. We are all Americans and love our country and our flag together."

And then the Chief dances for them, sings them lullabies and tells them stories. He shows them how the Indians walk and dance, using his own still-dancing body to demonstrate. "The Indian men dance like this; the buffalo dance is this way, the women dance another way, but the old grandma's can't lift their legs." And the Chief becomes the old grandma, dragging his feet and scrunching his face up, and soon the children are laughing.

Then he shows them a tom-tom.
The Chief: "And what is this?"
Children: "A drum."
The Chief: "No, that's not its name. Now Listen (starts to play it—tom-tom, tom-tom)
(Children listen)
The Chief: "What'd it say?"
Children: "Boom Boom."
The Chief: "No, listen—tom-tom."
Children: "Oh, tom-tom!"

He also teaches them about nutrition and safety:

"The big rock here, big uprooted tree here; the little Indian girl and boy that come to that big rock, come to that big tree, they stop; they look; they listen. Look for the red eyes of the bear, they play, safety first. Poor little white girl, poor little white boy, automobile here, automobile there, automobile coming, automobile going. Little white girl and boy, they don't stop; they don't look; they don't listen; they run. Mother cries, father cries, little child is hurt. Play safety-first, look for the red light, like the Indian looks for the red eyes of the bear."

He upgrades the show for the different ages: "This is how a tepee is built, these are the dance steps, these are the songs," he explains and demonstrates to the 2nd and 3rd graders.

For the big kids—4th, 5th, and 6th graders, he sits down and recites the stories; how the tepee came to be, for example:

"There was once an old man who had a problem to solve. His people were hunters, following the buffalo. And they didn't know how to provide themselves with shelter; they needed something to keep out the rain, snow and wind.

"The old man was sitting under a tree when an oak leaf floated down. He took the leaf and scrunched it into the ground, as the snow would, and it stood up. He told the women to sew together the hides using the pattern of the oak leaf. Nature had given the old man the solution—the tepee could easily travel with the Indians as they hunted the buffalo."

Thirty years ago, the Chief began putting together a children's book. The Chief's books have been written by hand. "I wrote a beautiful hand because when I went to school, if you didn't, those teachers would bust you across your knuckles with a ruler. This book is educational, no folk stuff. I want them to illustrate me standing in the center and children all around me. Beneath that it says, 'We're in the Council.' "

The Chief, with his own crayon drawings, details the great diversity in Indian culture, trying to simplify it for the children down to the least common denominator of wigwam and arrow. Every Indian nation had a different way to do things—even down to their moccasins. The variety of dwellings goes way beyond wigwam. He explains about longhouses, tepees, pueblos, and even shows the children how to cut out a tepee.

In his book, he explains about the different colors and different races of peoples:

"Some little girls and boys say when they see an Indian, 'Oh, he is not red; he isn't an Indian.' No Indian was the color red. When the white man came he called the Indians the red man or the red race, like you call yourself white, but you are not the color white. You are of the white race. There is also the yellow race which are the people of Asia, China and Japan. The Negro is known as the black race. Many are black, but many are brown and some are very light in color, but they are the black race. Now let us learn why we call the Indian red man. Many of the Indians painted their face and body with red clay, and the stain of bark of the tree or berries of the forest, so we are known as the red race. Some Indians are very dark and some are very light just like the white race. So don't be disappointed when you see an Indian for he will not be red."

He explains how the Indians named the different moons:

"In the long ago, the Indians had no calendar as we do now, so they used the moon for that. First the January snow moon, deep snow. February, the hungry thing or raccoon moon—that's when the animals would come out and eat and drink, then go back and go to sleep. The raccoon is the best furbearer. March, wild goose moon. That is when the wild geese return to the north. April, crow moon. The crow comes to the field. May, dogwood moon. The dogwood tree sends forth its bloom. June, the rose moon. That is when the wild roses bloom. July, corn moon. The Indians have fresh corn. August, the berry moon. The berries are ripe. September, the nut moon. The moon of the Indian summer. October moon, harvest moon, when they gather their crops. November, feast moon, the time they gather food and have their feast. December moon, long night sleep moon, longest night of the year."

He explains how and why the mother carried her baby on her back:

"The Indian mothers carry their babies on their backs. They call the carrier a woolapy, meaning cradle. A lot of little boys and girls say, 'Oh, I just would not want to be carried on my mother's back.' Let us find out why the Indians carry their babies that way. In a woolapy, the papoose was carried on the back because they only had one thing to ride, a canoe or dugout they were called. The Indians had a long way to walk at times and if they carried the papoose in their arms as your mamas, their arms would tire and they could not walk so far. When the papoose was carried on her back, the mother would not get tired and the papoose would not get sick. They would have sunshine and fresh air. Do you like fresh air and sunshine? The mother kept the papoose in the woolapy so if the enemy came she could pick it up and run. She would hang the woolapy on three poles like this or in a tree to keep the papoose from getting stung by ants or bitten by bugs or worms."

The Chief relates a Sioux fairy tale that all little Sioux Indian boys and girls were told when they were very young:

"When I was a little boy I would sit and listen to older people of my tribe. They told me the story of how the sunflower got its name. A long time ago there was a little Indian boy who loved the sunshine. He would always stand in one place and look to the smile of the Great Spirit. One day he was heard singing a song of the sunshine and the clouds. On days when it was dark and cloudy and the sun didn't shine, he was very sad; but when the sun was shining and the day was bright and clear, he would sing his song of the sun. He would run and stand in the same spot and look at the sun. He was happy again for the sun was shining and it was very bright. Because of his love for the sun they named him Standing Boy That Watches The Sun. As he grew older his eyes were growing very weak. One day he lost his sight and after he lost his eyesight he would go to the place where he always stood and would raise his head and sing to the sun, but everything around him was black. He would sing praises to the sun and the sunlight would shower on him in praise.

"One day after the sun had set in the west and day was gone he failed to return to his home. Ena, meaning mother, and Otang, meaning father, went to where they found him looking to the west. The spark of life had gone from him as the sun went from the sky. His mother and father buried him where he always stood to look at the sun. When the sun came in the sky the next day and all the people of his tribe came to pray and sing their songs to the Great Spirit that is God, they found a beautiful tall yellow and brown flower growing from his grave.—The place he had stood and looked at the sun. So that, my friends, is the way the sunflower got its name. It grows tall and slender and sometimes the blossoms are as large as plates. In the morning the flower is turned to the east and follows the sun across the sky, and as the sun sets in the west the flower is facing the west and the sunset."

This is just a sampling of the Chief's children's books. The children's book is bound to be a success because children will want to know the truth. The Chief has been collaborating with a young friend, Evelyn Silvertooth. He's going to let her get the royalities out of the book. "I don't want to be bothered with income tax no more."

At 105 the Chief's schedule is busy. When he was 100, he was afraid he was wasting his life sitting at home. As soon as his eyes improved from near blindness to long-distance vision, he started going, as he'd always done. The Chief knows you have to get out and do things and keep active. "I do my push-ups yet." He entertains in nursing homes, as well as giving demonstrations in the schools. Evelyn chauffeurs him to his various lectures throughout Texas. She says, "He's a prompt man with no time to waste. If you say eight, eight it is. He sits on the porch, hat in hand. He's ready to go."

While the Chief loves to visit the nursing homes, he wouldn't want to stay. "In nursing homes there's lots of groaning and grunting and dying." He prefers his shared existence with his fine dog, Jock. "He's 14 years old, he's my buddy and I take Jock lots of places, always did. One day, they were having a contest and the people was dancing the polka, and I grabbed old Jock, and he stood up and I went to swing him around and I almost fell on him."

Together, Jock and the Chief brave the Corpus Christi winds to take their walks. The Chief's been living in Corpus since 1932, when Corpus was just cotton fields. For the Chief, home was a stopping-off place between travels. Like an eagle, he was married for 60 years to one mate, Georgia, who also worked in the 101 circus. In her act, she could ride six horses at one time. In fact, the Chief and Georgia were married on horseback. She was part Cherokee and part Irish, with beautiful red hair and a temper that sometimes flaired. After she left the circus, she became a midwife and horse trainer. When Georgia died several years ago, the Chief became the "lone eagle."

The Chief has never stopped dancing or explaining. (He's been dancing for a hundred years.) "We hear the tom-tom; we keep rhythm with our feet. Now with the Indian women we circle, and we always dance from the east to the south, south to the west, west to the north, as the sun rises and sets. All of our homes, the tepees, the wickiups, the wigwams, the pueblos, whatever we live in, the door always faces east, to the rising of the sun, the beginning of day, like the beginning of life. And when we die, we bury the head to the east, and the feet to the west, because we fear not death. We do not die, our body goes to rest, but our soul goes on. And we dance to all those things, not to. . . .oh, like you see the war dance. That ain't before the war, it's after—the victory! Look what you did in 1918, the First World War, how everybody went crazy because it was over—dancing, singing, marching down the street—the same way the Second World War. But we dance the Victory Dance and the people think we dance that before we go to war—we'd be all out of wind! Wouldn't be able to fight the enemy."

The Chief would appear to have a secret fountain of youth and memory hidden somewhere in his modest house with its small vegetable garden. A salient thing about his garden is the mounds of cigar butts that seem to fertilize it and nurture the Chief. His appetite may also be a clue to his vitality. His love of food has not diminished over the years. Evelyn helps him with the marketing.

"I'm an expensive cook. My spaghetti sauce takes me $8 and all afternoon to make." He uses the very best olive oil and buys his steak and has it ground. He also makes wonderful fried chicken. "I've been in every crack and corner in Kentucky and I've never seen any chicken fried like that crazy Kentucky Fried Chicken, never with no batter. Now my chicken, I clean it well, wipe it dry, get a half pint of cream and soak the breasts and thighs, dip that in the pure cream and let the air dry it, then put flour in a sack and shake it. Get some fat and let the chicken simmer. Then you got some chicken."

His seafood gumbo is also a specialty, made with crabs, chicken, shrimp, flounder, oysters and stock from them. "People cook the seafood too long. You only want to cook the shrimp about 20 minutes." When he uses filé he remembers that it was the Indians who took the leaves off the sassafras tree and showed the settlers how to use the seasoning. "The white men have become millionaires on stuff that those people whom they called savages gave to the world—corn, beans, pumpkins, rutabagas, parsnips, turnips, asparagus." And so on and so forth—the Chief simmers in all of his knowledge.

The Chief is not a bitter man, just persistant and thorough. Occasionally a troublesome neighbor will complain of one thing or another. The Chief does not bother with grouchy people and gripes. "I just look at 'em and laugh to myself. 'Thank God, He hasn't made me that way.' Put the spirit of love behind what you're doing. I keep happy. If you're all the time frowning and complaining, you can't do your job. Success ain't to make millions. Lots of 'em that are millionaires, if their grandparents ain't left them a lot, they couldn't buy a loaf of bread. They ain't capable.''

The Chief has seen all kinds of people over the world. His exposure to different cultures has made him tolerant. He meets people one-to-one. ''There are good and bad in all races, and there are selfish people in all races, and the selfish one is the one who causes misunderstanding, causes hatred and puts a fear in the hearts of mankind.''

The Chief wishes that we could go back to a time when neighbors were neighbors and friends were friends. ''A woman would get sick, why, everyone would help her take care of her children; a farmer would get sick and we'd all pitch in and help to reap his crops. Today the great grandsons of those men who built the West and built Texas, now they say, 'Well, if you pay me a hundred dollars, I'll send you my combine over to help you cut the grain.' 'Sorry, why don't you have insurance to send your wife to the hospital?' ''

Religion, which can bring men closer to God can also, in practice, separate man from man. The Chief's religion is dominated by the Great Spirit and an accumulation of all his experiences. The Chief, who rode the railroads, borrows the trains to explain how religion is like a railroad system, where we all take different lines to the same destination.

''Well, say we're at the Mayflower Hotel in Washington, D.C., and I'm paying the cashier. And I pay her and turn around and you butt into me. 'Why Red Fox, I didn't know that you were here.' 'Neither did I, we could have had dinner together.' 'Where are you going?' 'I'm going to St. Louis.' 'So am I. I'm going to St. Louis.'

''So the bellhop takes your bag and puts it in a Yellow Cab, see. And we go down to Union Station and we split the fare; you pay 50 cents and I pay 50 cents. So we go in and we buy our tickets. And we walk to the gate and the man at the gate punches your ticket; he punches my ticket. I say, 'Why you're going on the B & O. Well, I'm not. I'm going on the Pennsylvania. You leave 15 minutes before I do.' So the bellhop goes to work and takes your grip and puts it in the train compartment and then he takes mine and puts mine in my roomette.

''And we sit on the observation deck and talk across the platform. Your train pulls out and goes by way of Cumberland, Parkersburg, Addison. But at Marion, Ohio, your train crosses mine because I go by the way of Baltimore, Harrisburg, Pittsburgh, Altoona and all those towns up in there. So when we get to Illinois, my train crosses yours and runs on the left-hand side, see. But when we get into St. Louis there's only one bridge across that great Mississippi River, and your train goes across 15 minutes ahead of me. But the same man pulls the switch and backs you into the berth at the depot where there are twenty-five tracks. And here I come and go over the same bridge and the same man pulls the switch, so I can back in there. Now if we don't derail on the journey, I'll meet you at the Statler Hotel down on Washington Street. But if we go in the ditch, like a lot of people is doing in religion, we won't meet each other there.''

"And we always dance from the east to the south, south to the west, west to the north, as the sun rises and sets."

On February 6th, 1976, 1700 schoolchildren were waiting in Brownsville to see the Chief in their school. He had to disappoint the children, for he entered the hospital, a gravely ill man. He had every intention of getting well and told his friend, Evelyn, "Go tell the principal I can't make it, but I'll be back in two weeks."

In his other previous hospital visit, a few years before, when he had spilled hot grease on his foot, he had ended up entertaining the patients. But this visit was different. He tried home remedies—boiled onions and honey, graveyard soup with milk and bread. Neither the remedies nor the chemotherapy worked.

On the twenty-second of February, he was planning on going to the Fat Stock Show in San Antonio as he always did. He already had his box seat ticket. He'd been going to rodeos in San Antonio since 1909 and, in his day, was considered one of the best riders. He could stop a horse by spinning a rope and catching its tail. He bragged and complained in the same breath: "I still spin the rope, but I can't jump through. I used to ride the broncs to a standstill. Now the cowboys take 'em eight jumps. They've got a union." The Chief had to postpone his appearance at the rodeo, too.

On March 1 at 3:30 a.m., during the transition from the hungry moon to the wild goose moon, Chief William Red Fox died in Corpus Christi, as the wild geese were returning to the north.

However the Chief was transported to the beyond—horse, sailing ship, railroad—he came to death via a full and magnificent life. The Chief once explained Sioux burial customs.

"We buried the dead with their head to the east, where the sun rises, because we believe in everlasting life. It's just like the smoke from the fire; it goes from the seen to the unseen, and in that fire the wood burns to ashes, like bones turn to dust. And the things that belonged to the Indian who died were buried with him, not because we believed that he was going to wear them or use them, but because they were his. They belonged to the one who died, not to the ones who still lived, and we did not want any sorrow with sisters and brothers trying to grab this or that."

The Chief gave of himself while he was alive, so that the only sorrow will be for the silence that has fallen like a shroud where once the Chief spoke vibrantly of times gone by.

Papa Louie

by Jamie Frucht

Louis V. Cranek exchanged his first name for the initials L. V. when his son Louis grew up and settled half a mile east of him near Columbus. On the driver's license with the bow tie picture of Mr. Cranek, it says L. V. But the name he is called by his family is Papa Louie. And his wife of 60 years is Mama Julie.

On his only visit to Las Vegas, he was messing with a slot machine when two women looked up and pointed at him. "You're LBJ." "No Ma'am," said Papa Louie emphatically. "I'm old man L. V. Cranek from Garwood, Texas. I'm an old rice farmer."

The resemblance is there. Papa Louie is 6'4" tall, and that's tall on him because he stands straight and smiles straight all the time.

Papa Louie doesn't know a lot about history. Some important history in his neck of the woods was the Colorado County feuds that raged in the late 1800's, early 1900's, with the Staffords, the Townsends and the Reeses shooting it out. Skull Creek was full in those days. But Papa Louie only had a walk-on role in that drama. It happened this way: .

"Once upon a time, my Grandma Geistman had false teeth and broke the lower part. I went to the dentist in Columbus to get them fixed. My second oldest sister Amelia went with me. She had a few hollows; the dentist would grind them out and put cement in.

"While I was sitting at the dentist's window waiting, I looked down and a fellow drove up with a pair of bay horses and a buckboard and a Winchester side of him and watered them horses at the water trough. I told the dentist, 'I sure hope someday I'll have two horses like that and a buckboard. That fellow even got a big Winchester side of him.'

"When the dentist heard that, he told me to close the blind and leave his office. The next day I heard there was a shooting feud. The dentist shot the man through the back and heart. That's all I know about that story. I don't know who they were. I don't know where anyone would get such a notion that I'd know something about that. History's too long ago. I'm too young a man for that."

Papa Louie was born December 24, 1894 in Frelsburg, 15 miles north of Columbus. His mother's people—the Geistmanns were Prussian and Grandma Geistmann was Holland Dutch. The Craneks way back were Czechs from Moravia. Louie's father was born in the 'sandy little land over yonder' called Pisek, no more than a flag station on the Missouri-Kansas-Texas Railroad.

There were nine children in Louie's family. Louie's world was mostly folk and kinfolk. Way back yonder when it was foot and horseback, people stayed put. Everyone lived at home. Home was almost self-sufficient with enough food and enough people to grow and eat the food. "We had a big patch of Irish potatoes and a big patch of sweet potatoes. We milked as many as 13 cows and, from the sweet milk and clabber, Grandmother Geistmann made cottage cheese.

Daddy made his own sugar and syrup.'' He could also make baskets out of ash wood by cutting strips, soaking them in water and then bending them any way. Louie has some 70-year-old baskets that have been active all those years holding eggs and corn. Others fell apart with the years. Louis says, ''I should be ashamed of myself — using those baskets up when they was antiques.'' But they were made to be used to gather eggs, not to gather dust as antiques.

Everyone had his chore. ''Brother Eddie slopped them hogs and I hauled the corn in a wheelbarrow. That's the only way we ever fed hogs—with kitchen slop and corn.''

''You are what you eat'' fits Papa Louie. His memories of daily meals are as precious and uplifting to him as another's account of great historical moments might be. The heart of the house was the kitchen, where the old wood stove radiated heat and cooking smells. The artifacts of Papa Louie's life include the ''big old frying pan where Grandma Geistmann could break 16 eggs at one time. Such a big family.'' Papa Louie remembers the dimensions of Grandma Geistmann's rice pudding cake—20 inches long, 14 inches wide. He likes his rice cooked the German way in sweet milk. He remembers the good ham and shallots, the milk gravy made with flour, the milk soup with dumplings.

Papa Louie went to ''a little Catholic Nun school with a little Sister and a little certificate and about 65 pupils. Everyone walked in those days—the Schmidts, the Gullys, the Ordners, the Buxkempers—the two-and-a-half to three miles along the pastures to school.''

Louie's formal education was lacking but he was educated. Everyone he met in his life took a liking to him and shared what they knew. ''I just about opened the fifth grade reader; that's all the schooling I had.'' When he left school, the Sister said, ''Louie you've been so wonderful. I want you to light a vigil and never be ashamed of your shadow.'' Louie lit the candle and learned the lesson by heart. ''Do you know all of my days if you'd have been behind me with your camera, I'd let you take every picture I went through in my life.''

Once with his Uncle Ed Geistmann, Louie remembers going horseback to Wharton County to visit two maiden school teachers. Louie was nothing but a boy and it was one of the first times he'd been away from his folks. At the ladies' house they sat down to a meal with homemade cottage cheese. ''I was a little bashful, holding back all the time and just ate a little bit. The second day, I was hungry like a young puppy.'' Louie realized his foolishness and took a big helping of cottage cheese. ''I'm going to eat,'' said Louie, and after his first bashfulness with the cottage cheese, Louie has never held back. ''I don't know the name of what scared me.'' He was a 'brave-o' all right.

With the appetite of a puppy and the disposition of a frisky pony, Louie was a natural to get into mild trouble. He recalls once with three other lads helping the local priest to dig a grave in the Catholic cemetery for old man Swoboda. The priest wanted to have a space where he could walk when he blessed the graves with holy water. While they were digging, they came upon some old bones of a big man. ''The priest came out and said, 'Just dig them out and lay them bones on the side, and I'm going to go to Frelsburg and get you all a quart of rotgut whiskey.' It was just 65 cents in them days.

"Well we were four young men digging that grave, and we got through about 4 o'clock. It was summertime and we was feeling good. We were kind of brave-o's, you know how such young men are. Well my partner said, 'What about let's ride into town and drink us a schooner of beer over the counter.' I said 'Let's **do** that.'

"I had my spurs and boots on and I spurred my horse on and rode into the saloon with my big bay horse 'bout 16½ hands high. The other fellow, his young horse reared up and broke a board so he couldn't ride it in then. I was by myself in there. And I rode up to that bartender and said, 'Let me have a schooner of beer.' I had a little dime in my pocket and he said, 'Yes Sir.'

"When I got through, he said, 'I'll tell you what Louie, why don't you ride this horse out and go tie it up and you come back. I want to talk to you.' I said, 'Yes, Sir.' So I rode my horse out. And he took me around the counter in back where he was tending bar. 'Say, Louie, you know you got the best Mama and Papa in the world and they sure wouldn't like that if they would see that.' Well, do you know, that broke me of drinking. I didn't drink for 30 years after it."

Louie didn't come from a drinking family. "My Daddy had a quart of whiskey on the shelf just for a purpose. He put two tablespoons of whiskey in some hot water and added sugar and that was medicine, a toddy for a sore throat."

Louie's second chance to be involved in some Texas history came when he was offered a job on the King Ranch. While Louie was helping a friend drive cattle to Ulm, they met a man who was looking for some young men to come down to the King Ranch to stop the cattle rustling. The man wanted to know if Louie was as good as he looked.

"I had a big old pistol on me and I put a dime on a post, stepped back about ten paces and I shot that dime off. Well, then he wanted me. So when I got home, I told my mama about it. She started crying, 'No I wouldn't let you go for anything in the world. You'll get killed for sure! No!' Since his mother absolutely wouldn't let him go, that was that. (Papa Louie is still a fantastic shot, but has had to be satisfied aiming at ducks instead of rustlers.)

The King Ranch didn't get Louie; Mama Julie did. She was from a Czech family that had immigrated to Fayetteville in 1884. Like Louie's family, hers had nine children.

The young people in those days had once-a-month dances and "play parties" in between for entertainment. They would walk two or three miles to their entertainments. At those "play parties" they played games such as Drop the Handkerchief and Frog in the Middle. Mama Julie can still chant it: "Frog in the Middle, can't get out, take a stick and punch him out." It was while playing Frog in the Middle that Romeo met his Julie.

Mama Julie was the frog. Everyone had his eyes closed and was singing. "Papa Louie must have kept his eyes open 'cause when I crawled out, he grabbed me."

The following week they met at a dance in Pisek. It was a kind of date. They danced the first and the last Home-Sweet-Home dance to the accompaniment of a push fiddle (accordian), a little violin and a cornet. That was May 1916, and after a six month's courtship, they were married on the 25th day of November.

Friends later asked her, "How come you got married so young?"

"He was such a handsome boyfriend. I was afraid someone would get him."

To which Papa Louie adds joyfully, "Awful, awful handsome."

Grandma Geistmann gave her grandson some advice for his wedding. "Louie, I'm going to leave two thoughts with you. Don't you never worry about anything. It just make an old man out of you. And if you don't die, you're going to live a long time." Papa Louie heeded that advice. "I guarantee you. She was so right. My good grandma, she was tricky. She was wonderful."

At 82 neither his joy nor his person is stooped. And Mama Julie is every bit as joyous as he is. They have five children—a girl, Earlyne, and four boys, Lester, Leon, Louis Jr., and James whom everyone calls Fritz. She had all the babies at home by natural childbirth. Did Papa Louie help her with the births? "No, he just looked on and cried." Papa Louie beams at their good fortune. "She was that lucky. She laid that egg just like a chicken. We was so blessed."

Though their marriage has been with them for 60 years, it's not taken for granted, but praised and cherished all the more. "If you find a companionship, it's the greatest thing in the world." He learned about love from his own family. My daddy was a Christian man. He wasn't too much of a church man." Nevertheless, he taught his sons practical religion that they could use every day of the week.

"Man ought to always remember that God made man and he thought he was lonesome and put him to sleep and took his left rib and made him a woman. **You sure don't want to fight your rib.**" That's the Bible according to Louie and his daddy.

Looking at his marriage, you know Louie's interpretation is right. "Whatever two people agree on together, that's the most important thing—to have a mutual understanding. But ain't two people who ever lived together who didn't squabble a little bit. If they said they didn't, they're just a big storyteller."

When there is disagreement, Papa Louie mends it. "If we, as human beings, really believe that we have a God and that man has a soul, then you are the only one that has to give an account of yourself. No one can do that for you. My belief was this all the time. If I offend you or offend my little wife, I'm going to come to her and ask her for forgiveness. Then I'm forgiven before man and God."

Papa Louie's religion is like his language, is like his person— immediate. Nothing mediates between him and his love. "My daddy always said, 'There's no man in this world that knows your business better than you do.' "

His daddy also taught him lessons of fellowship which Papa Louie passed on to his own sons. "You had better never say anything about anyone's belief because my daddy would run you out of the house. He

"Do you know, all of my days if you'd been behind me with your camera, I'd let you take every picture I went through in my life."
(photos by Mary Sherwood)

was just that kind of man. I came up that same way with my family. Don't never say that you're going to hate somebody because they don't go to the same church or sit in the same pew where you worship. The churches are all good. And if we are all God's children, if we really culture that, then I never will have that crazy idea that I will want to take a man's life.''

For 59 years he and Mama Julie have lived on the old Altair road with a buffer zone of grass separating their home from the flow of two lane traffic.

It's not a fancy house but it serves its purposes—to give Mama Julie a nice kitchen to concoct her kalaches and cheeses and other delicious daily specialties of the house. (Louie is lucky, his grandmother was a cook, his mother was a cook, and so is his wife.) The house also serves as a place for the large family to gather. With four sons, one daughter, four daughters-in-law, one son-in-law, twenty-three grandchildren and eleven great grandchildren, Papa Louie is satisfied to live simply. All his children live near him—in Columbus, El Campo, Nada, Altair. One of his sons is a judge in Colorado County. Papa Louie farms with two of his sons. Two of his grandsons have college educations, and have come home to be rice farmers.

As you enter the house, there's a transition room of old pine wood. This room between the inside and out is like a dream before waking, comfortable but faded. It is where Papa Louie keeps his hat and a souvenir machete. The "old timers," as he addresses his rockers, wait for him. He wants to share their comfort like old friends. "Sit down in that chair and see how it sets." There is a sink in the room where the men can wash up when they come home dirty and late from the rice harvesting.

Then the room steps up to the kitchen, the highlight of the house. After that all the other rooms drift off into grandchildren's and great grandchildren's sleeping quarters. At Christmas only the family was there—that was still 45 people.

Papa Louie also entertains dogs. They don't "live in," but play with the outside. He remembers a dog named Boddle—"had sense like a man; that was a smart dog, would crawl up on a 24 foot stepladder and just back down slowly." He's got a dalmatian dog now, a "coach dog," that claimed and guarded the white pick-up as his own, sleeping on it, worse than the RCA Victor dog and his victrola. When the pickup was sold, the dog mourned. He's also got a blue heeler pup and other dogs of mixed denomination.

A weathered barn, with eight half-wild cats (give or take a dozen) and a conglomeration of farming gear, sifts the sunlight through its walls' many cracks. And there's also 26 head of cattle that Papa Louie takes care of. And 100 acres of rye grass planted.

Mama Julie and Papa Louie raised their children without the aid of a doctor. There were no doctors in the little towns. And as with his religion, which seems a little like a home remedy, the Craneks concocted cures handed down from their parents. With coal oil, turpentine and a little lard, Mama Julie would make a salve and grease the baby's chest to cure a cough. For sore throat, she'd take a slice of bacon, rub a little bit of coal oil and turpentine on it, and tie the bacon around the neck of the ailing child. Next morning, there would be no sore throat. And the old standby was castor oil given by the tablespoonful. "And our big Leon, who got castor oil in soupspoons, to this day he can't drink soup with that big spoon, he got to have one of them little spoons. Such a big man like that," laughs Papa Louie, seeming to taste the joke.

They also grew up with well water drawn in a cedar bucket "with such a hook" and everyone drinking out of the same dipper and none the worse for it. Now all the great grandchildren, germ-conscious, have to have separate glasses.

"We got oh, such **big** boys," beams Papa Louie. Papa Louie himself is as fine a man as you could imagine. Mama Julie, who probably deserves some of the credit for the nourishing and nurturing she gave, says, "Papa Louie's been sick in his day, but he always got out of it." Part of his health is his own hard working.

Papa Louie's father was a cotton farmer. Mama Julie says, "That was our life. We had a garden; we had chickens; I picked 350 pounds of cotton a day; when we were first married, we lived at home." Papa Louie, after dry farming to supply his own family and help his father, became a rice farmer in 1944. The transition was not difficult. "Once you know how to work, the only problem is getting the right machines."

"When I got married, I had four mules and heavy rope lines and that's how I plowed, with doubletrees. And people say, 'Them good old days.' I don't believe in that. If it'd be the good old days, I still be seeing my boys with ropes over their necks with four mules and a walking plow. Give me tomorrow."

Combines replaced the mules and the binders in his rice harvesting operation. "When the combines all come together, about eleven machines, it's something to see." The miraculous machine does everything but plant the rice. It reaps the rice and at the same time, separates it with the seed going in the hopper and the straw going back on the ground. Then a grandson, as young as seven, in an Argue cart, comes alongside the combine and takes the seeds.

During rice harvest, Papa Louie wouldn't stop till he had rolled 110 acres of rice. He'd haul five loads a day, 500 barrels worth, the 55 miles to the drier. His day started when the dew evaporated; it didn't end till he was done, about 10 or 11 at night. Up until last year, Papa Louie rode the tractor with his two sons and hauled the rice. "The boys fired me last year."

Just as Mama Julie keeps her good china and old heirlooms in the china closet, so Papa Louie keeps his out in the yard. There all his history is spread about—an acre's worth of old machinery. The cab of an old Ford truck, rusting spring tooth, an International Farm-all middlebuster, used to bust the ground, now living with lichen. Everything's there in the field but the mules, and those he gave away to the "Negroes who live down yonder."

The Craneks lived without electricity till 1940. They got by with a wood and coal stove, heating warm water for their bath. In 1940 some of the Danish settlers in the area organized a rural electrification co-op to bring electricity to their farms. At that time the federal Rural Electrification Administration (REA) was encouraging farm families to form such co-ops, which could borrow federal money at two percent interest to build and operate rural electric systems. In Louie's co-op, a manager and seven directors were appointed. For 22 long years Papa Louie served as one of the directors from the Wharton County Electric Co-op.

He remembers how difficult it was to service the electric poles which were often in the middle of fields. When lightning would hit a pole, it was an all night ordeal to replace it. "We were eight men who had to pack a pole at 1 a.m. from the road into the rice field, dig the hole by hand. The boys would splice the wires." Later the poles were moved to the roadside to make repairs easier.

As a director, Papa Louie had the opportunity to travel to REA conventions all over the country. Mama Julie went too. Together they took full advantage, visiting many states. "We had a grand time all the time."

In Solvang, California, Papa Louie visited a man who had 500 hogs and a mechanized trough where the feed would flow by gravity down the mountainside. Papa Louie said, "Those mama and papa hogs—that was just a wonderful sight to see."

In San Francisco, he looked through a telescope at Alcatraz. "I was all duded up like a cowboy and I said as I looked through that thing, 'Uh-oh Al. If you'd conducted yourself like I done, you'd be looking through here, not me looking at you." He was so convincing that he had a crowd of believers around him. In the corn belt he talked German to the Iowans who were astounded—"Whoever would believe that you speak German in Texas?"

Papa Louie in fact speaks four languages—German, English, Czech and Spanish. That may seem incongruous with the old rice farmer who's lived in the same place for 82 years. But Papa Louie has a gift of language that follows from the good feelings he has toward people. He uses language to get closer. One of his common phrases is "I got to tell you all"—and he's not kidding. Energy guides his words that come from deep within him, welling up, gushing out, in their own rhythm, with their own rules.

Papa Louie was raised speaking German and learned English in the cotton fields from the Negroes. His English is entirely his own, spoken with more soul than most native speakers. He pounces on words like a dog on a rabbit, than prances around with the sounds.

Fifty-nine years ago when he moved to Garwood, he couldn't speak any Czech, but after living in the area he picked it up from working with so many Czech people. If he likes people and wants to speak to them, then he will learn their language. He used to take cattle to Louisiana with a friend and picked up the Cajun lingo. "But I done lost it because I don't practice it."

He doesn't speak any of his languages by the book. They were all learned naturally and are spoken naturally—farm language not formal language. "The most important thing in any language is if you can understand each other." Words that pertain to work and the farm he can pick up easily. "Now city doings would be a different story." He learned by doing with his hands and his heart. "Anybody can say **dummer asel** or **hulope mul,** you dumb mule, but if you're looking at the animal, at the actual dumb mule, then that will stay with you." Berlitz could do no better.

Using his language ability, Papa Louie became an interpreter for the German prisoner-of-war camp that was set up in Colorado County during World War II. The Rommel bunch was brought to Camp Swift in Bastrop. The prisoners from all over Germany spoke a variety of dialects, but Papa Louie could break through any barriers.

In addition to acting as interpreter, Papa Louie helped build two barracks near Garwood for the 86 prisoners-of-war. Because of the war, there were no young men left and much work to be done around harvest time. "In those days we didn't have any combines. We cut our rice with binders which we used to pull with mules and later, with tractors. The binder would reap the rice, tie it in bundles and kick it out. Then we had to shuck the bundles." Papa Louie showed the prisoners how to pile the bundles into "sombreros." Then the bundles would stand 14 days to dry, and be hauled to the threshing machine where the rice was separated from the straw. The prisoners became the labor force.

At the prisoner-of-war camp he saw the bitter fruits of propaganda and lies begin to rot. The Germans had told their soldiers that over in America the guards would throw the food to them, like to dogs. "The German prisoners, tears roll down their cheeks when they see the long tables with tablecloths on them and dishes to put the Irish potatoes and the meat and the gravy on. And there's cups, saucers, silverware. Who would ever believe it." And the Germans would even get sugar in their tea, which was more than the Craneks could get during the war. And if an American guard had one cigarette in those days, he'd give everyone a puff till the cigarette was smoked out.

Papa Louie was sorry to see all the bad propaganda and false expectations, but understood its reasons. "The Germans had to say those things to wage a war. They couldn't tell the troops, 'There are the best people in the world in America, don't kill them.' Just like our boys, they shoot to kill in a war. That kind of hatred got to die out slowly." All of Louie's sons have served in wars but he does not talk about their bravery and medals, but about their nightmares from seeing children devastated by war. "You take war. That's the worstest word in the world. That's worse than hell or anything."

Papa Louie and Mama Julie are big-hearted people who, despite living in a small place all their lives, have not distanced themselves from the world. Papa Louie always had a brave streak that made him embrace life and accept all life's dares. Age is just one more dare.

When he was young, Louie remembers the day in 1925 when he saw a barnstormer landing his biplane in a nearby field. Papa Louie tied up his mules and went to investigate and take a ride.

Barnstormers were a brave breed, but Papa Louie could outdo even them. He was in his own league.

"I didn't weigh but about 165 pounds. I was lanky and real super and a brave-o." He had just had his first son and was feeling sassy. He couldn't be contained. As the barnstormer and Papa Louie circled the garden on the right side, Papa Louie thought maybe Mama Julie might be looking out the window, so he got out of the plane and straddled the fuselage. "I rode the plane just like a cowboy." (Until the pilot saw him and told him to get back in.) That pilot crashed on his way home to Alabama. Mama Julie took care of him in her home for two weeks, dressing his wound in flax meal to draw the poison out. "He looked like one of my brothers and he had no one else to care for him."

It is the bravery and responsibility combined in one man that is so appealing. In addition to being a director of Wharton County Electric Co-op, Papa Louie has been a school trustee for 26 long years and helped annex schools. In the Knights of Columbus, he's helped to build a church.

But Papa Louie's best accomplishments are day to day. Rising at 5 in the morning, he lets Mama Julie sleep, while he makes his own breakfast. "Cereal, two slices of toast, a cup of coffee and one egg that looks you in the face." The love he feels for his family is a palpable energy and force that has no boundaries between life and death. His God is personal—living not only in his "Catholic organization" but out there in the fields where Papa Louie's worked hard all these years.

Papa Louie sits on a rocker that he gave his wife for a wedding present. He remembers Grandmother Geistmann and rocks while holding an imaginary child in his arms, perhaps himself as a baby rocked by his loving Grandmother. He says softly but strongly, "If Grandma isn't in heaven, I don't want to go there."

Later he is eating a dewberry kalache that Mama Julie has made. Friends are with them. He's said no formal grace, but his whole life is a praise and thanksgiving to God's creation, whether it be Papa and Mama hogs or brave, great grandchildren. Smiling at the friends and family congregating at the kitchen table, he observes simply, "You can make this world and your life heaven, right here and this is a part of heaven. Ain't this wonderful? God Almighty."

No, Papa Louie doesn't know a lot about history. Just everything about living.